Wise Moves

Wise Moves

Checklist for ☑Where to Live, ☑What to Consider, and ☑Whether to Stay or Go

SALLY BALCH HURME and **LAWRENCE A. FROLIK**

Cover design by Jill Tedhams/ABA Design

24 23 22 21 20   5 4 3 2

A catalog record for this book is available from the Library of Congress.

Discounts are available for books ordered in bulk. Special consideration is given to state bars, CLE programs, and other bar-related organizations. Inquire at Book Publishing, ABA Publishing, American Bar Association, 321 N. Clark Street, Chicago, Illinois 60654-7598.

www.ShopABA.org

CONTENTS

INTRODUCTION

As the hikers descended the trail in the hot late afternoon sun, a tall man found himself walking behind a woman more than a foot shorter. They were in a group of about 20 hikers taking a respite from an intensive National Academy of Elder Law Attorneys conference held at a resort on the edge of the Tucson desert.

The tall man was Larry Frolik, a professor of law at the University of Pittsburgh School of Law who had been teaching and writing about elder law for many years. The petite woman was Sally Hurme, an elder law attorney from Washington, D.C., who worked for AARP and taught elder law at George Washington University Law School. As they walked and talked, they realized they had both heard of the other and, by the time they got to the hotel, had decided to collaborate on an article or book.

Years went by. Both were very busy. No joint article or book was written.

In 2018, both were retired when the American Bar Association's Senior Lawyers Division and AARP approached them about a book on housing for older Americans. Where to live can be confusing, they explained. People needed someone with knowledge and experience to help them choose among all the options. Stay at home or move? Downsize to an apartment, condo, or co-op? Try independent or assisted living? What's an active retirement community? Continuing care retirement community? How to select a memory care or skilled nursing community? What about a move abroad? It's a lot to sift through, with no resource to help people figure out what would be a wise move.

Sally and Larry were the obvious pair to coauthor the book. Larry had recently written the ABA's *Residence Options for Older and Disabled Clients*, directed at lawyers, while Sally had written several ABA/AARP books including *Checklist for My Family* and *Get the Most Out of Retirement*. And, like others of their generation, they had made many housing choices for themselves and their families.

* * *

We, Sally and Larry, are delighted for the opportunity to finally coauthor a book, just as we had discussed many years ago on that hike. Based on our own experience and research, as well as conversations with friends and colleagues, we aim to help you examine the wide range of options available, to make wise choices at different stages along the way, and to feel confident that you have chosen the best path for yourself and your family for wherever you might call home.

A Very, Very, Very Fine House

Sometimes it might take a crystal ball to predict what lies ahead, but we've found that what happens in the future has more to do with planning than magic. Foreseeing where you might be living five, ten, or even twenty years from now takes forethought. That's what we hope this book helps you do—envision where you might be and take the steps to get there.

You might start with some big-picture thinking. What do you want, what do you like, and what do you need—for now and, as far as you can envision, for the long term? We help you through that process in Chapter 1, "A Crystal Ball."

In Chapter 2, "Should I Stay or Should I Go?," we help you think about the type of housing as well as the community where you live—the two components critical to your satisfaction. Whether you decide to stay in your home or move, look at AARP's factors for "livable communities" and the checklists in this chapter.

If you like where you live and want to stay there, in Chapter 3, "Make Your Home the Home of Your Dreams," you will find a host of suggestions on how to make your home the best home for you now and in the years to come. We walk you through how to look at your home to make sure it suits you so you can successfully "age in place." You will likely need some home modifications, but fortunately most are relatively inexpensive. We address that in this chapter, too.

If you'd like to make your home work for you financially, turn to Chapter 4, "Your Home: Your Biggest Asset." You'll find ways to make or save money by downsizing to a less expensive home and community, renting out extra space, or trying your hand as an Airbnb or VRBO host. We also explain some legal options with how you own your home that might develop more income, including putting your home in a trust, creating a life estate, selling and leasing it back, and taking out a reverse mortgage. You may be able to reduce your living expenses by taking advantage of government benefits programs.

If you want to stay in your home but need some assistance taking care of it or your-self, turn to Chapter 5, "Getting Help at Home." Just because you need help doesn't mean you have to move. Having someone come in a few hours—or more—a week, getting food delivered, or arranging ways to get where you need to go without a car can go a long way to ensure a comfortable life right where you now live.

Considering living with your adult children, other family members, or someone else? Look at Chapter 6, "Happy Together: Living with Others." Doing so can be very rewarding, as long as everyone works together as a team. And you can share expenses, chores, and caregiving for young and old. This chapter will help you avoid some common pitfalls and allow you to live harmoniously. A newer trend in living with others is cohousing. These made-from-the-ground-up neighborhoods bring together people who want to downsize into new, smaller homes built around a community center. There they interact with their neighbors, sharing meals, social events, laundry facilities, lawn tools, and more. These intentional communities focus on neighborliness, mutual support, and consensus management of the common property.

If you still want to live independently but want to move, you have many choices. Chapter 7, "Live on Your Own Somewhere Else," lays out what you need to know about renting an apartment, buying into a condominium, or being a shareholder of a cooperative. And Chapter 8, "Living in Age-Specific Housing," describes the many options you have in active adult communities, where you can enjoy activities in the company of others your age, no matter your budget.

Those who can no longer live on their own can turn to Chapter 9, "When You Need a Little More Help: Assisted Living." This chapter covers—and explains in detail—assisted living facilities and smaller board and care homes as well as congregate living. We explain what to look for, what to expect, and what they cost so you can find the best community for you in your area, in your price range. Chapter 10, "When You Need Memory Care," describes where people with dementia, including Alzheimer's disease, can get their needs met with professionals trained to support them. When your memory fails you, you can still find a place where you feel part of a community and are treated with dignity and respect.

If your health has declined and you need daily medical assistance, we help you choose a high-quality nursing home where you're also treated with dignity and respect. In Chapter 11, "Nursing Homes," we discuss the types of nursing homes and lay out what you need to consider when choosing one that meets your needs.

In Chapter 12, "All in One: Continuing Care Retirement Communities," you'll learn about these campuses that offer independent living, assisted living, memory care, and nursing care in one place. Continuing care retirement communities can be expensive, but those who can afford them value the assurance that their needs will be taken care of no matter what happens.

Care—whether at home or in assisted living, memory care, and nursing homes—can be expensive. In Chapter 13, "Paying for Care," you'll find critical information about how you may be able to pay for some of that care, including through long-term care insurance, Medicare, and Medicaid.

If you think one home is good but two are better, look at Chapter 14, "Twice as Nice: Second Home." Many people enjoy having more than one home, perhaps to take advantage of different climates or to be close to family part of the year. You will find insights and suggestions on the advantages and possible disadvantages of owning two homes. Two homes can be nice, but there are some legal consequences that we discuss. When it comes to death and taxes, as we explain, you can have only one legal residence. This chapter also goes into the ins and outs of timeshares and how to determine if that's a good investment for you.

For the adventurous, what about a move abroad? You'll find a road map of how to approach living outside the United States in Chapter 15, "Living Abroad." We have tips on what to think about before debarking to another country. It can be fun, but we help you make sure you have thought through all the options and contingencies, so you're prepared.

Our hope is that all the details, anecdotes, and suggestions we provide throughout this book will help guide your way. Each chapter also has checklists. Fill them in using a pencil or erasable pen so you can use them more than once and over time, should your situation change. Or download the electronic files from http://ambar.org/WiseMoves. If you complete the checklists electronically, you may want to print them out and place the pages in a three-ring binder, keeping a backup folder on your computer.

A word to the wise: Even the best planner may stumble, as you'll read about in our own and others' stories. Don't be surprised if you have to go through this process more than once. We aim to prepare you for that, too, so you can feel confident and knowledgeable each step of your way.

CHAPTER 1

A CRYSTAL BALL

A decade ago, Sally and her husband, Art, gazed into the future about where they were going to live. They were comfortably living in the suburban community where they had raised their two children, driving into the city to work. On the weekends, they had an old stone farmhouse about an hour away where they spent time renovating, gardening, and enjoying being in the country. Once it was fixed up, it could be a good place to live after they retired. Then retirement came along, and the farmhouse still needed lots of costly work. But instead of being able to concentrate on major renovations, they started noticing that Art was developing health issues. Maybe moving to the farm wasn't such a good idea. They had gazed into the future but hadn't considered all the contingencies. So they pivoted, making some minor modifications to their suburban home to make it a better fit.

That worked for a while, but as Art's physical and cognitive health continued to decline, they realized they needed to move closer to family for support. Neither the farmhouse nor the suburban home met their needs. They decided to sell both and buy a large multistory house to share with their daughter, her husband, and their two kids. Moving closer to family was a great idea, but moving in with family, not so much. Living with two preteens, five dogs, a few goats, pigs, chickens, and cattle on a working farm was a little too close for comfort.

Sally and Art carefully evaluated their long-term needs: stay close (but not too close) to family members for the invaluable support they provide; downsize to a small, one-floor house that wouldn't need much maintenance or housework; and live in a walkable neighborhood close to health care and services. And so they moved again.

Gazing into her crystal ball all those years ago, Sally never envisioned living in a 1,750-square-foot cottage in a little town she'd never heard of. But it's working because the house and surrounding community are ideal for their current needs. She and Art are comfortable and happy there. It's the right fit. For now.

———————————

Our home. This book is about how you can create a home that brings you comfort and happiness as the years pass. It may be the house you have now or the home you may move to. You may make one move, or maybe more. To have the best possible home, think about

1

what you now have, what you want, what you need, and what you can afford. Then, as best as you can, predict what you will want, need, and be able to afford in the future. The assessments in this chapter will help you examine your current situation and identify your priorities.

We can't anticipate all eventualities. There is no right answer as you gaze into your crystal ball, but we intend to help you tease out what's important to you and think through your housing options and your choices, step by step.

Some situations will be clear. You love your home, you can still walk down the stairs to the laundry and up to the bedrooms, and you're close to your loved ones. So no move for you. Or perhaps you don't want to drive or take care of house maintenance, so you figure it's time to move. Even if the next move seems clear, take these assessments to help you anticipate future needs and see the choices for now and the long term.

Or you may not be clear on what to do next. In the following chapters, we set out all the variables and options to help you make the right decisions. But for this chapter, let's start at the beginning.

As you're going through these checklists, be as thorough as you'd like. Leave blanks where something doesn't apply. And if you have a partner, have that person fill out the checklists separately. Later, come back to look at your responses together; where you disagree, find common ground.

The following checklists are in Chapter 1:

- ❏ *Living Arrangements*
- ❏ *My Current Home*
- ❏ *Community: What's Important to Me*
- ❏ *My Future Home and Community*
- ❏ *Where I'd Like to Live*
- ❏ *My Health and Health Outlook*

Living Arrangements

I currently live (check all that apply):

	Love it	Like it	Don't like it
By myself	❏	❏	❏
With spouse or partner	❏	❏	❏
With minor child/children	❏	❏	❏
With adult child/children	❏	❏	❏
With grandchild/children	❏	❏	❏
With sibling(s)	❏	❏	❏
With other relative(s)	❏	❏	❏
With roommate(s) or friend(s)	❏	❏	❏

	Yes	No
What I like and don't like about my current living arrangement:		
I feel connected at home and fit in with my community.	❏	❏
I have a satisfying home and social life.	❏	❏
I live with others but would prefer not to.	❏	❏
I live with others but feel isolated.	❏	❏
I live alone and feel lonely.	❏	❏
I'd like more help.	❏	❏
I have enough support.	❏	❏
What I want in a future living arrangement:		
To live by myself	❏	❏
To live with someone who can share expenses and experiences	❏	❏
To live with others who are of similar age	❏	❏
To live with others who have similar interests	❏	❏
If I need help or care—		
To live with family who can care for me	❏	❏
To live with others who can care for me	❏	❏
To live where I can get the support I need	❏	❏

My Current Home

	What I have	What I want	What I need
Single-family dwelling	❏	❏	❏
Duplex/triplex	❏	❏	❏
Apartment in a multilevel complex	❏	❏	❏
Garden apartment	❏	❏	❏
Condominium	❏	❏	❏
Cooperative	❏	❏	❏
"In-law suite" with family	❏	❏	❏
Small house on family property	❏	❏	❏
Shared housing	❏	❏	❏
Cohousing	❏	❏	❏
Retirement community	❏	❏	❏
Senior housing	❏	❏	❏
Rehabilitation facility	❏	❏	❏
Assisted living	❏	❏	❏
Nursing home	❏	❏	❏
Memory care	❏	❏	❏

What I like and don't like about my home:	Yes	No
I have all the space I need.	❏	❏
I have more space than I need.	❏	❏
I'd like more space.	❏	❏
It is well maintained and up-to-date.	❏	❏
It needs expensive updates.	❏	❏
It needs a lot of maintenance.	❏	❏
The lawn or grounds need too much mowing and maintenance.	❏	❏
It is convenient to services, stores, and health care providers.	❏	❏
I have to drive almost everywhere.	❏	❏
It is too isolated and requires too much driving.	❏	❏
It is too far from my children, grandchildren, or other family.	❏	❏
It is too far from my friends.	❏	❏
The neighborhood is not safe.	❏	❏

	Yes	No
Car services (taxis, Uber, Lyft, etc.) and public transportation are easily available.	❑	❑
Recreational facilities are nonexistent or too far away.	❑	❑
The weather is too harsh, too cold, or too hot.	❑	❑
I like my kitchen.	❑	❑
I have enough storage space.	❑	❑
I like my bathroom(s).	❑	❑
My heating/air conditioning keeps me comfortable.	❑	❑
My heating/air conditioning is energy inefficient or needs replacing.	❑	❑
My home's technology is up-to-date.	❑	❑
My home has too many steps.	❑	❑
The washer and dryer are conveniently located.	❑	❑
Parking is easy and convenient.	❑	❑

Community: What's Important to Me

	What I have	**What I want**
I have good neighbors.	❏	❏
My family is nearby.	❏	❏
My friends are nearby.	❏	❏
I feel safe in my neighborhood.	❏	❏
The neighborhood has sidewalks and streets that are easy to cross.	❏	❏
The neighborhood is bike friendly, is not too hilly, and has wide streets and bike lanes.	❏	❏
It's easy to drive around my neighborhood.	❏	❏
Parking is convenient.	❏	❏
Family, friends, or neighbors are available to take me where I want to go, if needed.	❏	❏
Public transportation is convenient, is affordable, and gets me where I want to go.	❏	❏
Taxis and ridesharing services (such as Lyft and Uber) are available when I need them.	❏	❏
It's easy to get to coffee shops or restaurants.	❏	❏
It's easy to get to entertainment.	❏	❏
I am near an exercise facility.	❏	❏
My place of worship is not too far away.	❏	❏
Volunteer opportunities are available to me.	❏	❏
It's near stores and pharmacies, or they deliver.	❏	❏
It's near my doctor, dentist, and other health care providers.	❏	❏
Public parks and playgrounds are nearby and easy to get to.	❏	❏
Public activity centers, like the library or swimming pool, are nearby and easy to get to.	❏	❏
Recreational facilities are available to me in the larger community.	❏	❏
Cultural opportunities are available to me in the larger community.	❏	❏

My Future Home and Community

	What I need	What I want
One level (no stairs)	❏	❏
Accessible entrance	❏	❏
Safe shower	❏	❏
Little or no maintenance	❏	❏
Less or no lawn care	❏	❏
Lower utility bills	❏	❏
Lower property taxes	❏	❏
More affordable rent or condominium HOA fees	❏	❏
Better weather	❏	❏
Closer to children/grandchildren	❏	❏
Closer to shops, restaurants, and other stores	❏	❏
Closer to health care providers and hospitals	❏	❏
Closer to activities I like to do	❏	❏
Less driving and more walking	❏	❏
More available and dependable public transportation	❏	❏
Supportive services available in my home	❏	❏
Necessary personal services available in my community	❏	❏
More opportunities for volunteer activities	❏	❏
More opportunities for socialization with neighbors	❏	❏
Better employment opportunities	❏	❏
Better sense of community	❏	❏

Where I'd Like to Live

Point ranking from 0 to 5, where 0 is not at all important and 5 is very important

Size and type of area

____ Population under 10,000

____ Population 10,000–50,000

____ Population 50,000–250,000

____ Population 250,000 or more

____ Many dense mid- or high-rise buildings

____ Many lower density, low-rise buildings

____ Strict zoning so that residences are separate from shopping and businesses

____ Shops and homes are intermingled

____ Planned community

____ Gated community

____ Age-restricted, adult community

Location

____ Northeast

____ Southwest

____ Southeast

____ South

____ Upper Midwest

____ Plains

____ Rocky Mountains

____ Northwest

____ Southwest

____ Far West

____ Near Atlantic Ocean

____ Near Gulf of Mexico

____ Near Pacific Ocean

____ Near desert

____ Near a lake

____ Near mountains

____ In another country

____ Four seasons

____ Mild weather

____ No cold winter weather

Activities

____ Near a golf course

____ Near public parks

____ Near tennis courts

____ Near a community recreation facility

____ Near a senior recreation center

____ Near a hospital

____ Near museums

____ Near a public library

____ Near my preferred place of worship

____ Near a comprehensive shopping area

____ Near public transportation

____ Near a grocery store

____ Near quality restaurants

____ Near lower-cost or chain restaurants

____ Near entertainment outlets

____ Near coffee shops

____ Near an airport

____ Near an interstate highway

____ Near a college or university

____ Where I can cross the street safely

____ Where I can walk or bike for exercise

____ Pet friendly

____ Where I can get around without a car

____ Where traffic is light and it is easy to get around

____ Near volunteer activities

____ Near work opportunities

____ Near a child

____ Within a day's drive of a child

____ Near grandchildren

____ Within a day's drive of grandchildren

____ Close to a parent

____ Within a day's drive of a parent

____ Close to other friends or relatives

My Health and Health Outlook

	Me		My partner	
	Yes	No	Yes	No
Exercise and mobility				
I exercise several days a week, including cardio and strength/resistance training.	❏	❏	❏	❏
I use my gym membership regularly.	❏	❏	❏	❏
I golf regularly.	❏	❏	❏	❏
I play tennis regularly.	❏	❏	❏	❏
I swim regularly.	❏	❏	❏	❏
I walk 30 minutes or more almost every day.	❏	❏	❏	❏
I regularly ride my bike at least a mile.	❏	❏	❏	❏
I ski as often as I can.	❏	❏	❏	❏
I get my exercise watching sports.	❏	❏	❏	❏
I've had hip or knee replacements.	❏	❏	❏	❏
I use a walker, wheelchair, or cane.	❏	❏	❏	❏
It's difficult for me to climb stairs.	❏	❏	❏	❏
It's difficult for me to walk long distances.	❏	❏	❏	❏
Diet				
I eat well-balanced meals.	❏	❏	❏	❏
I eat unhealthy meals a few times a week.	❏	❏	❏	❏
I eat out more than I eat at home.	❏	❏	❏	❏
I have special dietary needs.	❏	❏	❏	❏
I enjoy an occasional cocktail, glass of wine, or beer.	❏	❏	❏	❏
I drink more than I should.	❏	❏	❏	❏

	Me		My partner	
	Yes	No	Yes	No
Daily activities				
I need help getting dressed.	❏	❏	❏	❏
I need help moving around.	❏	❏	❏	❏
I need help with personal hygiene.	❏	❏	❏	❏
I need help doing laundry.	❏	❏	❏	❏
I need help shopping.	❏	❏	❏	❏
I need help getting to appointments.	❏	❏	❏	❏
I need help taking my medications.	❏	❏	❏	❏
I need help using a telephone.	❏	❏	❏	❏
I need help using a computer.	❏	❏	❏	❏
Health				
I smoke or vape.	❏	❏	❏	❏
I am underweight.	❏	❏	❏	❏
I am overweight.	❏	❏	❏	❏
I take medication for my heart.	❏	❏	❏	❏
I have had a heart attack.	❏	❏	❏	❏
I have a heart condition.	❏	❏	❏	❏
I have diabetes.	❏	❏	❏	❏
I have respiratory disease.	❏	❏	❏	❏
I have a cancer diagnosis.	❏	❏	❏	❏
I am a cancer survivor.	❏	❏	❏	❏
I have joint pain.	❏	❏	❏	❏
I have arthritis.	❏	❏	❏	❏
I have poor balance.	❏	❏	❏	❏
I have fallen in the past year.	❏	❏	❏	❏
I have short-term memory loss.	❏	❏	❏	❏
I have mild cognitive impairment.	❏	❏	❏	❏
I have dementia.	❏	❏	❏	❏

CHAPTER 2

SHOULD I STAY OR SHOULD I GO?

Back in 1982, the British punk rock group The Clash released "Should I Stay or Should I Go." While not about housing choices, that song's title sums up what this chapter is about.

How happy you are with where you live depends on both your home and your community. Of course, what works for you today may not be ideal in the future. In this chapter, we take a look at where you are living now to see if it is going to fit your needs for the next couple of decades, and we help you assess other places you are considering. We get you started thinking about what your present home and community offer and what you might need in the years to come. You can't predict the future, but in this chapter, we help you ask the right questions about what is best for you and what you can afford.

Why Stay?

The majority of people age 50 and older—76 percent—want to remain in their current home and community, according to AARP research. We want to live as independently as possible with the best quality of life for as long as possible. That means staying where we are until either our wants and needs change or the community changes. Staying in place, however, doesn't mean doing nothing. As we explain in Chapters 3 and 5, you can do many things to make your life more comfortable and satisfying right where you are. Don't just settle for good enough. Be proactive so you are glad you live where you do.

Why Move?

Only about 3 percent of those over age 50 move each year, compared to 15 percent of all Americans, according to the U.S. Census. While a small percentage, that still adds up to millions of people. Why do folks move? The U.S. Census reports that people move because they want better or cheaper housing, they have changed jobs or have been transferred, or they have retired. Other studies suggest other reasons: wanting a change in climate, to be closer to family, to provide caregiving, to reduce living expenses, or for health reasons.

Of course, everyone who moves has a particular reason. The reasons for moving later in life vary.

Larry and his wife, Ellen, moved from the house that they had owned for more than 30 years to a co-op apartment just four blocks away. Their two children were grown. The three-story house with a full basement seemed too large for just the two of them. They were growing tired of stairs—up to the second-floor bedroom, down to the basement for laundry, up to the third floor for holiday decorations. Larry was tired, too, of mowing the lawn, shoveling snow, and maintaining a 90-year-old house. And Ellen found it a little unnerving to be alone in the large house when Larry was away on one of his frequent trips. But they loved their community. So they moved to a smaller place in the same neighborhood, near the university where Larry worked and not too far from downtown, where Ellen worked.

Sally and Art, her husband, had different reasons for moving. For 45 years, they lived in a house in the suburb of a metropolitan area. Because their kids were now married with their own kids and living in other states, they wanted to be closer to family. They were both retired, so there was no job-related reason to stay put. Art was developing mobility issues that would require extensive modifications to their home. Living in a metropolitan area was expensive, and ever-climbing property taxes took a big part of their budget. Their suburban location required getting in a car to get to almost anything, including driving to get to any public transportation. There were no sidewalks in the neighborhood. Even walking the dog was a safety challenge. So they moved to a smaller house in a much smaller rural community near their daughter, son-in-law, and grandkids.

Whatever your reasons for considering a move, be sure to think through what kind of living arrangement is right for you now and will leave you best situated in the years to come. Remember how, if you had young kids, a key factor in picking where you wanted to live was good schools? Now other considerations have become more important.

Think Long Term

To be ready for whatever happens, consider all your housing options. You may want to move into a condo or apartment so you can spend more time traveling without worrying about pipes freezing while you are gone. You may want to live closer to family or farther from snow. Ask yourself what you'd do if you experienced reduced income, declining health, or the death of a significant other. Exploring your options ahead of time prepares you for whatever may happen later.

Think of all the changes that happened in your life between when you were 20 and 40. You probably left home. Maybe you went to college, joined the military, got married, had kids, moved at least a couple of times for work or for a new job, rented a number of apartments, and bought a house. For both of us, as our wants and needs changed, so did our housing. In those early decades, Larry lived in multiple apartments in three states until he married, and then he and his wife bought a house. Sally lived in five states with her parents, then with roommates, and ultimately with Art and their two kids. She lived in furnished and unfurnished apartments and a succession of larger houses.

There is every reason to think that our housing wants and needs are going to be just as fluid over the next decades. Larry hopes that his co-op apartment will be his last independent home. He loves his neighborhood, but he has his eye on a continuing care retirement community (CCRC) a few miles away, just in case. (See Chapter 12 for more on CCRCs.)

Sally took three tries after age 60 to find the right place. That first dream retirement home—that stone farmhouse fixer-upper—turned out to be too far from stores, doctors, and especially the grandkids. Scratch that idea. Living with a daughter's household of two preteens and five dogs—nope, a little *too* close to family. Scratch that idea. Her current cottage, in a small town close to her daughter, son-in-law, and grandkids, was never on the former want list, but it's perfect for her and her husband's needs right now. And she's already scoped out the nearby assisted living facilities, just in case another move becomes necessary. She's determined to make this house her last but is ready for the possible time that her husband, who has now been diagnosed with dementia, may need more care than she can provide at home. And she is realistic about possibly needing care herself in the future.

Figure Out What You Want and Need in a Community

People want to live in a great variety of places: in the city or in the country, where it is always warm or where seasons change, or in the mountains or at the beach. How close do you want to be to family or others you care about? Do you want to move to a smaller home to save money so you can travel more? Do you want someone else to do the maintenance and mow the lawn? Do you want to downsize to an apartment or condominium?

In Chapter 1 you had the opportunity to assess what matters to you and those you live with. It may be that you are just fine where you are now, or perhaps you have identified shortcomings that point to a need to find a community that is a better fit. The process to find a better fit can be challenging if you and the rest of your family have differing ideas. If you don't agree, talk together about your priorities to come to an agreement. One of Sally's friends always thought she wanted to live at the beach, while her husband wanted to stay in town. The discussion about where to look went on for over a year and got pretty heated at times. They both did a pro and con list for each of their preferences and finally decided to live in town and take longer vacations at the beach.

Checking the Livability of a Community

Home is more than the roof over our heads. So much of the satisfaction—or dissatisfaction—about where we live is based upon the community around us: the collection of people, places, and services.

Whether it is in the heart of a major metropolitan city, in a suburb of commuters, in the midsized town where you grew up, or out in the country, your community should provide the services you need and activities you like to keep you engaged. It's where we buy our groceries, do our banking, get our medical care, educate our children, cut our hair, fix our car, volunteer, and meet with our friends. It's where we attend religious services, walk the dog, picnic in the park, go to the gym, cheer at Little League softball games, and celebrate the Fourth of July at a neighborhood block party.

But what if your community has serious shortcomings? It could be that the neighborhood is becoming unsafe, friends are moving away, or property taxes are rising. Maybe you've stopped driving, but stores, restaurants, and medical services are far away and public transportation is limited.

AARP has made it easy to assess what it calls the livability of your community and those you are considering. Go to the AARP Livability Index (www.AARP.org/livability index), where you can search by address, zip code, or community name. The index provides a livability score based on seven key factors:

1. Housing: affordability and access
2. Neighborhood: access to life, work, and play
3. Transportation: safe and convenient options
4. Environment: clean air and water
5. Engagement: civic and social involvement
6. Health: prevention, access, and quality
7. Opportunity: inclusion and possibilities

You can customize the index to place greater or lesser emphasis on the features that are important to you.

You can also check to see if the community you live in or are considering has committed to becoming more "age-friendly" by joining the AARP Network of Age-Friendly States and Communities. These are towns, cities, and counties where the local leadership has committed to explicitly consider the needs of older adults as they make decisions about housing, transportation, and public spaces, in the name of better serving the needs of all residents. Learn more at www.AARP.org/agefriendly.

We'll walk through a few of the seven livability factors here.

Transportation

How we get around in our community can be an important factor in deciding where to live. Most Americans rely on their cars to get them where they need to go. We drive to work, the grocery store, doctors' appointments, restaurants, movie theaters, civic meetings, volunteer activities, the gym, the park, religious services, and friends' houses.

For most of us, our car is the answer to our transportation needs. That's how it was for Larry's parents. At age 80, they lived on the edge of town, miles from the nearest store and public transportation. Up to then, it was not a problem because they had two cars and each drove to wherever they needed to go. By age 85, though, Larry's mother developed macular degeneration and could no longer drive. Larry's father took on the task of driving her to the grocery store, where she had to put up with him second-guessing her grocery choices. He drove her to the mall, to her doctors' appointments, and to visits with friends. She didn't want to pay for taxis. She couldn't even take a walk safely because the neighborhood had no sidewalks. She was totally dependent on her husband. She hated that. And he wasn't happy about spending so much time "carting her about," as he put it.

Eventually—especially when Larry's dad realized that someday he, too, might be unable to drive—Larry's folks decided it was time to move from their single-family home to some place they'd need to drive less. They settled on an apartment in a continuing care retirement community (CCRC)—a pricey option, but one that fit their budget and needs (see Chapter 12). It was across the street from a grocery store and much closer to their church. The CCRC provided an evening meal so his mother didn't have to cook every night. His father also admitted that he was happy to be free of the large lawn and garden. They came to love their apartment, with its large dine-in kitchen, two bedrooms, and two bathrooms. They made new friends and enjoyed the clubs and gatherings at the CCRC. A move that they had dreaded became a move that met both their wants and their needs.

One of the key reasons Sally retired was to end her daily work commute. She'd spent at least an hour and a half driving to and from work every day for decades. Traffic was a nightmare and parking a growing expense. Even after she stopped working, she still had to get in a car to get anywhere.

Finding a place less car-centric was key to Sally's latest move. She wanted someplace where she could safely walk. Now, her little town has just four stoplights! And sidewalks! She walks to the bank, hardware store, restaurants, dentist, post office, library, and public ice-skating rink. Her new office is one block from home, so she can walk home to check the mail, fix lunch, and quickly retrieve the phone she inadvertently left charging in the kitchen. Larry's co-op apartment is one block from his favorite restaurant, two blocks from a great deli, three blocks from his pharmacy, and four blocks from the main public library.

If you drive, you probably haven't given much thought to the need for other ways to get around. Here are some questions to ask yourself, even if you want to stay in your present community:

1. How much time do I spend in my car getting around?
2. How much more time will I spend in my car if I have a greater need for health care?
3. How much do I spend on auto insurance, car payments, gas, maintenance, and repairs?
4. If I can't drive, how will I get around?
5. Are there places I could walk or bike to?
6. Can I save money by using public transit, taxis, or ridesharing services?
7. If I plan to depend on my spouse or partner, how will that work for both of us?
8. If my spouse or partner no longer drives, how will we get around?

Even if you spend a lot of time in your car, that doesn't mean you should move. Larry has a cousin who at age 72 lives on a farm. She is 30 minutes from the nearest town of any size and an hour from a city where she shops, goes to the movies, and visits her doctor and dentist. She is fine with those long drives. She also knows that someday she won't be able to continue to drive as much. But for now, she is so happy living on her farm, seeing deer and wild turkeys, that she is willing to put up with the long drives.

If you are thinking of moving to a new community, think seriously about much driving you will have to do, particularly in bad weather, in snow, or at night. Living outside the city where you can get away from the neighbors may be appealing. But is it worth the trade-off in the hours spent driving? Even if you don't mind all that driving now, in a few years you may not like it so much.

What happened to Larry's parents is just an example of how our wants may remain constant—in Larry's mother's case, to be independent, go to the store, and to visit friends—but our needs may change. If you are willing to move as your needs change, you can focus on your present wants rather than your future needs. But will you want to move again when the time comes? If you move now to a community that is far away from your children, will you be willing to move again closer to your children when your health declines and you need their assistance? Of course, you can't be sure what you will be willing to do, but at least you can recognize that the community that is best for you today may not be the best for you tomorrow.

Also imagine how much more driving you may need to do if your health declines and you need more medical appointments. If it is snowing, you can just skip going to that little café for lunch, but you can't skip going to the doctor. Is there another way to get there?

That brings us to the next questions: What are the alternatives to driving? Is there public transportation—buses, subways, trolleys, or trains? Where are the stops, and where does it go? How often and during what hours and days is public transportation available? Are there taxis available? What about ridesharing services such as Uber or Lyft? If so, you might be able to cobble together taxis, ridesharing services, and public transportation. You could use a bus for routine trips but call a ridesharing service for destinations not well served by a bus or just to ensure that you get to your doctor's appointment on time.

Can you walk or bike to some destinations? Are there clearly marked and safe paths and bike lanes? Are there safe places to park a bike? Does your community have bike-share stations where you can rent a bike as needed? Would an electric bike be a good investment?

Neighborhood

In the past, people thinking about relocating had to give serious consideration to the availability of stores, professionals, and other services. Today with the Internet, those concerns have diminished. With almost anything you want deliverable within two days, who cares if there are few stores near where you live? Still, before picking a new community, it makes sense to investigate whether the services and shops important to you are available. The Internet hasn't replaced local restaurants, coffee shops, and dry cleaners. If you like to shop in person, be sure the stores you like to frequent, whether a national big-box chain store or a local boutique, are near enough so that you can get to them on a regular basis.

More than shopping and eating, you want to make certain you'll find the things you like to do. When Sally's mother moved from a small town to a large city, she was glad that her favorite activities—opera and concerts—would be much easier to get to. If opera doesn't excite you, what about a major league sports team, recreational activities, historic sites, museums, or national parks? Are the things you love to do nearby? Check out work and volunteer opportunities that excite you and help you contribute to the issues you care about, and in the case of work, add to your income.

You should also be satisfied that services you need, such as lawyers, accountants, and dentists, are located within a reasonable distance of your potential new home. A good way to find out if they are near is to ask your current accountant and dentist if they can recommend a counterpart in your new neighborhood. If you are moving to a smaller community, you may find it difficult to locate quality professionals within a reasonable radius. You may still want to move there, but at least you know what you are getting into.

You should also consider whether you can get quality personal care, such as an in-home nurse or caregiver, should you need that. Even if you are quite healthy now, you need to be realistic. Many of us will need medical help and personal care later in life. It makes sense to inquire before you move. If you don't know who to contact, look at the website for the National Association of Area Agencies on Aging (www.n4a.org). It represents the 622 publicly funded Area Agencies on Aging (AAAs) located across the country. AAAs receive funds from the federal and state governments to provide information, support, and services in their area. They are a resource center for all older people without regard to their income. The local AAA should be able to tell you whether supports such as personal caregivers or adult day care are readily available.

Health

Before settling on a new community, check into the availability of health care that you need. Of course, you may be willing to drive some distance to get it, but you should know that before you move. You should consider both the health care you now need and whether you can find specialized care that you might need in the future. Where is the nearest hospital? Research its quality and specialties. Are there doctors' offices and urgent care and outpatient treatment facilities in the vicinity? How many physicians are there? Are there physicians who specialize in treating older patients? In short, get an idea of what is available and how close the medical providers are that you need now or may need in the years to come.

A good way to learn about the availability of health care is to talk to local residents. Ask them about their regular physician and any other medical specialists you see. Where are they located? Are your neighbors satisfied with the quality of care? If they must go to a hospital, where would they go? Where would they go if they needed rehabilitative services or memory care? Are there therapists who come to their home? Is the local pharmacist helpful and knowledgeable?

You can also use the Internet to see how many doctors practice in the area. How many rehabilitation providers and home health care providers serve the community or are located within a reasonable distance? Check on cancer specialists and geriatricians, if those are providers you may need. In terms of health care, what is okay when you are 65 may not be okay when you are 85. The availability of health care may not be determinative, but you shouldn't move without at least knowing what health services are in the area. If you have Internet access and are far from a medical center, telehealth access may be available.

Engagement

Some of us find ourselves so busy that we almost have too many friends and too many social obligations. We long for more time alone. Others live near families and get all the social interaction they need with their children and grandchildren. For some, sitting down with a good book or taking a solitary walk are great ways to spend time. But many of us, as we age, experience a decline in social life as we spend less time interacting with others.

We're no longer working. Our friends move away, become ill, or die. We become less involved with social groups as our health declines or our driving skills diminish. We no longer want to drive across town at night to that monthly book club meeting. If our spouse dies, we may find that we lose some of our social contacts.

Before you move, ask yourself, what kind of social life will I have? How will I meet new people? Are there clubs and organizations that we want to join? Are volunteer activities nearby? Are there religious entities that we might attend or join? Is the community welcoming to outsiders? Gather information. Some will be factual, such as what religious groups are active in the community. Some will be subjective—for instance, how welcoming the community is to new residents.

You may be able to gather facts about the civic or gardening clubs from the local chamber of commerce or other community groups. As you collect such information, you should get a picture of whether the community will have the organized groups and volunteer activities that satisfy you. Some of us really enjoy getting together in an organized fashion. If line dancing, a book group, or volunteer work sounds great, see if the community has those types of activities.

The subjective question—Is the community open to outsiders?—is difficult to answer. You need to talk to others who have moved recently into the community. Ask them whether they felt welcomed into the neighborhood. Are they invited to the homes of longtime residents, or do they find themselves mostly mingling with other newcomers? Is it a place where you make your own fun? A place where, if you want to be alone, others won't bother you?

Where the Kids Are

Another factor to consider is whether the location of the community will help or hinder your relationships with children and grandchildren. Will they be glad to visit you there? Life in a small town may suit you, but will they want to spend their vacation time there? How difficult will it be to travel to where they live? Some of us want to be able to drive to see our children, and even more importantly, our grandchildren. Larry's college classmate has no intentions of moving from her Massachusetts home despite the long winters because she's close to family. She lives ten miles from one son and three grandchildren and eighty-five miles from her other son and three more grandchildren. No moving to Florida for her. Another friend from law school moved to Tampa from Chicago even though his only grandchildren live in Chicago. He prefers to live in the sun and fly to visit his grandchildren. And, as he expected, they are happy to visit him in the winter.

Keep in mind that your children may not always live where they live today. If you move to be close to them, you better either accept that they may move away or be willing to move again to stay close to them. Another of Larry's college classmates retired from Omaha, Nebraska, to Tucson, Arizona, because he and his wife wanted to be able to enjoy the outdoors and be closer to their daughter who lived in Scottsdale. Later their daughter took a new job and moved to San Diego. At first, they wondered if they should move to San Diego to be near her and their new grandchild. Ultimately, they decided not to because they had become integrated into the life of Tucson. Rather than move, they have accepted that they will just have to drive the 400 miles several times a year to see their grandchild.

If you are willing to move far from your children, consider how easy it is to take the train, fly, or drive from your new home to where your children live, or for them to visit you. If you move to Denver or Atlanta, for example, you have access to large airports with lots of connecting flights. It's pretty easy to get to almost anywhere. But many attractive retirement locations are not close to a busy airport. Any trip is likely to involve an extra stop or two and often at an unwelcome departure time very early in the morning. One of Sally's regrets about her move away from the city is that she has a more than two-hour drive just to get to an airport.

An isolated location can also discourage visits by children. On the other hand, moving into a condo on the beach may be an attractive vacation spot. Your children may not be able to visit very often, but they may want to plan their vacation to be near you—and the beach.

Safe at Home

As we grow older, our health status and that of our partners can impact our choice of housing, as Sally's story shows. She and Art always figured that they would continue to live in their suburban home where they had raised their two kids. The plan to age in place was fine until Art developed significant health issues. They decided to alter that plan and move closer to family members who could help with caregiving and to live where they had ready access to coordinated health care.

For many of us, our home no longer fits our needs due to changes in our physical abilities. According to Harvard University's study *Housing America's Older Adults 2018*, mobility challenges increase sharply with age. Some 43 percent of those 80 and older experience issues getting around, compared to only 11 percent of those ages 50 to 64. Navigating stairs can become difficult or impossible as our joints and muscles don't support us the way they used to. Losing physical strength and vigor makes home maintenance and yard work more of a burden. Decline in our ability to see as well as we used to increases the risk of slips and falls as we navigate even the familiar spaces in our homes. Sally's mother ended up with a broken hip—and a permanent move to assisted living—when she tripped over a table leg in the dark.

Dementia often is the reason for moving. In 2018, 5.7 million people had Alzheimer's disease or other dementias, according to the Alzheimer's Association, and that number is expected to grow to 14 million by 2050. As dementia progresses, people may require more and more assistance. Living alone becomes difficult and finally impossible. Larry's neighbor has dementia. He and his wife moved into the co-op apartment from their house because of his declining mental condition. She simply couldn't continue to maintain the house and look after him. He is safer in the apartment, and she has the support of the neighbors in caring for him and taking care of herself.

Safety concerns may require home modifications, which we discuss in Chapter 3. You may need to bring in services to help make sure the person with dementia has the care needed at home. You'll find more about this in Chapter 5. Moving nearer to or even living with family members is an option covered in Chapter 6. You may need to move to where personal care assistance is provided; we devote Chapter 9 to this. The pros and cons of age-specific communities, assisted living facilities, memory care, nursing homes, and continuing care retirement communities are also discussed in later chapters.

Going It Alone

The death of a spouse or life partner can affect the survivor's housing wants and needs. People react to the death of a spouse in different ways. Some find it too depressing to remain in the same house or apartment. They seek new housing to avoid painful memories. Others, comforted by memories of the deceased partner, want to remain in the same house. For many, the practical considerations of newly living alone—such as the space being too big, too difficult to maintain, too lonely, or too far from other family—may spur a change in residence.

For some, the financial changes that come with the death of a partner are paramount. The loss of a spouse almost always means a reduction in income. If the partner was working, there may be an immediate income loss. There will also be a reduction in Social Security benefits. Here are the basics of what you need to know about Social Security survivor benefits:

- Social Security stops upon the recipient's death. In fact, you may need to return the last-received benefit payment.

- Surviving spouses who were receiving a benefit equal to 50 percent of the deceased spouse's benefit get instead an amount equal to 100 percent of the decedent's benefit.

- Surviving spouses who were receiving benefits on their own work record can get the same amount they were receiving or 100 percent of their spouse's benefit, whichever is higher.

- Social Security may pay a death benefit of $255 to the surviving spouse or next of kin.

Couples living off a private pension plan or 401(k) plan may not see a drop in income at the death of one of the spouses. Almost all pension plans are calculated to pay out the same amount until the death of the surviving spouse. The 401(k) benefits will automatically continue to be paid to the named surviving beneficiaries.

In time, the surviving spouse may want to evaluate whether to keep the home that was too large even for two. Experts advise spouses to not make a major decision or move until at least a year has passed. It took Sally's mother about two years after her husband's death to decide to leave the small town she called home for over 45 years, pulling up roots to move to an age-restricted condominium in the city where a daughter lived. It was a big decision and a big move, but she thrived in her new environment. She rapidly made many new friends, many of whom were recently widowed like she was. A major plus was that she could now enjoy season tickets for the opera. Larry's mother-in-law waited over two years after her husband's death to move from the large family home in a small town to a condominium next to a university in an urban area. She, too, bloomed in the new environment. She took university courses that were designed just for older students—no homework, no tests, and just five weeks long. She joined a travel club that made day trips together. She kept her car, but she usually took the subway because she lived only three blocks from a station. When her health deteriorated, she was only four miles away from a world-class medical center. In many ways, her last years were some of her best years.

Figure Out Finances

Naturally, finances play a significant role in where we live. Most of us, when we retire, have less income than when we worked. The nonprofit American Consumer Credit Counseling recommends spending no more than 35 percent of your income on housing costs, including mortgage or rent, utilities, insurance, furniture, and maintenance. If your income during retirement is less than it was when you were working, then that 35 percent is a lesser amount that you can spend on housing. You may have to decide whether to devote a greater percentage of your income to paying for your housing or reduce your housing costs. Which should you do?

First, you need to figure out how much you spend a year on housing. Track your expenses for six months or a year to find out what it really costs to live where you do. You may not think of transportation costs as a cost of housing, but they can be. Where your home is located can have a big impact on your bottom line. A home in a city where you can walk and take public transportation is going to use up less of your budget than a home in the suburbs where you need a car to get you to where you need to go.

Second, if you're not already retired, estimate your anticipated retirement income (we explain how in the text that follows) or, if you are already retired, look at your current income. According to the U.S. Census American Housing Survey, the median cost for utilities is $202 a month, and an average of $500 a year is spent on routine home maintenance. You should also factor in additional expenses you might face in the future. When will you need to replace the aging washer and dryer? Will the house need a new roof in the next few years? Are your property taxes likely to rise in the coming years?

Third, calculate the percentage of income you spend on housing. Ask yourself if that percentage is okay or too high. Will it or does it prevent you from doing other things that are important to you? If the answer is yes, it is time to think about whether you can reduce what you spend on your housing, reduce your other expenses, or increase your income.

Estimate Your Retirement Income

Let's go back to how you can estimate your retirement income.

Social Security

To calculate your and your spouse's expected Social Security benefits, look at your annual Social Security statements that come in the mail in your birthday months. You can also estimate your future retirement benefits at www.socialsecurity.gov/estimator or view your statement online at www.ssa.gov/myaccount/. The amount you get depends in part on the age at which you retire—the older you are when you claim Social Security benefits, the higher the payment—as well as how much you have earned each year in the past and how much you will earn each year until you retire. Whatever the amount, the good news is that the annual payment is adjusted upward for inflation so that your buying power remains about the same no matter how long you live.

Pension

For our parents, a reliable and secure pension after working 30 to 40 years was a sure thing. Today, however, fewer and fewer of us will get a lifetime pension. In 2018, only 23 percent of workers participated in a defined benefit company pension, according to the Bureau of Labor Statistics. For those lucky enough to have a private pension, the payments vary greatly, from a few dollars a month to generous benefits. But most pensions are not indexed to inflation. Retirees who depend on a private pension without an inflation factor will find their disposable income declining as the years go by.

Retirement Savings Account Plans

A little over half of the 135 million full- and part-time workers in the United States participated in retirement saving account plans in 2018. Unlike a pension that guarantees fixed monthly payments for life, retirement plans such as 401(k)s provide employees a lump sum amount when they retire. The retiree must then invest that amount to make it last during the many years of retirement.

The following checklists are in Chapter 2:

- ❑ *What Makes My Community Livable*
- ❑ *My Housing Budget*
- ❑ *What Can I Afford?*

What Makes My Community Livable

First, go to www.aarp.org/livabilityindex to find out the livability of your current community and every community you're considering. Record the scores here:

Livability index of my community: _____

Livability index of _____: _____

Livability index of _____: _____

Livability index of _____: _____

Livability index of _____: _____

Next, make your own assessment of your community with these criteria. Check the items it has.

Housing: Affordability and access
- ❏ Affordable housing options
- ❏ Multifamily dwellings (duplexes, townhouses, apartment buildings)
- ❏ Subsidized housing
- ❏ Vacancies or listings of affordable housing options

Neighborhood: Access to life, work, and play
- ❏ Grocery stores
- ❏ Farmers markets
- ❏ Public libraries
- ❏ Parks
- ❏ Exercise opportunities
- ❏ Volunteer opportunities
- ❏ Compact neighborhoods
- ❏ Streets and homes that are free of crime

Transportation: Safe and convenient options
- ❏ Public transportation
- ❏ Bus stops and transit stations
- ❏ Low traffic congestion
- ❏ Safety for pedestrians/bikers
- ❏ Low accident rates for drivers
- ❏ Walkable destinations

Environment: Clean air and water
- ❏ Clean air
- ❏ Clean water

Engagement: Civic and social involvement
- ❑ Social connections
- ❑ Fast Internet
- ❑ Civic involvement
- ❑ Voting
- ❑ Culture, arts, and entertainment

Health: Prevention, access, and quality
- ❑ Exercise opportunities
- ❑ Healthy foods
- ❑ Health care professionals
- ❑ Hospitals and urgent care facilities
- ❑ Quality health care

Opportunity: Inclusion and possibilities
- ❑ Age diversity
- ❑ Income equality

My Housing Budget

Current home	Amount
Fair market value:	_____
Assessed value:	_____

Housing expenses

Mortgage payments:	_____
Remaining amount of mortgage:	_____
Years left to pay off mortgage:	_____ years
Interest rate on mortgage:	_____ percent
Property taxes:	_____
Homeowners' insurance premium:	_____
Homeowners' association (HOA) monthly fee:	_____

Home equity loan

Monthly payments:	_____
Remaining amount of debt:	_____
Years left to pay off loan:	_____ years
Interest rate on loan:	_____ percent

Home equity line of credit (HELOC)

Monthly payments:	_____
Total credit available:	_____
Total credit used:	_____
Interest rate:	_____ percent

Reverse mortgage

Amount borrowed to date:	_____
Total amount available:	_____
Interest rate:	_____ percent
Total debt including interest:	_____

Rent

Monthly payments:	_____
Monthly utility costs:	_____
Renters' insurance premium:	_____
Remaining months on lease:	_____ months
Outstanding assessments:	_____

Total housing expenses: _____

Home service expenses

House cleaning: _____

Security: _____

Snow removal: _____

Yard/landscaping: _____

Total home service expenses: _____

Utilities

Electricity: _____

Heating: _____

Propane: _____

Sewage: _____

Water: _____

Wood: _____

Total utilities: _____

Total housing-related expenses: _____

Other expenses

Monthly

Other debt

Car payment: _____

Credit card payment: _____

Student loan payment: _____

Food

Groceries: _____

Dining out: _____

Transportation

Auto maintenance and repair: _____

Gasoline: _____

Public transportation: _____

Taxis and ridesharing services: _____

Services

Cable television and streaming services: _____

Cell phone: _____

Housekeeping: _____

Internet: _____

Landline telephone: _____

Security system: _____

Insurance

Auto: _____

Dental: _____

Life: _____

Long-term care: _____

Medical premiums and deductibles: _____

Vision: _____

Entertainment/Recreation

Club memberships: _____

Entertainment: _____

Fitness: _____

Gifts: _____

Hobbies: _____

Other: _____ _____

Total other monthly expenses: _____

Total × 12 months: _____

Yearly

Federal income taxes: _____

State and local income taxes: _____

Charitable donations: _____

Clothing: _____

Dental: _____

Medical copayments and deductibles: _____

Medication copayments and deductibles: _____

Season tickets for sports and entertainment: _____

Subscriptions: _____

Vacations: _____

Vision: _____

Other: _____ _____

Total yearly expenses: _____

Occasional

Car purchase: _____

Dream vacation: _____

Home appliances: _____

Major home repairs: _____

Recreation items or equipment: _____

Other: _____ _____

Occasional expenses: _____

Total housing-related expenses

+ Total other monthly expenses

+ Total yearly expenses

+ Occasional expenses

Total annual expenses: _____

Income (anticipated or actual)

Monthly

Earnings: _____

Social Security

At age 62: _____

At full retirement age: _____

At age 70: _____

Pension: _____

Annuity: _____

Investment income: _____

Rental income: _____

Other: _____ _____

Total monthly: _____

Total × 12 months: _____

Required minimum distribution: _____

Total annual income: _____

Minus total annual expenses: _____

Balance: _____

What Can I Afford?

Current annual income: _____

Current monthly income: _____

    Average monthly housing costs: _____

    Total annual housing cost: _____

Percentage of monthly income spent on my home: _____

Percentage of annual income spent on my home: _____

Anticipated annual income

    Wages: _____

    Social Security: _____

    Pension: _____

    Retirement savings: _____

    Required minimum distribution: _____

    Investments: _____

    Rental income: _____

    Other: _____ _____

    _____ _____

    _____ _____

    _____ _____

Projected decrease in monthly income: _____

Projected decrease in annual income: _____

If my income declines, can I still afford my present home? ❑ Yes ❑ No

CHAPTER 3

MAKE YOUR HOME THE HOME OF YOUR DREAMS

In the unforgettable words of Dorothy in *The Wizard of Oz*, "There's no place like home." It's true. Researchers time and again report that people of all ages want to stay in their homes and communities for as long as possible. More than three in four people agree with the statement "I'd really like to remain in my current residence for as long as possible," according to AARP's 2018 Home and Community Preferences Survey.

If you want to stay in your home just as long as you can, we can help you plan ahead. After all, in 20 years, both you and your home will be 20 years older. Now is the time to assess whether where you live today will continue to be a good fit in the years ahead. You started this assessment in Chapter 1. In this chapter, we help you think about making your home the home you want to and can live in for the long term.

What do you like? Dislike? What do you need that you don't have now? Do you need to make room for a home office, visitors, or entertaining? Do you have too much space? Is it too costly to maintain? Does it need expensive repairs such as a new roof or furnace? To make your home more livable for now and into your later years, can you make minor adjustments, or do you need major renovations? What changes will enhance the safety and comfort of your home, for yourself, your family, and visitors—from children in strollers to the skier with a broken leg to people who use wheelchairs or walkers?

The 2018 AARP survey also found that more than a third of respondents—36 percent—said they plan to modify their homes so they can stay as they age. Perhaps just a few simple changes to your existing home could keep you comfortable and safe. Based on the work AARP has done to help us make our homes fit, we offer tips on how to make your home safer and more comfortable for years to come. We also look at the technology that's making home life easier and more energy efficient.

Are You Ready?

Step back and look at your home. Does it meet your needs today, or have your family circumstances changed so that your house is no longer a good fit? The architect Roland Mace coined the term "universal design." By that he meant that buildings should be usable and accessible to all regardless of our age, ability, or needs.

At the end of this chapter, we have a comprehensive checklist of the design features that make homes accessible, but here are a few. How many are in your home?

- Is there at least one step-free entryway?
- Are the halls and doors wide enough to accommodate those who use a walker or wheelchair?
- Is there at least one bathroom that is large enough for those who use a walker or wheelchair?
- Are the door handles easy-to-use levers rather than doorknobs, which are difficult for people holding a baby or packages?
- Are the light switches easily reachable?
- Are there grab bars in the bath and shower?
- Is there a laundry room, bedroom, and bathroom on the main level?
- Are the contents of kitchen cabinets and other storage easily accessible?

Many of our homes won't meet our needs as we age. In 2017, more than 19 million older adults were living in housing that didn't provide them with the best opportunity to live independently, and only about 1 percent of the nation's present housing is equipped to meet their needs. Use our checklist to take a look at your home and note what needs to be changed to make it more accessible for you and your guests. Even without major remodeling or new construction, there are many projects you can do to make your home safer and more comfortable. For ideas, see the slide show at www.aarp.org/livable-communities /housing/info-2015/lifelong-home-slideshow.html.

Slips and Falls

Among people age 65 and older, falls are the number one cause of injury and death from injury, the Centers for Disease Control and Prevention reports, and the number of falls is surging. Depressing, yes, but there are steps you can take to make your house safer. Get rid of or tape down throw rugs. If you have bare floors, install carpet—not deep-pile plush, but a firmer surface. Place nonslip mats in the kitchen. If you have a cat or dog, keep the feeding and watering dishes off to the side, away from where you walk. Eliminate clutter from stairs. Larry's old house had a basement with stairs that turned 180 degrees halfway down. He noticed that he used the wide turn point to store things such as the vacuum cleaner. Not a good idea. It was always in the way when he or his wife carried a large laundry basket down to the washing machine in the basement.

Grab bars and handrails can make moving and getting up and down easier and safer. Permanently installed bars by the front door give you something to hold on to when trying to balance grocery bags. The two steps down to the garage also need a grab bar. All stairs, inside and outside, should have a handrail far enough from the wall to get a good grip.

Handrails on both sides double the safety. If you have a one- or two-step drop between rooms, make sure there is a visual contrast. These small changes in level often catch people by surprise. Stairs should be well lit. Sally's son-in-law installed a ramp to make it easier for his grandfather to get in and out of the house. He doesn't need a wheelchair or use a walker, but the steps were just too steep and the risk of falling too great to not add this safety feature.

Bathrooms are notoriously dangerous. When Sally's husband began having mobility issues, he found it difficult to safely climb in and out of the bathtub. Sally had a Certified Aging-in-Place Specialist (CAPS) walk through their home to pinpoint risks and suggest strategies to make it safer. He recommended grab bars in the bathroom: suction-held hand-holds on the bathroom wall and toilet safety bars. Sally did it herself for less than $100. The consultant installed a sturdy handrail next to the kitchen steps and recommended that a small table blocking a walkway be moved. CAPS is a designation for home remodelers, builders, and consultants who have been trained on how to make homes more livable. Take advantage of their expertise. You can find a CAPS in your area through the National Association of Home Builders, www.nahb.org.

It's easy to understand why so many falls occur in the bathroom. The combination of hard surfaces and water makes it slippery. Grab bars in the bathtub and shower are one obvious answer. Other simple, inexpensive measures can also help reduce bath-related falls and injuries:

- Provide a transfer bench or secure swivel seat to get in and out of bathtubs.
- Provide a shower chair or bath seat so you can sit while showering or bathing.
- Install a wall-mounted soap dispenser so you don't have to bend down to pick up a dropped bar of soap.
- Install a handheld or adjustable-height showerhead.
- Apply no-slip strips to bathtub and shower floors or provide a slip-resistant mat.
- Provide a toilet safety frame with armrests or a toilet seat riser to make it easier to sit down and get up.
- Install and always use a nightlight or replace the light switch with an illuminated switch that can be seen in the dark. Sally's bathroom ceiling fixture comes with a dimmer switch, so she can keep on a low light as a night light and have a bright light for putting on makeup.
- Secure bathroom rugs to the floor with double-sided carpet tape.

If you have only an old tub, a more permanent but expensive solution is tearing it out and replacing it with a walk-in shower. Prefabricated kits can easily convert the space where your tub is located into a shower. The shower can either have a very shallow lip or be barrier free with a floor that slopes to the drain. Kits can run $800 to $2,500, depending on size and quality, according to the home improvement website www.bobvila.com. This can be a do-it-yourself project if you are very knowledgeable about plumbing and framing. Hiring a professional can add another $2,000 to $15,000. When Sally and Art lived with their daughter, they added a walk-in shower to a first-floor half-bath by bumping out a wall into an adjoining room. Her son-in-law was able to do the framing and plumbing to install a shower kit at a cost of about $2,000. It became very useful when everyone else was getting ready for work and school. Plus, it was great for washing dogs!

Let There Be Light

Lights are important for both safety and comfort. Is there enough light in your house?

When he finally admitted he needed reading glasses, Larry noticed he was more comfortable reading with a strong light over his shoulder. He bought a special reading light that he can pull right over his book or newspaper. Sally's sofa used to face a big window, but the morning glare made it hard to read the newspaper. She adjusted the angle of the sofa, so the sun shone on the paper instead of into her eyes.

You may notice that you are more comfortable reading if you increase the wattage in the light or buy a lamp with more bulbs. Replace your old light bulbs with LED lights that provide more light and last for years. Sally has installed battery-operated lights that automatically turn on when she opens the closet door. It sure makes it easier for her to find the shoes she's looking for.

And for safety, lights are critical. Be sure you have plenty of light around doorways and stairs, so it is easier to see what you're doing and highlight any tripping hazards. Larry had a light over his front door on a timer that turned it on as the sun set. He never again had to fumble in the dark to insert his key.

Sally has motion-sensor lights in her driveway and on her back porch to make sure she has plenty of light when she gets out of her car or goes outside. You might enjoy having a large rocker light switch in your garage that can be turned on with a fist or elbow when your arms are full of grocery bags. Get table lamps that come with a push-button switch on the lamp base or lamps that turn on with a foot switch.

Plug-in night lights in sleeping areas can make you safer whenever you get up in the night. You might want to use small lights with motion sensors that light your path down the hall to the bathroom.

Fire Safety

Fires can occur anytime, without notice. Be prepared.

- Install smoke detectors on every floor of your home, test them frequently, and replace their batteries as needed. You should have a set date to replace the batteries every year—and the fire department may remind you—perhaps on the day that daylight savings ends. Many experts recommend hard-wired smoke alarms with a backup battery for a power outage. They may require professional installation, but they last longer and you don't have to remember to change the batteries as often. Maryland recently passed a law requiring that all residential smoke detectors last 10 years without needing a battery change.

- Make a fire escape plan and practice it with all members of your household. Make sure escape routes are clear of clutter and doors and windows are in good working order.

- Consider installing anti-scald faucets on bathtubs, showers, and sinks.

- Have the dryer vent duct cleaned yearly by an appliance repairperson or chimney sweep. Fires can occur when lint builds up in the dryer or the exhaust duct.

- Be sure extension cords have the UL and OSHA labels on them and are in good shape:

  - Inspect them regularly for signs of wear and tear.

  - Replace old extension cords that are cracked or frayed.

  - Use only exterior extension cords for outside use.

  - Pull the plug, not the cord, when disconnecting it from the socket.

  - Use extension cords only when they're absolutely necessary and not for long-term purposes.

  - Never put extension cords under carpeting or furniture.

Make Your Home Smart

Technology is devising all sorts of systems and gadgets that can make our homes more livable. We've come a long way from the adjustable furnace thermostat. We thought it was neat that we could set the timer on a furnace to automatically cool down when we were gone during the day and warm up by the time we came home. And who could forget The Clapper: Clap and your light goes on; clap and it's off. Today, we can do so much more.

Smart homes are no longer just for the super tech-savvy and rich. Home automation has become affordable and consumer friendly. It can save you money and make your home more accessible and secure.

Basically, anything that runs on electricity can be at your command via your smartphone. The list of available smart gadgets grows longer every year. There are smart smoke detectors that, when they go off, sound an alarm and also send an alert to your phone. You can install a water sensor that will tell you that the second floor washing machine is flooding before it ruins your ceiling. A smart irrigation system with a moisture sensor can automatically adjust how much it waters your lawn. How about a text alert when your dryer cycle is finished? You can get a smart thermostat that can detect when you are home and which room you are using so that your HVAC only operates when and where it is needed.

You can have the porch lights with a motion sensor so they will come on when the pizza delivery arrives. Your garage door will automatically open as you pull up. A smart home can notify you when it's time to take medicine or alert emergency services if you fall and can't get up. Alexa or the Google Assistant can tell you the weather and turn on your TV.

Your doorbell can ring on your phone, show you a video of who's at your door, and let you talk with a visitor when you're in a back room or not at home. Sally's friends monitor their cat sitters' visits when they travel. Once they were in Costa Rica and the cat sitter failed to show up, so they called to remind her. The rest of the week, she said she stayed a half-hour every visit, but the doorbell clocked her at eight minutes tops. They never hired her again. On another trip, a stranger loitered at the front door. The chime went off on the phone, and they talked to him as if they were home and scared him off.

Voice-activated speakers, such as Amazon Echo and Google Home, can also be a good way to communicate. Just by speaking into the device, you can talk with friends or family, send out an alert in an emergency, turn on and off lights, and get the news and weather, all without getting up from your chair. Every day more devices and apps are created that can make our homes safer and more livable. Find out all about smart homes with AARP's *My Smart Home for Seniors*, available at www.AARP.org/TechBooks or where books are sold.

Be Prepared

Sally grew up in Kansas, so she knows what it's like to have the tornado warning sirens go off when the sky turns a weird greenish color and the winds begin to pick up. By then it's too late to figure out what you should take along.

No matter where you live, you need to be prepared if you suddenly must leave your home. It might be an approaching hurricane, wildfire, flood, earthquake, or tornado. According to The Hartford Financial Services Group, 75 percent of all U.S. households are at risk for one or more natural disasters. Some disasters may come with little advance warning, leaving little time to grab some things and get out to safety.

Don't be scared. Be prepared.

Any planning—however much or little—will help make such distressing situations easier to deal with. How will you find out about an approaching disaster? Many communities have a system to receive alerts. You just need to sign up to get texts, phone calls, or e-mails. Do you know how you will evacuate if you need to? Do your emergency responders maintain a list of residents who may need assistance getting safely out of their homes? What will you do about your pets in case of an emergency? Sally posts a small sticker on her front door that says in case of a disaster, she has two cats that need to be rescued. In case of a power outage, does the utility company know that your medical equipment depends on power?

If you haven't already, create an emergency evacuation plan and pack an emergency preparedness kit. To do both, use the Emergency Preparedness checklist in this chapter, which is based on guidance from the Federal Emergency Management Agency (FEMA). Go over the plan with your family to make sure you can stay calm—as best as you can—in any emergency and know what to do to be safe. Pay close attention to any special needs, including an escape chair that can be used to get down steps if someone in your family uses a wheelchair or walker, extra hearing aid batteries, food for a service dog, backup power for oxygen units, and a list of all prescription medications for everyone in the family.

Now is a good time to make sure you have copies of important information readily accessible. You could have paper copies in a folder or scan them to a file on your computer or phone. Use the Documents to Go with You checklist to make sure that in an emergency you'll be able to easily put your hands on what you need. Larry has a friend who lives in Southern California. Because of the danger of a wildfire, he keeps a bag of important documents near his front door, ready to take with him on a moment's notice.

Paying for Modifications

Some of the costs of major home modifications that are medically necessary may be deductible from your income taxes. Check with your tax advisor. If, for example, you need to install an entrance ramp or elevator, widen doors and hallways, or create a roll-in shower to make it easier for a wheelchair user to live at home, these costs may be deductible if your doctor recommends the modification because of a medical condition and the amount deducted is reasonable. If the improvements increase the value of your home, you can deduct only part of the cost. The total amount of all your medical expenses must be over 10 percent of your adjusted gross income, as of 2019. Here's an example:

Say you have $55,000 in adjusted gross income. You pay $6,000 in out-of-pocket medical expenses for doctors and medications and $3,000 to install a ramp so you can get to the front door in your wheelchair. You'd need total medical expenses over $5,500 (10 percent of $55,000), so with $9,000, you qualify. You can now deduct $3,500 in eligible medical expenses ($9,000 minus $5,500).

The Department of Veterans Affairs (VA) may help cover costs for home modifications for veterans. When his amyotrophic lateral sclerosis (ALS, also called Lou Gehrig's disease) advanced, a friend was able to hire a contractor, with the help of the VA, to create an accessible bathroom, with wide doors and a roll-in shower. Check with the VA.

The following checklists are in Chapter 3:

- ❏ *Signs It May Be Time to Relocate*
- ❏ *Home Safety Checklist*
- ❏ *Home Technology*
- ❏ *Emergency Preparedness*
- ❏ *Documents to Go with You*

Signs It May Be Time to Relocate

	Yes	No
Does your home need expensive major repairs?	❏	❏
Is it difficult for you to do or arrange for basic home repairs?	❏	❏
Is it difficult for you to arrange for or do yard care such as mowing the lawn, cleaning gutters, or shoveling snow?	❏	❏
Has someone you lived with died or moved away?	❏	❏
Do you lack a family support network nearby?	❏	❏
Do you feel increasingly lonely?	❏	❏
Do you need a car to get around but are driving less or not at all?	❏	❏
Is parking unsafe?	❏	❏
Is walking unsafe?	❏	❏
Are stores, services, and medical professionals far?	❏	❏
Do you have trouble climbing the stairs in your home?	❏	❏
Are renovations to make your home the home of a lifetime (see the AARP HomeFit Guide) too costly?	❏	❏
Do you find the weather unpleasant?	❏	❏

Home Safety Checklist

For more detailed home safety checklists, tips on do-it-yourself fixes, and resources for improvements that may take a trained professional, check out the AARP HomeFit Guide and downloadable worksheets at www.aarp.org/homefit.

	Yes	No
Steps/Stairways/Walkways		
Are steps free of slippery treads or loose carpeting?	❏	❏
Do stairs have safe, nonslip surfaces?	❏	❏
Are there handrails on both sides of the steps and stairways?	❏	❏
Are there light switches at the top and bottom of the stairs?	❏	❏
Is there grasping space for both knuckles and fingers on railings?	❏	❏
Are the stair treads deep enough for your whole foot?	❏	❏
Would a ramp be feasible in any of these areas if it became necessary?	❏	❏
Are all stairs free of clutter?	❏	❏
Are outside walkways well lighted?	❏	❏
Is your house number visible from the street?	❏	❏
Is it easy for you to unlock, open, close, and lock the front door?	❏	❏
Floor surfaces		
Are surfaces nonslip?	❏	❏
Are there unsecured throw rugs or doormats that might slip underfoot?	❏	❏
Is carpeting loose or torn?	❏	❏
Are changes in floor levels obvious or well-marked?	❏	❏
Do you have to step over any electric, telephone, or extension cords?	❏	❏
Are there electrical cords under carpeting?	❏	❏
Driveway and garage		
Is there always space to park?	❏	❏
Is parking convenient to the entrance?	❏	❏
Does the garage door open automatically?	❏	❏
Does the garage door stop automatically if something is in the way?	❏	❏
Is there adequate lighting in the driveway and garage?	❏	❏
Is the driveway surface smooth and level?	❏	❏
Is the garage connected to the house?	❏	❏

	Yes	No
Windows and doors		
Are windows and doors easy to open and close?	❑	❑
Are window and door locks sturdy and easy to operate?	❑	❑
Do doorways accommodate a walker or wheelchair?	❑	❑
Is there space to maneuver while opening and closing doors?	❑	❑
Does the front door have a view panel or peephole at the right height?	❑	❑
Does the screen or storm door operate smoothly?	❑	❑
Does the door open with a lever-type handle?	❑	❑
Kitchen/Appliances		
Can you easily open the oven and refrigerator doors?	❑	❑
Are stove controls clearly marked and easy to use?	❑	❑
Is the counter the right height and depth?	❑	❑
Are cabinet doorknobs easy to use?	❑	❑
Are faucets easy to use?	❑	❑
Can you sit while working in the kitchen?	❑	❑
Are the items you use often on reachable shelves?	❑	❑
Do you have a step stool with handles?	❑	❑
Is a fire extinguisher within reach of the stove?	❑	❑
Is the microwave easily accessible?	❑	❑
Bathroom		
Can you easily get in and out of the tub or shower?	❑	❑
Do you have a handheld shower head?	❑	❑
Do you have a bath or shower seat?	❑	❑
Does the tub or shower have nonslip strips or mats?	❑	❑
Are there secure grab bars in the shower?	❑	❑
Can you easily reach the soap and shampoo in the shower?	❑	❑
Are faucets easy to use?	❑	❑
Are faucets clearly labeled "hot" and "cold"?	❑	❑
Is the hot water heater regulated to prevent scalding or burning?	❑	❑
Are items you use often easy to reach?	❑	❑
Can you easily get on and off the toilet?	❑	❑
Are there secure grab bars next to the toilet?	❑	❑

	Yes	No
Lighting/Alarms		
Are there enough lights?	❏	❏
Are the lights bright enough?	❏	❏
Do you have night lights where needed?	❏	❏
Can you easily turn switches on and off?	❏	❏
Are outlets properly grounded to prevent a shock?	❏	❏
Are extension cords in good shape?	❏	❏
Do you have smoke detectors in all key rooms?	❏	❏
Do you have an alarm system?	❏	❏
Do you use a personal emergency response system?	❏	❏
Does the telephone have volume control?	❏	❏
Can you hear the doorbell ring all throughout the house?	❏	❏
Are working flashlights available in multiple rooms?	❏	❏

Home Technology

	I have	I want
Smartphone	❏	❏
Motion-sensor lights	❏	❏
Dimmer switches on lights	❏	❏
Programable thermostat for HVAC	❏	❏
Monitor or camera to see what's happening while away or in other parts of house	❏	❏
Camera at entrance	❏	❏
Outdoor security camera	❏	❏
Buzzer system to remotely unlock door	❏	❏
Remotely controlled lighting	❏	❏
Remotely controlled ceiling fans	❏	❏
Curtains that adjust to light or temperature	❏	❏
Power-operated window shades	❏	❏
Robot vacuum cleaner	❏	❏
Moisture-sensing lawn irrigation	❏	❏
Push-out alerts to your cell phone for fire, water, and carbon monoxide warnings	❏	❏
Home entertainment remotely adjusted	❏	❏
Central hub system	❏	❏

Emergency Preparedness

Preparation steps

❑ Check insurance policies for wind, flooding, fire, or other storm damage coverage.

❑ Determine an evacuation plan and make sure everyone knows it.

❑ Designate a primary contact person for your family, preferably outside of the area.

❑ Know the locations of emergency shelters.

❑ Plan for special assistance if mobility is an issue.

❑ Register with a utility company if using electrical medical equipment.

❑ Store cold packs for medication that needs refrigeration.

❑ Store food for special dietary needs.

❑ Plan for care of pets.

❑ Have a supply of food for service dogs.

❑ Maintain a supply of water.

❑ Prepare an emergency kit.

Emergency kit items

❑ First aid kit and manual

❑ Moist towelettes

❑ Portable battery-powered TV or radio

❑ Cell phone charger

❑ Flashlight and extra batteries

❑ Matches in waterproof container

❑ Medications (five- to seven-day supply)

❑ Cash and coins

❑ Blank checks

❑ Credit/debit/ATM cards

❑ Change of clothing and sturdy shoes

❑ Blankets and pillows

❑ Books, games, puzzles

❑ Toilet paper

❑ Contact lens solution

❑ Hearing aid batteries

❑ Extra pair of glasses

❑ Incontinence supplies

Documents to Go with You

Contacts

❑ List of family members and emergency contacts

❑ Telephone tree of emergency contacts

Medical

❑ List of medications

❑ Copies of prescriptions

❑ List of health care providers (names and phone numbers)

❑ List of allergies or special needs

❑ List of type and model numbers of medical equipment

❑ Copy of health insurance and Medicare cards

❑ Copy of medical directives

❑ Medical records

Financial

❑ Homeowners' insurance policy (cover page)

❑ Auto insurance policy (cover page)

❑ Personal property inventory

❑ List of credit/debit/ATM card numbers

❑ Copy of Social Security card

❑ List of financial accounts

Personal

❑ Birth certificate

❑ Driver's license

❑ Social Security card

❑ Passport

❑ Marriage certificate

❑ Financial powers of attorney

❑ Health care powers of attorney

❑ Copy of will

CHAPTER 4
YOUR HOME: YOUR BIGGEST ASSET

Your house is more than just a place to live. For many of us, our house is our most valuable asset. It may be worth more than all our other savings, investments, and other property put together. If not the most valuable asset, it is probably right up there. In this chapter we consider how you can use your home to make you more financially secure.

One way is to sell it. We go into different ways to sell your home, including ways you can do so and still live there. We also go into other options. For example, you can rent a room, share your house, put it into a trust, or get a reverse mortgage. And if you just want to save on some household expenses, we tell you about government programs to help with that, too.

How Much More Money Do I Need?

If you're reading this chapter, you're probably interested in increasing your income. That doesn't necessarily mean you're ready to sell your house. Let's step back and consider whether you need more income to have a satisfying life—and if so, whether to use your house as a way of creating more income.

To start, you need to know how much and where you are spending. The My Housing Budget checklist from Chapter 2 will help you map your current housing costs. Then compare that amount to your income. Next, consider the needs and wants you can't afford. How much more income do you need to satisfy those needs and wants? Finally, look through this chapter to learn the many ways that you might use your house to create more income and satisfy those unmet needs and wants.

If your income exceeds your expenses, you can either save and invest that amount or spend it on your unmet needs and wants. If your expenses exceed your income, you may need to use your house to create more income. How much? Naturally that depends on what you need or want. Perhaps you need more income to help pay for medical expenses, pursue a degree, or take a cruise every year. If it would cost, say, $7,000, and you just don't have that amount, let's look at how you might use your house to get it.

Determining the Value of Your House

The first step is to determine the value of your home. Remember, it is worth what someone else will pay for it—that is, the market value. It's not what you think it's worth or what you wish it would sell for. How do you determine the market value of your house?

Don't make the mistake that some people make: believing your house is worth the appraised value for your local property taxes. In most communities, the appraised value is far below the actual market value.

Without taking that big step of putting your house on the market, you can get a reasonable estimate. Go online to sites that offer free estimates of house values. Some of the more popular sites are www.Redfin.com and www.Zillow.com. Many local governments have online databases showing sales data that you can look at as well. These websites focus on characteristics such as location, square footage, and number of bedrooms and bathrooms, and they depend heavily on the sale prices of comparable houses (called comps) in your neighborhood and community to provide an estimate of what your house is worth.

Look at more than one website and assume the average value is in the ballpark. If you want a more accurate estimate, you could engage a local real estate agent who will help you determine a reasonable sales price. If you are thinking of selling the house, the agent will be glad to work with you. If you are not interested in selling, you may have to pay the agent a fee.

The local agent has the advantage of an in-person understanding of your home. The agent can factor in your home's appearance or its curb appeal. The agent knows about any upgrades you've made, such as a new kitchen, or any upgrades that it needs, such as new carpeting. Finally, an agent likely knows buyers' preferences in your community. For example, in areas with a harsh climate, an attached garage adds value to a house.

Once you have an estimate of what your house is worth, you can begin to think about how you might turn that value into more income.

Selling Your House to Create More Income

Larry has a friend who lived in Minneapolis. Divorced and newly retired from his job as a high school teacher, he realized he no longer wanted to live in a big city. He decided to move to a small town in the Ozark Mountains. He sold the Minneapolis house for $370,000 and bought a smaller house in Missouri for $200,000. Result? He had, after expenses, more than $150,000 to invest, which he put into a mutual bond fund. He earns about $6,000 a year from his investment—additional income that he spends on travel.

Suppose you have finally paid off the mortgage on your house. It's yours, free and clear. It's worth $500,000. That $500,000 is equity that you have accumulated in your house. If you sell it, you still need somewhere to live. But suppose that you sell your house for $500,000 and downsize. Maybe you don't need a four-bedroom house anymore. Two bedrooms are enough. You buy a smaller house for just $300,000. Maybe, like Larry's friend, you move to a different town where housing prices are lower. In your new town, a $300,000 house is not much smaller than your old $500,000 home. Or perhaps you move into a condominium. It's a lot less space, but you can buy a pretty nice condominium in your town for $300,000. Or you could just pocket the entire $500,000 and rent an apartment.

No matter how you manage it, if you sell for $500,000 and buy a new home for $300,000, you have $200,000 (give or take after expenses) to invest. If it earns 3 or 4 percent in after-tax income each year (although that rate isn't guaranteed), you could have additional income of $6,000 to $8,000 a year for the rest of your life. Your annual property taxes might be lower, too. When Sally traded her big house in suburban Virginia for a little house in rural Virginia, her property taxes went from over $6,000 a year to just about $1,000—a most welcome savings.

Be Aware of Possible Tax Consequences

Next you need to calculate the possible federal tax liability should you sell your house. You are taxed only on the gain in the value of the house. In the language of the Internal Revenue Code, your gain is the difference between your adjusted basis and the sale price. Some states also tax the gain on the sale of a house. Be sure to see if that might apply to you.

Your adjusted basis is the amount you paid for the house plus the cost of any capital improvements such as a new addition, a renovated bathroom, or a new fence. Let's say you purchased your house for $100,000, made no capital improvements, and sold it for $200,000. Your gain is $100,000. If you paid $100,000 for your house and renovated the kitchen at a cost of $15,000, your adjusted basis is $115,000. You can also add any closing costs. For example, if closing costs are $4,000, and you sell your house for $200,000, your basis is $100,000 + $15,000 + $4,000 or $119,000, and your gain is $81,000—that is, $200,000 minus $119,000.

Even if you sell your house and have a gain, it may not be taxed because the gain may be, in IRS language, excluded. Here's what that means.

If, at the time you sell your house, you had used it as your principal residence for two out of the previous five years and if you are married and file a joint return, you can exclude up to $500,000 of gain; a single person can exclude up to $250,000. Any gain beyond those amounts is taxed as capital gains. Details of the tax consequences of selling a house can be found in the Internal Revenue Service Publication 523, "Selling Your Home," at www.irs .gov/pub/irs-pdf/p523.pdf.

As you can see, if you sell your house, in most cases you won't owe any federal income tax on the sale. You can keep the profit, invest it, and use it to supplement your income.

It Costs Money to Sell a House

In addition to taxation on capital gains, you'll also want to factor in costs associated with selling a house.

You likely will need to make some repairs and cosmetic upgrades. When Larry and his wife sold their house, they had several small projects they had let slide: fixing a broken window in a garage door, painting the dining room, and replacing some roof tiles. Not a lot of money, but those repairs and modest upgrades added up.

Next, unless you sell your house yourself, you will have to pay the real estate agents' commissions, typically 5 to 6 percent of the sale price, split between the listing agent and buyer's agent.

You may also have closing costs that run from 1 to 3 percent of the sales price to pay for attorney's fees, title transfer costs, surveys, and other expenses. A home inspection may reveal repairs that need to be made. Larry's friend Janet sold her house contingent on a home inspection. Unfortunately, the inspection turned up a problem with the home sewage line. That cost her almost $1,800 to fix.

Finally, you will have moving costs. The average moving cost is $2,300 for an in-state move and $4,300 for interstate, according to the American Moving and Storage Association. Larry's move—even only four blocks away, and even after getting rid of books, much of their furniture and clothing, and moving everything but the larger furniture themselves—cost nearly $1,000.

Check How the House Is Titled

Before you call a real estate agent and ask about selling your home, you need to be able to answer one question that the agent is sure to ask: Whose name or names are on the title? You can find that on the deed.

Sole Ownership

You may own the house individually. That's probably the case if you are single or if you bought it before you married and didn't retitle it in the names of you and your spouse. If you are an individual owner, you have complete control of your house. You can live in it (in legalese, occupy it), rent it out, sell it, give it away, or leave it to someone in your will. If you die without a will specifying who inherits the home, state law—called the law of intestacy—will decide who gets the house. Intestacy laws have a priority list of those the legislature presumed you'd want your property to go to, such as your spouse or children. Tip: If you own a house, make a will! That way you, not the state, decide who inherits your house when you die.

Joint Ownership

If you were married at the time you bought the house, the house is likely titled in the names of both spouses. Joint owners, however, do not have to be spouses. You can jointly own a house with anyone—a sibling, a child, a friend, or an unmarried partner. Depending on the state where the house is located, the deed may say that the house is owned as either "joint tenants with right of survivorship" or "tenants by the entirety." There are subtle differences in the rights of a spouse between these forms of joint ownership. Regardless of which form of joint ownership is on the deed, both spouses must agree to sell, mortgage, or rent it. Both forms of ownership protect the other owner. When one owner dies, the survivor automatically becomes the sole owner of the house.

Tenants in Common Ownership

Some houses have multiple owners who are listed on the deed as tenants in common. This is often the case if the owners are not spouses, such as siblings or a parent and a child.

The main difference between joint ownership and tenants in common ownership is what happens when one of the owners dies. Unlike joint ownership, where the surviving owner automatically becomes the sole owner of the house, with tenants in common, when one owner dies, his or her share of ownership goes to whomever he or she gave it to in the will. If the deceased owner did not leave a will, the ownership share goes to whomever the state law of intestacy provides.

Unlike a joint tenant with the right of survivorship, tenants in common can sell their ownership interest to whomever they please. In reality, not many folks want to buy a common tenant's ownership. Imagine, for example, that siblings Ann and Bob inherited a family summer home as tenants in common. If Ann decides she can't afford the expenses and wants to sell, a stranger is unlikely to want to buy her share in the house because Bob has an equal right to occupy the house. Ann is more likely to sell her interest in the house to Bob or perhaps give her interest to her daughter, Deidre.

If you own a house with one or more tenants in common, you should keep in mind that the other owners can sell, give away, or leave by will their interest in the house at any point. Maybe Bob was fine owning a summer home with sister Ann, but he's not as happy owning it with his niece, Deidre. His only alternative is to buy her out or get her to buy his share. If she won't sell her interest to him and won't agree to jointly sell the house or if they agree to sell but can't agree on a fair price, he can go to court and force a sale by what is called partition action. A court can order the property to be put on the market and sold to the highest bidder. If Deidre does not want to lose the property, she can submit a bid and buy the property. Usually, merely threatening a partition action is enough to cause a co-owner to offer a fair price and buy out the other owner or agree to jointly sell the property.

Community Property

In the nine states that recognize community property (Arizona, California, Idaho, Louisiana, Nevada, New Mexico, Texas, Washington, and Wisconsin), how the house is titled does not determine who owns the house. Instead, under state law, spouses have rights in the house. The right depends upon specific state law, but basically each spouse has an equal interest in the house if it was purchased after the couple married. At the death of one spouse, his or her half of the house goes to the surviving spouse. A house that was owned by one spouse before the marriage or was inherited during the marriage is considered separate property. The other spouse has no legal ownership unless the couple agrees to a different ownership arrangement. If you live in a community property state and are unsure about who owns what, you should consult a lawyer.

Think Carefully before Putting a Child's Name on Your Deed

Some co-ownerships of houses result from a parent adding a child's name to the deed. Parents do this for a variety of reasons. Often the child is named as a joint tenant with the right of survivorship. This means that if the child survives the parents, the child will become the sole owner of the house. Of course, the parents could leave the house to the child by each writing a will that gives the house to the child. But that means that after the death of the first spouse, the surviving spouse could write a new will that does not leave the house to the child. For example, a surviving spouse who remarries might leave the house to the new spouse rather than to the child of the first marriage. To make sure that cannot happen, the couple can add the child to the deed as joint owner with right of survivorship.

We've also heard of a parent who adds a child to the deed as a joint tenant with right of survivorship to reward or pay the child for help as a caregiver. Once the child's name is on the deed, the child is assured of inheriting the house as payment or in recognition of how the child helped the parent. Sometimes, the parent puts the child's name on the deed to encourage the child to help. Of course, putting a child's name on the deed is a gift. Even if the child fails to help the parent, the child will inherit the house.

Based on our personal and professional experience, we encourage you to carefully consider the pros and cons before putting your child's name on a deed and consult with an elder law attorney. Once done, it can't be undone unless the child agrees to let his or her name be taken off the deed. Here are some factors to consider:

- *Consider all your children.* If you have more than one child, be sure to explain to the other children why you are doing it. If you don't explain why while you are alive, at your death the other children may protest and try to get a court to revoke the joint ownership by claiming it was the result of fraud or undue influence and not a valid gift.

- *Consider the implications for your financial security.* Putting a child's name on a deed can have an unexpected consequence because that action is legally a gift to the child. The value of the gift is equal to the child's ownership interest in the house. If the child and one parent are co-owners, the parent has given half the value of the house to the child. If, later, the parent applies for certain governmental bene-fits, that gift may disqualify, or disqualify for a time, the parent for those benefits. This is a particularly important consideration if the parent later needs to apply for Medicaid to help pay for the cost of a nursing home or other long-term care. The gift of co-ownership in the house to the child may for a time disqualify the parent for Medicaid benefits. (We explain Medicaid eligibility later in this chapter.) A gift may also affect eligibility for VA benefits.

- *Consider the tax consequences for your child.* While it may at first sound attrac-tive to your child that he or she is getting the house now rather than having to wait to inherit it after you die, the different tax consequences between getting it now and waiting until later may make the idea less inviting. Let's say you purchased the home for $250,000 and at the time of your death it's worth $500,000. If you leave your child the house by will, the child would have a basis equal to the value of the house when you died, $500,000. Your child could then sell the house for $500,000 and have no gain and no capital gains tax because the basis was equal to the sale price. When you make a gift of your home by adding your child as a joint owner, however, it's trickier—and potentially more costly. Here's how calculating your child's basis works: You originally purchased your home for $250,000. It has increased in value to $500,000 at the time you make the gift. You have made a gift of $250,000, half of the current value of the house. Your tax basis in the house was the purchase price of $250,000. After the gift, each of you has a basis of $125,000, or half of your basis before you added your child as a joint owner. At your date of death, the house is worth $500,000. Your child, as a joint owner by right of survivorship, inherits the other half of the house and your basis, which is stepped up to the value of your interest in the house when you died. Because the house was worth $500,000, your basis at death was one-half of $250,000. This makes your child's basis $125,000 from the gift plus your $250,000 or $375,000. Your child does not live in the house and decides to sell it for $500,000, resulting in a capital gain of $125,000. The gain is subject to the capital gains tax, which can be as high as 20 percent. The homeowner exclusion does not apply because your child did not live in the house.

Live with a Life Estate

Another way to create income is by selling your home but continuing to live in it. You do that by selling to someone—usually a child—the right to own your home after you and your spouse have both died. Until then, you can continue to live in it. This is called creating a life estate and a remainder interest. These two terms, *life estate* and *remainder*, describe how the ownership of a house is divided in two. A life estate gives the owner of the life estate the right to live in the house until death or, in the case of a couple, until the death of both spouses. The owner of the life estate is called the life tenant. The remainder interest is the right to own the house after the death of the owner of the life estate. In legalese, the person who owns the remainder is called the remainder person.

Let's say you're age 80, you're a widow, and you own a house worth $300,000 but need more money to live on. You can sell a remainder interest in your house to a child for, say, $150,000. You now have $150,000 to cover your expenses and can live in the house until you die. At that point your child takes possession and ownership of the house. Your child gets a house worth $300,000 while helping you financially.

Life estates are governed by state law, but almost all states require the life estate holder, not the remainder person, to pay property taxes, insurance, and ordinary repairs and maintenance of the property. The remainder person has the right to sell the remainder, but there are very few potential buyers of remainders because of the uncertainty as to when they could take possession. If, however, the life tenant and the remainder person agree, together they can combine their ownerships and sell the house outright. They need to agree on how to split the sale proceeds before they sell the house.

An estate for years is a possible alternative to the life estate. Your child can buy the right to own and occupy the house after a set number of years, for example ten years. You have the right to live in the house for ten years. Your child gets it at the end of the ten years or sooner, if you die before then. During those years, you still have the right to sell or give away your right of occupancy to anyone you choose. Typically, you'd leave that occupancy right to the child who has the right of ownership after ten years have passed.

Why would a family do this? Imagine again that you're 80 and plan to leave your house to your son. Because you need more money to live on, you create an estate of years for ten years by selling the right to own and occupy the house to your son. He buys the future right to own the house as a way of financially helping you now. He protects his investment by knowing that in at least ten years (sooner if you die or move to assisted living or other housing with more support), he will own the house outright. If you want to stay in the house after the ten years have passed, he could let you live there for free or rent it to you. If he needs his money back, however, he has the right to sell the house and force you to move.

Sale and Leaseback

In the previous section, we discussed creating a life estate in your house and selling the remainder interest, keeping the right to occupy the house until you die. With a sale and leaseback, you can sell the house to anyone, including a stranger, and lease back the right to live in the house for as long as you like.

Here's how it works. In a sale and a leaseback, the owner sells the house and at the same time enters into a lease with the buyer that guarantees the seller the right to stay in the house until the seller decides to move out or dies. The seller, the original homeowner, pays rent to the buyer, paying the rent out of some of the sale proceeds. For example, Gary, age 77, sells his house to his daughter, Gretchen, with a lease that guarantees him the right to rent and live in the house. Gretchen pays Gary $250,000 for the house. If he invested the full $250,000, Gary might get an after-tax return of 3 percent, earning $8,200 a year. Say he lives in the house and pays Gretchen rent of $350 a month or about $4,200 a year. This would give Gary an additional $4,000 a year in income (minus property taxes and other expenses of the house). Ten years later, Gary moves into assisted living. Gretchen sells the house for $260,000. That is not much gain on her investment, but then Gretchen bought her father's house to help him have additional income, not to make money for herself. Meanwhile, Gary still has what is left of $250,000 to help pay the cost of assisted living, which costs about $50,000 a year. With $250,000, Gary could afford up to five years in assisted living.

If Gretchen doesn't have enough savings to purchase the house, Gary could sell it to her and take back a mortgage. Gretchen would make monthly payments on the mortgage and, in return, receive monthly rent checks from Gary. Because the purpose of a sale and leaseback is to create additional money for the seller, the rent should be less than the mortgage payment. For example, Gary would pay $350 a month in rent while Gretchen might pay $850 a month as mortgage payments. This would net Gary an additional income of $500 a month or $6,000 a year. If Gary needs to move out of the house, Gretchen could sell the house to pay off the remaining mortgage. If the sale proceeds were not enough to pay off the remaining debt, Gary could cancel the unpaid portion of the mortgage debt. If Gary dies while still living in the house, his will could provide that the mortgage debt is canceled. This would let Gretchen sell the house and keep all the proceeds.

If you are thinking of using a sale and leaseback, you should contact a lawyer. Your lawyer will prepare a lease that sets out the monthly rent and other terms and gives the seller the right to terminate the lease. The lawyer will also advise on any potential tax consequences of the transaction and the necessary interest rate. For example, the IRS insists that you charge a minimum rate on intra-family loans.

The lease should specify who pays for what, including the utilities, property taxes, repairs and maintenance, utilities, and any capital costs such as new carpets, roof, or furnace. Usually the person who lives in the house pays most if not all these expenses. To create more income, however, the buyer could agree to pay the property taxes. If over time the lease does not meet the needs and financial abilities of the parties, they can negotiate new terms and sign a new lease.

As explained earlier, the sale of the house will likely not result in additional federal income taxes for the seller because of the $250,000 or $500,000 exclusion. For example, if Gary bought the house in 1990 for $100,000 and sells it to Gretchen for $250,000, he has $150,000 of gain. As a single taxpayer he would only be taxed on any gains over $250,000.

The lease, however, has federal income tax implications for Gretchen. The rent that Gary pays is income for Gretchen. However, she may have off-setting deductions for any expenses she pays, such as property taxes. An even larger deduction may result from taking an annual deduction for depreciation for what the child paid for the house. The annual depreciation is equal to the purchase price of the house divided by 27.5. The value of the land cannot be depreciated. For example, if Gretchen paid $250,000 for the house, and the land is worth $50,000, she can take annual depreciation on the $200,000 value of the house, which would be $7,273. If the rent was $500 a month, or $6,000 a year, the depreciation deduction of $7,273 would result in her having no additional taxable income. The annual depreciation lowers her basis by the amount of the deduction, in this example by $7,272. After five years, her basis would be reduced by $36,365 down to $213,635. If Gary died and Gretchen then sold the house for $240,000, she would have $26,365 of ordinary income gain on which she would pay federal income tax.

Putting Your House in a Trust

If you talk to an attorney about drafting a will, that attorney may suggest that you think about putting your house into a trust. Why? You could have a variety of reasons for creating a trust, but some people put their home into a trust as a way to arrange their finances in the event they need Medicaid to help pay the cost of nursing home care. With your home in a trust, your spouse wouldn't have to sell it to reimburse Medicaid for the cost of your care. Here's how it works.

Let's say a couple puts their house into a trust. They are the trust grantors, so they determine the trustee's powers and how the house is to be managed. Usually they will want to reserve the right to occupy the house for as long as they want to. They do this by naming themselves beneficiaries of the trust. The trust terms may say that it comes to an end when the grantors die. The trust grantors also need to name secondary beneficiaries who will receive the trust property after both spouses have died. Because the grantors are the trust beneficiaries, the IRS considers them to be responsible for income taxes due on any income created by the trust. If the trustee sells the house, the profit on the sale may create income tax liability for the grantors.

Medicaid, known in some states as Medical Assistance and in California as Medi-Cal, is a joint federal and state program that pays for the cost of a nursing home for those who don't have enough money, savings or income, to pay the costs. (See Chapter 13 for more information about Medicaid.) You become eligible for Medicaid assistance only after you have spent almost all your savings and income on the cost of your nursing home care. If you own a house, however, you are given a bit of a break. If a couple owns a house and one spouse enters a nursing home, the other spouse can continue to live in the house for as long as he or she likes. In the long run, however, Medicaid has a right to recover the cost of paying for the care of the spouse in the nursing home. To protect that right, Medicaid puts a lien on the house. Basically, a lien is an IOU that must be paid out of the proceeds of the sale of the house if it is sold or when the spouse who is living in the house dies.

If the house is owned by an irrevocable trust, however, Medicaid cannot put a lien on the house as a way to get paid back. Say the wife is in a nursing home. The husband can continue to live in the house for as long as he likes and never needs to repay Medicaid if the house is sold. When he dies, the estate does not have to repay Medicaid.

An attorney friend of Larry's told him about Marsha and Max, a couple who was in this situation and put their house into a trust, naming themselves as trustees. Max's health was deteriorating, and he feared that someday he would have to move into a nursing home. If Max went into a nursing home, Medicaid would pay $5,000 a month toward Max's nursing home care. Suppose Max lives in the nursing home for ten months and then dies. If the house wasn't in a trust, Medicaid would put a lien on the house for $50,000, the amount it paid for Max's care. Five years after Max dies, Marsha sells the house for $200,000 and moves in with her son. When she sells the house, she must pay Medicaid the $50,000. If Marsha had still been living in the house when she died, her estate would have to pay Medicaid the $50,000. Usually that means the estate would sell the house and use the sale proceeds to pay back Medicaid. With their home in a trust, however, Marsha and Max retained that asset and never have to pay Medicaid back.

Warning: The Five-Year Look Back

There is an important caveat to putting a house in an irrevocable trust. To be eligible for Medicaid, the nursing home resident or his or her spouse cannot have made any major gifts within the five years before applying for Medicaid. If Max moves into a nursing home and applies for Medicaid, he will have to report all such gifts. Under Medicaid rules, gifts do not include typical birthday or holiday gifts. When Marsha and Max put their house in the trust, Medicaid considers that transfer a gift that must be reported. If they made the transfer to the trust within five years of Max's Medicaid application, his eligibility for Medicaid will be delayed. The larger the value of the gift, the longer the delay. Basically, you are not eligible for Medicaid for a period determined by the amount of the gift divided by the monthly cost of a nursing home where you live. If you give away $100,000 and the average monthly cost of a nursing home is $10,000, you are ineligible for ten months. But if the transfer to the trust took place more than five years ago, the transfer does not have to be reported and does not affect Max's eligibility for Medicaid. That's commonly known as the five-year look back.

Of course, when Marsha and Max transferred the house to the trust, they had no idea if or when one of them might inevitably move to a nursing home. If either one does, they must be able to pay for the costs of the nursing home and not apply for Medicaid until five years have passed after they transfer their house to the trust. They and their attorney need to discuss how they might pay for a nursing home during that five-year period. For more information and advice about whether you should put your house in a trust, contact an elder law attorney.

Share or Rent out Your House

Sharing your home or renting out part of it are two ways of using your home to create income. Both ways have advantages and disadvantages.

House Sharing

House sharing is a term used to describe letting another person live in the house with the homeowner. You can invite a sibling, child, grandchild, or other relative or friend to move in. Usually the person does not pay rent. Instead, you agree to divide up some of the costs and responsibilities of the house. Whatever terms you negotiate should be in writing. In Chapter 6 we cover all the ins and outs of living with others.

Before you ask someone to share your house, check the local zoning laws. You may find that even if you live in a house that is zoned for a single family, you may be allowed to share your house with someone other than a family member. The only catch may be that you cannot charge rent. Still, sharing expenses can be very helpful. A housemate who shares expenses can be an excellent way to lower your housing costs. A good roommate can also provide social companionship: someone to share cooking, meals, and conversation. The number of older people living with nonrelatives is small but growing—over the last decade from 1.5 million to 2.6 million, according to Harvard University's Center for Housing Studies. The critical factor in sharing a house with a stranger is the homeowner's trust and comfort level with the stranger.

Some have called this growing trend the "Golden Girls," named after the 1980s sitcom about four older women living as housemates. The *Washington Post* featured the successful home-sharing story of Jane Callahan-Moore, who shares Stefanie Clark's condo in Chicago. Clark had extra space and appreciates having some additional money each month, but primarily she enjoys the companionship. The pair share both space and time. They cook meals together and provide support for each other. Callahan-Moore, who couldn't afford to live on her own in as nice of a neighborhood, finds home sharing with Clark an ideal solution.

Renting out a Room or Part of Your Home

To create more income, some homeowners rent out a spare room or perhaps an attic or a third floor to a relative or stranger. If you are thinking of doing that, your first step is to make sure that the local zoning laws permit you to do so. While the local zoning law may permit the homeowner to share the house and expenses, it may not permit renting part of a house to an outsider.

If it is legal to do so, renting a room or part of the house can be an excellent way to lower your cost of living. If you want to be a landlord, you will need to have your tenant sign a written lease that lays out all the terms. The written lease can be a standard lease that is easily found on the Internet or obtained from a real estate agent. Be sure to include the amount of the rent, when it is due, penalty fees for late payment, whether subletting is permitted, what events or behavior permit you to evict the tenant, specific quiet hours, and acceptable uses of the property, such as not operating a business. The lease should also state whether the tenant has a right to use other parts of the house, such as the laundry or garage. If you are not sure whether to include a clause, the best advice is to include it. Remember, you don't have to enforce a clause even if it is in the lease. But you can't enforce a clause if it is not in the lease.

Make sure you do due diligence for potential tenants. Ask for and check references and require a security deposit. Still, that may not be enough—even if you know the person socially. After all, the tenant will have access to your entire house. The potential dangers are so great that you should pay for a professional background check. Better to spend a few dollars before leasing than lose many dollars from a theft or assault by the tenant. For $20 to $30 you can use an online service that conducts tenant background checks.

One way to find a compatible roommate is to contact a community organization, such as a house of worship, that matches homeowners with a person the organization has vetted and can vouch for. Community organizations that match homeowners and strangers do so to address the shortage of affordable housing. The matching helps both homeowners who need financial help paying for the cost of their homes and someone who needs an affordable place to live. A potential housemate might be a college student looking for a homelike environment rather than a college dorm. A new arrival to a town could be looking for a stable place to live while getting acquainted with the community.

The New York Foundation for Senior Citizens has been running an intergenerational home-matching service since 1981. The community organization typically investigates the home sharer through background and credit checks to ensure the safety of the homeowner. It will try to match the homeowner and a sharer who have compatible interests, attitudes, and education. After the parties agree to share a house, the organization will probably have them sign a written agreement that details financial and other expectations for everyone.

You can look online for organizations that help match homeowners with those who want to house share. Senior Homeshares, www.seniorhomeshares.com, is a nonprofit that operates an online house-sharing site that matches older homeowners with older individuals seeking to house share. In the greater Boston area, Nesterly, www.nesterly.io, has a home-sharing platform that pairs households with empty rooms with students and younger people looking for affordable places to stay. Two other websites that may help you with house sharing are www.silvernest.com and www.sharinghousing.com.

Whether you're considering sharing with a relative, friend, or stranger, adequate insurance is a must. You should contact the insurance company that issued your homeowners' policy and explain that you are considering sharing or renting space in your home and that you want to make sure you have coverage for anything the home sharer or tenant might do that causes injury to the house, the homeowner, or third parties, such as a delivery person. You may be required to take out a new policy designed for landlords. Because the policy should go into effect the first day of the lease, be sure to nail down the insurance before the lease is signed.

Temporary Rentals

How about renting out a room or your entire house to tourists or others who need temporary housing? The most popular way of becoming a short-term rental host is through websites such as Airbnb, HomeAway, and VRBO. These online services connect your space with visitors wanting an alternative to a hotel, taking a percentage of the host's rent as their commission or charging a listing fee.

To use one of these online sites, you first create an account. In your listing you include an accurate description of the space and its amenities and post attractive photos. You decide what you want to charge for rent, although some sites that rent entire houses may determine what is an appropriate amount. To figure out how much to charge, be familiar with what other similar properties in your vicinity are charging. You can impose a minimum night stay requirement, but most hosts do not.

As a short-term rental host, you must maintain an accurate calendar of when your space is available for future rentals. Your guests will be asked to rate you as a host and, in turn, you will be expected to rate your guests. You will also incur expenses: cleaning after every guest; changing linens; and replenishing supplies, such as paper products, coffee, shampoo, soap, and laundry detergent—all the amenities a guest would expect at a hotel.

Be sure that local laws permit you to engage in short-term rentals. You need to know your local zoning restrictions. Many municipalities are imposing strict requirements on short-term rentals out of concern for changes in neighborhood characteristics, a squeeze on rental housing for locals, and the loss of hotel or occupancy taxes. Depending on where you live, you may be required to have a business license or permit, to be on the premises if you are renting for less than 30 days, and to pay city and state hotel or transient occupancy taxes.

Again, you will want to inform your homeowners' insurance provider that you are renting out a room or your house. What if your home gets trashed by unruly guests? What if a guest gets injured while on your property? What if a guest damages a neighbor's property by starting a fire that spreads next door? Your typical homeowners' insurance may not cover liability for commercial purposes. Check to make sure that your personal property and belongings that may be stolen or damaged by a paying guest are covered. If you don't tell your insurer that you are hosting, you may have your policy canceled or the claim denied. You probably should have business or commercial insurance on top of your homeowners' policy even if you rent out your place only once or twice a year. Some insurers now have special policies for homestay, bed and breakfast, home-sharing, or rental dwellings. Be straightforward with your insurance agent to get the coverage you need and be sure you understand all exclusions.

If you live in a gated or planned community, be sure that your homeowners' association rules permit you to host paying guests. If you live in a condominium or co-op, check to see if you are allowed to rent or sublet your unit. Even if you are not permitted to sublet your unit, you can ask to be allowed to operate as a short-term host.

You may have to pay local and state occupancy taxes on a percentage of the rent. Don't overlook federal and state income taxes. You must report the rental income on your federal income tax return if you rent your space for more than 14 days. You may also need to pay a state income tax on your rental income. If you report the income on your federal income tax return, you should also be eligible to deduct your rental expenses such as cleaning and linen costs. You may also be able to depreciate part of the value of your house. Federal income taxes and allowable deductions can be confusing. Check with an accountant as to federal and state income tax consequences of collecting income as a host.

Before you leap into becoming a host, research the whys and hows of being a short-term host. You'll find dozens of books as well as online advice that discuss hosting. Take both the positive and negative reviews with a grain of salt. If it seems that hosting might work for you, give it a try. If you don't like it, you can always quit doing it.

Note that if you have a reverse mortgage—see the next section—transient rentals are not permitted.

Consider a Reverse Mortgage under Special Circumstances

Let's say you can no longer easily afford your house, but you don't want to sell. You might want to consider a reverse mortgage, which is a way of getting additional money. With a reverse mortgage you borrow against the home's value and can use the money and the home until you and, if you're married, your spouse sell the house, move out permanently, or die. After death, your estate pays back the mortgage plus interest accrued. This can be accomplished by selling the house if there is any remaining equity or turning the house over to the lender if there is not. As with any mortgage loan, there are costs associated with taking out a reverse mortgage. Be sure you understand all those costs and the amount of interest that you will have to repay. You may decide a reverse mortgage is just too costly.

If you take out a reverse mortgage, you will likely have these costs:

- a loan origination fee of $2,500 to $6,000 depending on the house's value
- closing costs that will include expenses such as an appraisal, survey, pest inspection, flood certification, document preparation, and title insurance
- an initial mortgage insurance premium equal to 2 percent of the loan amount
- annual mortgage insurance premiums of .5 percent of the outstanding balance of the mortgage
- a monthly servicing fee that may be as high as $35 a month

After you have the reverse mortgage, you must reside in the home as your primary residence, pay the annual property taxes, have homeowners' insurance, and maintain and repair the house. If you do not occupy the home as your primary residence or if you can't keep up with those expenses, the reverse mortgage must be paid in full. If you fail to pay, the loan can go into foreclosure. And, of course, every month that passes means you owe more interest and mortgage insurance on the amount of money that you have borrowed.

Is a reverse mortgage right for you? It is a way to increase your monthly cash flow or to help you make a one-time payment of your bills. But be careful. Remember, some day you or your estate will have to pay it back. Suppose with your reverse mortgage you withdraw $200 a month to help cover your bills for ten years. Then your health declines, and you want to move in with your daughter. You sell your house. That means you owe all the money you borrowed, plus the interest and mortgage insurance premiums that have compounded monthly.

Applying for a Reverse Mortgage

The amount that you can borrow as a reverse mortgage is determined by your house's value. Reverse mortgages are obtained from private lenders, such as banks. Almost all reverse mortgages are insured by the Federal Housing Administration (FHA) through the U.S. Department of Housing and Urban Development's (HUD) Home Equity Conversion Mortgage (HECM) program. A HECM is insured by the FHA and is available only through an FHA-approved lender.

To ensure that you will be able to meet your ongoing financial obligations, HECM lenders must first complete a financial assessment. The financial information you provide will determine whether the bank can approve the loan. As a potential borrower, you must show that you will be able to pay the property taxes, homeowners' insurance, and possibly flood insurance during the life of the reverse mortgage. In some cases, the lender may be required to use some of the reverse mortgage proceeds to set up an account that will cover these payments. Before you can apply for an HECM, you must meet with a financial counselor from an independent HUD-approved housing counseling agency, who will explain the obligations, costs, and alternatives to a reverse mortgage.

To be eligible for an HECM, the borrower must be age 62 or older. That means if a couple owns a house, at least one borrower must be age 62 or older (with one exception, discussed on the next page). The house must be their primary residence, which means they reside there for at least six months every year. If they fail to use the home as their primary residence, the full amount that they owe on the reverse mortgage, including interest and mortgage insurance, must be paid back.

Loan Amount

The maximum amount you can borrow depends on several factors:

- the appraised value of your house up to $726,525 (as of 2019), increased annually for inflation
- interest rates
- the principal limit factor (set by HUD)
- the age of the youngest borrower (whether or not he or she is on the loan or under age 62—see "Who Are the Borrowers?" on the next page)

For example, in 2019, if your appraised home value was $726,525, the interest rate was 3.5 percent, and the younger spouse was age 65, the reverse mortgage limit was $379,973; if the younger spouse was age 80, the limit was $445,360.

Although you can take out all the money from the loan in a lump sum, you can also use the loan as a line of credit. This means you take money out only as you need it to pay bills or living expenses. You may also elect the monthly option that pays you a fixed monthly dollar amount for as long as you live in the house. No matter how you arrange the payouts, interest begins to accrue only on the amount paid out, not on the total potential amount of the reverse mortgage. That is one reason it may be better to take out money as you need it, instead of a lump sum.

Who Are the Borrowers?

HECMs are available only to borrowers age 62 and older. If you are married and both spouses are age 62 and older, usually you will put both names on the reverse mortgage. But what if one spouse is younger than age 62? HECM loans are underwritten to the age of the younger spouse, even if he or she is under age 62 and not listed as a borrower. The younger the spouse, the lower the amount the couple can borrow.

HUD rules permit the younger, nonborrowing spouse to remain in the house and not have to immediately pay off the mortgage loan upon the death of the borrower. The following conditions must be met:

- The surviving spouse was married to the borrower at the time the mortgage was taken out, remained married for the rest of the borrower's life, and still lives in the house.
- The marriage is disclosed at the time the mortgage is taken out.
- The nonborrowing spouse is included in the loan documents.
- The loan is in good standing at the time of the borrower's death.

If all these requirements are met, the nonborrowing spouse has 90 days to establish legal ownership after the spouse's death. If that is done, the mortgage is not due until the death of the nonborrowing spouse.

What Is the Interest Rate?

You might think that you don't have to worry about the interest rate because you don't have to make monthly payments. But the interest does have a big impact on how much you can borrow and how far you can stretch your loan amount. The lower the interest rate, the more you can borrow. Because you are not making monthly payments, your loan balance grows each month as the interest, mortgage insurance premium, and servicing fees accrue on top of the interest and fees that were previously charged.

The interest rate on a reverse mortgage is set by each lender, so it pays to do some comparison shopping. As with traditional mortgages, both fixed rate and adjustable rate reverse mortgages are available. A fixed interest rate stays steady over the life of the loan, but it is only available if you take out a lump sum reverse mortgage. An adjustable rate is tied to a market index and can increase or decrease as market interest rates change. It's less predictable than a fixed interest rate, but it offers more flexibility in how you take out money from your loan. In addition to interest, lenders add a margin—or additional percentage amount—to the variable interest rate. The amount of the margin is set at the time the loan is originated and does not vary over the life of the loan.

Paying Back the Reverse Mortgage

The reverse mortgage plus accrued interest and fees must be paid back when one of the following happens:

- The last borrower or eligible nonborrowing spouse dies.
- You stop using the house as a principal residence (usually 12 months after you move into a nursing home or other supported residence).
- You fail to return the annual certificate that the home is your primary residence.
- You sell or transfer ownership of the house.
- You stop paying the property taxes or homeowners' insurance on the house.
- You let the house fall into disrepair.

Borrowing from a Child

An alternative to selling your home or getting a reverse mortgage from a bank is to borrow money from a child with the understanding that the loan doesn't need to be repaid until you die or sell your house. This is sometimes called a private reverse mortgage. Loan terms should be put in writing. To not run afoul of tax complications, the interest rate needs to be at least the rate set by the IRS as the Applicable Interest Rate. Keep in mind, however, that borrowing money from children can put them at financial risk if you become unable to repay the loan. Because of the legal and tax complications, be sure you and your child get expert advice on how to safely make this transaction.

Government Programs That Can Help Lower Your Home Costs

Homeownership means paying property taxes and the cost of utilities. For some, these costs become unaffordable. Fortunately, there are government programs that may help lower or defer those expenses.

Property Tax Relief

Property taxes can be so costly that some homeowners have to cut their spending or consider moving into a less expensive house that has significantly lower property taxes. Recognizing the burden that property taxes can have on homeowners with limited incomes, many states and localities offer property tax relief. These are the most common types:

- tax deferral
- homestead exemptions

- circuit breaker programs
- property tax freezes
- abatement of increase in taxes due to home improvements

Eligibility for these state and local programs varies. Some are based solely on age, with all homeowners past a certain age eligible. Other programs have both a minimum age and an income test to qualify.

If you think you might qualify for property tax relief, investigate whether your state, county, or local taxing entity has such a program and whether you qualify. Do an Internet search for "property tax relief for seniors in _____ (state, county, or locality where the house is located)." Many local and state governments provide detailed information online about available programs. The Lincoln Institute of Land Policy has a database listing many available programs in every state at www.lincolninst.edu/research-data/data-toolkits /significant-features-property-tax/topics/residential-property-tax-relief-programs.

Tax Deferral

As the name suggests, property tax deferrals do not reduce property taxes but only delay when the tax must be paid. Some states pay the property taxes to the local taxing authority, such as a school district. The state then expects repayment from the homeowner at some later date. Most such programs have a minimum age requirement. For example, the state of Washington has a minimum eligibility of age 60. Many states also have a maximum income cap. The deferral may or may not include the annual interest that accumulates over the years that the taxes are deferred. The taxing authority, or the state if it pays the taxes on behalf of the property owner, places a lien, an IOU, on the house in the amount of the unpaid taxes. When the house is sold or the homeowner dies, the taxes must be paid along with any accumulated interest. How much in taxes can be deferred depends on the home's value, either the assessed value for property tax purposes or the actual market value.

Many eligible homeowners do not take advantage of tax deferral programs. Some may wrongly fear that the state will foreclose to collect the lien for the deferred taxes. Others are not comfortable shackling their homes with debt, even if they won't have to repay it until they sell the home or die. They are simply uneasy with burdening the house with a debt that would reduce the value of their estate at death. If the payment of property taxes seriously reduces your quality of life or is forcing you to sell, we recommend that you investigate the option of property tax deferral. Doing so may literally save your house.

Homestead Exemptions

In some states, homestead exemptions are used to reduce the property tax burden for older homeowners. The exemptions provide for a reduction in the assessed value of the home, which reduces the property tax. The exemptions may be a fixed dollar reduction, such as $20,000, or a percentage reduction, usually with a dollar cap on the amount.

States differ on which property tax is reduced. Some states apply the reduction to all property taxes, such as the county, the locality, and the local school district. Other states limit the exemption to a specified tax, such as the local school district property tax.

Eligibility requirements vary from state to state. Some limit the exemption to those of a minimum age, such as 60 or 65. Some states also impose an income limit. In a few states, where there is only an age requirement, the exemption is automatic. Other states require the homeowner to apply for the exemption.

Because the exemption may apply to anyone who meets the state's minimum age requirement without regard to income, if you are age 60 or older, you should investigate to see if you might qualify for a homestead exemption and thereby lower your property taxes.

Circuit Breakers

Some states and a few localities provide property tax relief through state-financed payments to localities or school districts that take the place of the homeowner paying the property tax. The state steps in to pay enough of the taxes to reduce the tax burden on the home-owner to a manageable level. The state payment is called a "circuit breaker" because like an electric circuit breaker, the state payment protects the homeowner against an "overload" of property taxes. Typically, the state pays some portion of the property taxes of homeowners who meet minimum age requirements and whose income is below a designated amount. The lower the income of the homeowner, the greater the share of the taxes paid by the state. Other states merely provide a set amount of tax relief to older homeowners who meet the state income requirements. There is typically no requirement that the homeowner ever repay the property taxes paid by the state.

Almost always, circuit breaker relief is granted only if the homeowner applies for it. If you think you may qualify, go online to your state's home page to see if your state or locality has a circuit breaker plan and whether you qualify.

Property Tax Freezes

Some states bar or limit any increase in property taxes for eligible older homeowners. The tax is frozen as of the year the homeowner becomes eligible for the program. As an alternative, a few states and some localities freeze the assessed value of the home. The property tax may still increase if the taxing entity raises the tax rate, but the homeowner is at least protected against an increase in property taxes because of a rise in the property's market value. A freeze in the assessment value can be very helpful for homeowners who live in an area that is subject to gentrification or rapidly rising home prices.

Abatement of Tax Increase

A major home improvement, such as renovating a kitchen or adding a garage, can result in an increase in the home's value and possibly in its assessed value. That, in turn, increases the property tax. Some local taxing authorities have a law or ordinance that bars certain improvements from causing an increased assessment in the home's value for qualified homeowners. This is commonly referred to as a tax abatement.

The abatement of an assessment increase is usually available to all homeowners, not just older homeowners. Most programs do not have an income requirement. Not all improvements qualify. For example, the addition of an in-ground swimming pool may still result in an increase in assessed value. A few abatement programs may be limited to designated areas, such as a recognized historical district. To qualify, you'll probably have to apply for the abatement.

Help with the Cost of Utilities

If you're having trouble affording the cost of heating and cooling your home, there may be help. The federal government provides funds to states through the Low Income Home Energy Assistance Program (LIHEAP) to help homeowners (and also renters) pay some of their home energy bills. The program may also provide weatherization assistance to fix leaky doors and windows, add insulation, or fix broken furnaces or air conditioners. Crisis grants are available for households in immediate danger of being without heat or cooling.

LIHEAP funds are provided though state-operated energy assistance programs. To find your local LIHEAP office, contact the National Energy Assistance Referral (NEAR) at 1-866-674-6327, TTY 1-866-367-6228, or e-mail energyassistance@ncat.org. You can also use the state map at www.acf.hhs.gov/ocs/liheap-state-and-territory-contact-listing.

Federal regulations allow states to set their own income eligibility requirements within 110 to 150 percent of the federal poverty level. In 2019 the maximum income that a state could allow was $18,735 for a single-person household and $25,635 for a couple. Larger households can have higher incomes. The amounts are adjusted annually to reflect changes in the federal poverty level. You need to check your state's income eligibility requirements. States also have the option of allowing families participating in the Temporary Aid for Needy Families (TANF) and Supplemental Nutrition Assistance Programs (SNAP, commonly known as food stamps) to automatically qualify for the program. In many states, older homeowners receiving Supplemental Security Income (SSI) are eligible for a Special Reduced Residential Service Rate Program, which can provide an additional 20 percent off electric and/or gas bills.

It is important to note that because funding for LIHEAP is limited, qualifying for assistance does not guarantee that you will receive it. If you're eligible and funds are available, LIHEAP provides a cash grant paid directly to the utility company or fuel provider. Cash grants range from $200 to $1,000 based on household size, income, and fuel type.

Application requirements depend upon your state. You commonly need to provide a recent heating bill and the names of all who live in your household along with their dates of birth, Social Security numbers, and proof of income.

In some states, the utility companies have special programs to help with energy costs. The company may have a "round-up" option for customers to add a bit to their regular bills that goes into a fund to assist other customers with high energy bills. United Way charities may also have programs to help those threatened with shutoffs, especially during extreme weather. See all the programs available in your state at liheapch.acf.hhs.gov/snapshots.htm.

The following checklists are in Chapter 4:

- ❏ *My House as an Asset*
- ❏ *Estimate of My Home's Value*
- ❏ *House-Sharing Expense Allocation*
- ❏ *Is a Reverse Mortgage Right for Me?*
- ❏ *Community Resources to Lower Housing Expenses*

My House as an Asset

Home address: _____

Property taxes I pay

    City or municipality: $_____

    School district: $_____

    State: $_____

    Other: $_____

    Total property taxes: $_____

Location of the deed to my home: _____

Name(s) on the deed: _____

My ownership interest in the home

❑ Full ownership

❑ Joint with right of survivorship

❑ Tenant in common

❑ Life estate

❑ Other

If I am a co-owner

What happens to my ownership share if I die? _____

Can I leave my share by a will? _____

Do I have a will that does that? _____

What are the limitations on co-owners selling their shares (such as right of first refusal of the other co-owners)? _____

Do all the co-owners have to agree to another co-owner selling or giving away his or her share? _____

What happens to the shares of the other co-owners if they die? _____

What are the co-owners' occupancy rights? _____

What are the restrictions, if any, on my use of the property? _____

What are the limitations, if any, on who I can leave the property to? _____

Is how I use my home restricted by covenants or easements? _____

Do the local zoning laws permit me to share my house or rent a room? _____

If I want to house share, what rooms of my house am I willing to share? _____

If I want to rent part of my home, which room(s) do I want to rent and will the renter have the use of other rooms, such as the laundry room? _____

If I want to be a short-term rental host, which parts of my house do I want to be available to guests? _____

Estimate of My Home's Value

Date of construction: _____

Date of purchase: _____

Purchase price: _____

Zip code: _____

Square feet: _____

Lot size: _____

Type of house:

   ❑ Single family

   ❑ Duplex

   ❑ Condominium

   ❑ Cooperative

   ❑ Other: _____

\# Rooms: _____

\# Bedrooms: _____

\# Baths: _____

Basement	❑ Yes	❑ No
Finished	❑ Yes	❑ No
Garage	❑ Yes	❑ No
Carport	❑ Yes	❑ No
Off-street parking	❑ Yes	❑ No

Age of heating/air-conditioning systems: _____

Age of roof: _____

Professional landscaping	❑ Yes	❑ No

Major updates or remodeling

  Type: _____

  Date: _____

  Cost: _____

  Type: _____

  Date: _____

  Cost: _____

  Type: _____

  Date: _____

  Cost: _____

Zillow estimate: _____

Redfin estimate: _____

Other online estimate: _____

Real estate agent estimate: _____

Tax-appraised value: _____

Recent sales of similar houses in area:

    Address: _____

    Date of sale: _____

    Days on market: _____

    Sale price: _____

    Address: _____

    Date of sale: _____

    Days on market: _____

    Sale price: _____

    Address: _____

    Date of sale: _____

    Days on market: _____

    Sale price: _____

    Address: _____

    Date of sale: _____

    Days on market: _____

    Sale price: _____

    Address: _____

    Date of sale: _____

    Days on market: _____

    Sale price: _____

    Address: _____

    Date of sale: _____

    Days on market: _____

    Sale price: _____

House-Sharing Expense Allocation

If you're thinking about sharing your house, consider who will pay for what. Make sure you have your agreement in writing.

Item	Percentage paid by house sharer	OR	Dollar amount
Mortgage:	_____		_____
Property taxes:	_____		_____
Homeowners' insurance:	_____		_____
Water/sewage:	_____		_____
Gas/oil:	_____		_____
Electricity:	_____		_____
Cable:	_____		_____
Internet:	_____		_____
Housecleaning service:	_____		_____
Lawn service:	_____		_____
Household products:	_____		_____
Newspaper:	_____		_____
Magazines:	_____		_____
Cleaning supplies:	_____		_____
Groceries:	_____		_____
Other:	_____		_____

Is a Reverse Mortgage Right for Me?

My current monthly income (refer to your calculations in Chapter 2)

Social Security: _____

Pension: _____

1/12 of required minimum distribution from retirement plan: _____

Investments: _____

Wages: _____

Supplemental Security Income (SSI): _____

I receive Medicaid ❑ Yes ❑ No

My cost of living (refer to your calculations in Chapter 2)

Current monthly living expenses: _____

Annual expenses, including property taxes: _____

Other, including one-time expenses: _____

Reason I want to tap into my home's equity through a reverse mortgage

❑ Pay off a mortgage

❑ Pay down debts

❑ Pay medical bills

❑ Pay for home repairs

❑ Pay for in-home support or service

❑ Pay family to provide caregiving help

❑ Pay for monthly living expenses

❑ Have more income for a more comfortable life

❑ Help family member with debts

I plan on living in my house for the next _____ years.

I live in my house _____ months each year.

The people who live in my house and their ages

Age

❑ Myself: _____

❑ My spouse: _____

❑ Child: _____

❑ Grandchild: _____

❑ Sibling: _____

❑ Other relative: _____

❑ Friend: _____

My home is a
- ❑ Single-family dwelling
- ❑ Duplex
- ❑ Manufactured home
- ❑ Condominium

I own my home

Individually   ❑ Yes   ❑ No

Joint with right of survivorship with: _____

As tenant in common with: _____

Life estate with: _____

Appraised value of my home: _____

Date of most recent appraisal: _____

Amount of property taxes: _____

Homeowners' insurance coverage   ❑ Yes   ❑ No

Amount of possible reverse mortgage: _____

Interest rate on reverse mortgage

Fixed rate: _____

Variable rate: _____

Lump sum amount that I need to borrow

Pay off mortgage: _____

Pay off debts: _____

Pay off medical bills: _____

Pay for home repair: _____

Monthly amount I want to borrow to help pay for my living expenses: _____

Number of months I can borrow that amount before reaching the limit of the reverse mortgage: _____

Costs of a reverse mortgage

Loan origination fee: _____

Closing costs: _____

Initial mortgage insurance fee: _____

Monthly mortgage insurance fee: _____

Ongoing costs to maintain residence

Property taxes: _____

Homeowners' insurance: _____

Homeowners' association fee or condo fees if applicable: _____

Repairs and maintenance: _____

Monthly mortgage servicing fee: _____

Community Resources to Lower Housing Expenses

If needed, these community resources may be available to lower your expenses. Check with your local taxing authority about these resources:

- ❑ Tax deferral

Age requirement	❑ Yes	❑ No
Income requirement	❑ Yes	❑ No
I am eligible	❑ Yes	❑ No

  Amount of tax deferred: _____

- ❑ Homestead exemptions

Age requirement	❑ Yes	❑ No
Income requirement	❑ Yes	❑ No
I am eligible	❑ Yes	❑ No

  Amount of reduction in assessed value: _____

- ❑ Circuit breaker programs

Age requirement	❑ Yes	❑ No
Income requirement	❑ Yes	❑ No
I am eligible	❑ Yes	❑ No

  Amount of taxes paid by state: _____

- ❑ Property tax freezes

Age requirement	❑ Yes	❑ No
Income requirement	❑ Yes	❑ No
I am eligible	❑ Yes	❑ No

  Home assessment frozen at: _____

- ❑ Abatement of tax increase due to home improvements

Restriction on type of improvements	❑ Yes	❑ No

  Cost of improvements: _____

Restriction on locality	❑ Yes	❑ No
Age requirement	❑ Yes	❑ No
Income requirement	❑ Yes	❑ No
I am eligible	❑ Yes	❑ No

The energy assistance program in my area is administered by _____.

Check your eligibility for these energy assistance programs:

- ❑ Paying my energy bills
- ❑ Weatherization
- ❑ Energy repairs to furnaces or air conditioners
- ❑ Emergency assistance to stop fuel cut-off
- ❑ Fuel cost reduction for those receiving Supplemental Security Income
- ❑ Volunteer repairs by civic organizations

CHAPTER 5
GETTING HELP AT HOME

You don't have to move just because you need extra help to take care of yourself or your house. You can stay comfortably and safely in your home thanks to the many services that come right to your door. If you realize it is time to cut back on your driving, especially at night, public and private transportation services can help you get to the places you need to go. Pharmacies can drop off your prescription drugs at your house. Restaurant meals—from pizza to five-course dinners—as well as groceries and easy-to-prepare meal kits can be delivered to your door. If you're homebound, just about every community in the country has a Meals on Wheels program, where volunteers deliver prepared meals to your house.

Similarly, if you need help with your personal care such as getting dressed, taking a shower, or remembering to take your pills, someone can come to your home. You can hire someone on your own, go through a home health care agency, or pay family members to provide care. Sally tried them all when she needed extra help to care for Art when she went out of town. Here she shares with you the benefits and complications of each.

This chapter sets out what's available, how to find it, and any legal documents you might need—we are both, after all, attorneys. The assistance you can get depends on the resources in your community. One of the best places to find out what is available is your local area agency on aging (AAA). Find your local AAA by going to the National Association of Area Agencies on Aging at www.n4a.org. Another great tool is the Benefits CheckUp (www.benefitscheckup.org), a database of 2,500 benefit programs available nationwide, hosted by the National Council on Aging. Some programs have age or income restrictions, but you may be pleasantly surprised about what services you can get right at home.

Transportation

Getting to where you want to go can be a big hassle—with or without a car. If you cut back on driving, or stop driving altogether, reliable transportation is essential for doctors' appointments, shopping, visiting friends and family, and being independent. But having to arrange rides with neighbors, friends, and family can lead to feelings of frustration. And public transportation may not be convenient. Fortunately, lots of towns are working on improving transportation services for all ages. Some services are free; some are not. But if you sell your own car, you're saving on maintenance and insurance. You can use those savings to pay others to get you from here to there.

Transportation around Town

Your town may still have traditional taxis, which is one option. A cab company in Sally's area sells coupon books for discounts, which she purchases in advance.

Ridesharing programs such as Uber and Lyft are available in more and more areas. If you haven't used these before, here's how they work: You set up an account using your computer or smartphone, supplying a credit card number so you never have to fuss with cash—even for tips. Everything's billed to your credit card. You download the app to your smartphone ahead of time. When you want to go somewhere, you hail a ride by opening the app and typing in the address of your destination. The app, which knows where you are, connects with a nearby driver and provides the rate and wait time. You then can watch a map on your phone to see the driver approaching and follow the route the driver takes until the ride is over. When Sally returns to the Washington, D.C., area for a medical appointment, she often uses her Uber app to get from the train station to the doctor's office. She enjoys never having to worry about carrying cash. Larry likes to use Lyft at the airport when he and his wife return from a trip so they don't have to lug their bags back to their car that is parked in some distant airport parking lot.

A company called GoGoGrandparent has come up with an alternative for those who want to use ridesharing services but don't have smartphones or aren't comfortable using apps. Once you sign up and put your credit card on file, you call GoGoGrandparent's phone number to request a ride. For a small surcharge, it will find an available Uber or Lyft driver for you and accommodate any special needs you might have. GoGoGrandparent will call you back as the driver is arriving and monitor your trip to make sure you safely get to where you're going. If you want, it will also send a confirmation e-mail to your family. You can even schedule trips in advance.

In addition to taxis and ridesharing services, you may find publicly operated or subsidized ride services in your area. Explore these options with your local AAA. The list might include rides offered by volunteers arranged by a nonprofit organization. In some communities, ride services are free or subsidized by a supporting organization. Typically, these rides need to be scheduled in advance. Some communities have free mini-buses or vans that circulate through town on fixed days, times, and routes. They don't offer door-to-door services, but if you are near a route, it may be just what you need to get to the library, medical office, or coffee shop. Also check with your faith community for programs that use volunteers to help you get where you need to go.

Once you find potential publicly operated or subsidized transportation options, you'll want to find out how they work. Here's what you need to know:

- the hours they are available
- how far in advance you need to schedule your ride
- whether you can request a ride ahead of time
- how to order the ride—by calling or through a website or phone app

- the level of assistance provided—for example, if you need help getting in and out of a car or even from inside your home, or you use a walker
- whether accommodations for wheelchairs, if you use one, are available
- how you pay for the ride

Another solution is to hire someone, perhaps a relative, to drive you, whether with your or his or her car. Check with your auto insurance company to see whether your insurance will cover someone you hire driving your car.

Transportation to Medical Appointments

If you need to get to a medical appointment, find out about your local non-emergency medical transportation (NEMT), sometimes called paratransit. These services can drive you to and from your doctor or other medical provider. Even if you generally drive, you might have had surgery but can't drive until you are cleared by the surgeon. Perhaps you're on pain medication that makes driving illegal and unsafe or have a cast on your leg that prevents you from safely pressing the gas and brake.

Many areas have transportation brokers who use specialized software that locates available and qualified non-emergency transport providers and schedules the appropriate trips. Others may be coordinated through your local hospital. NEMTs use a variety of vehicles, including vans and wheelchair-accessible vehicles that can accommodate mobility needs. Some services will wait for you until you need a ride home. In Sally's area, NEMTs don't wait; they charge a separate fee to get you back home.

While the law requires private health care insurers to cover emergency transportation, most insurers won't reimburse you for non-emergency transportation. Fortunately, in many areas, state and local programs, departments of aging, and hospital systems help fund NEMT transportation. These funders understand that it's less expensive to provide the necessary transportation to keep people healthy than to treat them later after their medical issues have worsened.

Two new companies, Circulation and Roundtrip, coordinate with some health care providers and hospitals to arrange for ridesharing programs to transport you. If you are not in good health and are concerned that you don't have a way to get to your doctor's appointment, you can arrange with your care managers and health care providers, who in turn can arrange the ride. The health care providers who use these programs can follow your progress to make sure you get to your appointment on time and return home safely. Some may even pay for the ride or charge a discounted price.

States are required to make sure there are qualified NEMTs to transport people on Medicaid, but not everyone has Medicaid coverage. Medicare, on the other hand, does not pay for transportation for routine medical care unless you have a medical diagnosis and other forms of transportation will endanger your health. Some Medicare Supplement plans, however, include NEMT as an extra benefit.

Transportation costs for medical appointments may be deductible as a medical expense; check with your tax advisor.

Food Delivery

It's no longer just pizza! Many restaurants deliver to your door, everything from a deli sandwich to a fully prepared gourmet meal. Your meal might be delivered in person or even by a robot. Food delivery robots—knee-high remote-controlled coolers on wheels—have been seen on the streets of Washington, D.C. According to one source, neighboring George Mason University, in the Virginia suburbs, was the first university to include in the student meal plan robot-delivered food to any place on campus. More conventional food delivery services include BeyondMenu, DoorDash, Grubhub, UberEats, and, for those in New York City, Seamless. These cell phone apps let you select your meal from the menus of local restaurants and have it delivered to your door.

But it's no longer just meals that can be delivered. Major supermarket chains now offer online shopping where you place your order and have it delivered to you or you can pick up your already-bagged groceries at the store. Before choosing a grocery delivery service, check out how it works and the cost on the store's website. It might be free if you order more than $35 or $60 worth of items, or it might be free the first time you use it (with a minimum order). Lesser amounts could run $5 or $10 per delivery. Some chains offer a membership or monthly fee that reduces the cost per delivery. Generally, the more you order, the lower the delivery cost. Having just a gallon of milk and a box of cereal delivered is probably not cost efficient. You'll also want to figure out if the prices online are the same as those in the store and if the online system honors manufactures' coupons and in-store sales. *Consumer Reports* has evaluated some supermarket delivery services, and The Penny Hoarder (www.thepennyhoarder.com/food/best-grocery-delivery-services) has helpful price comparisons of some major grocery delivery services.

Another option is having meal kits delivered to your door. Everyone from millennials to Baby Boomers is finding the delivery of easy-to-prepare, nutritious meals a benefit that saves time, hassle, and stress. Industry analysts say that the meal-kit business is expected to grow to $10 billion by 2020.

Dozens of companies offer these packages, with all the ingredients along with a recipe on how to cook your own meal. Just follow the directions, and soon your dinner is ready. Blue Apron was one of the first companies to offer meal kits you order online. Now Amazon and Walmart have joined in with Dinnerly, Every Plate, Freshly, Green Chef, HelloFresh, Home Chef, Maratha & Marley Spoon, Peach Dish, Plated, Sun Basket, Terra's Kitchen, veggie-oriented Purple Carrot, and many others to simplify meal preparation.

The convenience of meal kits comes at a cost, although competition among the companies is driving prices down. Many of the services cost about $10 a plate—on average about half of a restaurant meal and twice as much as purchasing your own ingredients and preparing your food.

If you're confined to your home, you have another option: Meals on Wheels, the meal delivery program. Volunteers in your local community deliver freshly prepared meals every weekday. Across the county, Meals on Wheels programs provide 225 million meals to 2.4 million people every day. The menu can be tailored to your dietary needs and preferences. If you live outside of the hot-meal delivery route, frozen meals may be available. Some communities make microwave ovens available if the program participant doesn't own one. An added bonus of Meals on Wheels is having someone check in on how you are doing each day.

The specifics of how the service works, who is eligible, and the cost depend on the local program in your area. In Sally's community, you need to be age 60 or older, not able to get to regular social activities, and unable to cook your own meals or not have someone else available to help you with meal preparation. There is no cost for the food, but donations are welcome.

Where Larry lives, there is no age limit. You just need to be either homebound or unable to regularly prepare nutritious meals. Those who are eligible receive one hot lunch and one cold dinner meal Monday through Friday. The cost of the meals is determined by what the recipient can afford. Some pay nothing.

To find out about the program in your area, go to www.mealsonwheelsamerica.org.

Hiring In-Home Assistance

At some point, you may find it necessary to hire someone to help provide care in your home. Your first step is to be clear about the care you need. Are you looking for someone to provide companionship and make sure you are safe? Do you need someone to help you get out of bed in the morning, take a shower, and dress, fasten buttons, zip zippers, and put dirty underwear and socks in the hamper? Do you need someone to shop for groceries and fix breakfast and lunch? Do you want someone to do light housekeeping, do laundry, take out the trash, and vacuum? Remind you to take your medications as prescribed? Check your blood pressure? Assist you with a catheter or wound care?

Once you've identified the services you need, you have options for finding in-home care. You can go through an agency that supervises a pool of aides who are employees of the agency. Or you can hire someone on your own through a registry or through your own networking. Another option is to pay a family member to take care of you. Each option has its pros and cons.

Hiring through an Agency

Hiring through a home care agency may be the easiest and safest choice. Agencies generally screen skills, check credentials and references, withhold Social Security and taxes, and arrange for a backup if the scheduled aide can't show up. But they are likely to charge a higher hourly rate (and pay the aide less) to cover the supervisory and administrative work they do.

Before selecting an agency, you'll want to make sure it has the proper licensing to deliver the level of care needed. For example, some home health care agencies may not be able to provide skilled nursing care or aides who can administer insulin injections. You should make sure the agency has staff that can give the type and hours of care you need or your doctor prescribed. Do you need daytime, nighttime, or weekend hours? Are the physical or speech therapists you need available?

Use Medicare's Home Health Compare tool at www.medicare.gov/homehealthcom pare/search.html to find Medicare-approved home health care agencies near you. You can also check with the local AAA; find your local AAA at eldercare.acl.gov/Public/Index .aspx. AARP's Caregiving Resource Center also maps local home care agencies at www .communityresourcefinder.org.

If you use an agency for hiring home care services, make sure you understand the services that will be delivered as stated in the agency's contract. The agency will assess your needs and match you to one or more of the aides it has available. You should insist that the agency works closely with you to find someone in its pool of aides who has the right skills and proper training. Also insist on the right to reject any aide with whom you are not compatible. The agency should also have backup aides who can substitute in case the regular aide can't make it.

All this and more should be set out in the contract. The agency will most likely have a standard contract that sets out the services it provides. We walk you through the agreement in our checklist for Home Health Care Agency Contracts at the end of this chapter.

Look for clear explanations of how the aides are supervised and how to request a different aide. The contract should include the services to be provided, the specific individual at the agency in charge of supervising care, the aides' schedules and pay rates, and the process for handling grievances and terminating the agreement. Ask questions about any terms you don't understand. Remember, however, that regardless of what the agency tells you, its only obligations are those set out in writing in the contract. To be sure you are getting what you want, have a lawyer review the contract with you.

Some of the costs may be covered by Medicare or Medicaid. If Medicare covers any part of the cost, the agency must be approved by Medicare and the care must be prescribed by an attending physician.

Hiring Directly

Hiring someone directly, rather than through an agency, may be a bit more affordable and the aide gets all the money. On the downside, the burden is on you for screening, doing the paperwork, withholding and paying Social Security and taxes, scheduling, and finding a backup if the worker can't show up. Some areas maintain registries or referral services of aides, private-duty nurses, and therapists who are independent contractors. You still will need to do the legwork to check out those professionals.

If you are hiring directly, check references, do a background check, and verify that the individual has the appropriate licensing. Use the Home Care Contracts checklist in this chapter to draft a written agreement. Be specific about the services the individual will provide, work schedule, pay, and benefits covered. It's best to have a lawyer review the agreement to make sure it's comprehensive and fully protects you.

Veterans Benefits

Sally's husband is a disabled veteran. He wants to stay home as long as possible, so she's been working with the social worker at his local Veterans Affairs (VA) office to explore services available. As you might expect if you've had any experience working with the VA, she's learned there are lots of details and many hoops to jump through. Some services depend on the percentage of service-connected disability while others depend on the extent of the vet's financial needs. Some depend on the availability of contract providers in the area. For example, Sally's husband is eligible for community adult day health care, but there is no contract provider near where they live. Right now, he doesn't need more help, but down the road he may be able to get other VA in-home services such as home health care or homemaker/home health aide services.

With the VA's Home-Based Primary Care program, a health care team supervised by a VA physician brings skilled health care services to veterans in their homes. This program is for vets who have complex health care needs that require more attention than they can get through routine clinic-based care, who live a long way from a VA clinic, or whose caregiver has trouble providing the level of care needed. A nurse practitioner, physician's assistant, or nurse provides the primary care. A social worker will coordinate therapy visits from a physical, occupational, or speech therapist; arrange nutritional counseling from a dietitian; and coordinate help managing medicines.

If you are a veteran getting a VA pension and you need financial assistance to pay someone to help you with basic tasks such as bathing, feeding, dressing, or toileting, you may be eligible for an increased pension through the VA's Aid and Attendance program. Aid and Attendance is available also if you have a disability that makes you bedridden or you have very limited vision. To be eligible, the vet must meet an asset limit as well as an income eligibility cap that is adjusted for unreimbursed medical expenses, such as insurance premiums and the cost of adult day care, assisted living, or nursing home care.

Veterans seeking the larger pension amount will be rated on the need for regular ongoing care based on their inability to dress and undress and keep themselves clean and presentable, their inability to feed themselves or attend to "wants of nature," a need for frequent adjustments of prosthetic or orthopedic appliances, or an incapacity that requires regular assistance to be protected from harm. In 2019 the most a single veteran with no dependents could receive was $23,209 a year. The Senior Veterans Service Alliance has helpful examples of how the Aid and Attendance allowance is calculated at www.veteransaidbenefit.org/eligibility _aid_attendance_pension_benefit.htm. You may also want to consult an attorney who is knowledgeable about VA benefits to help you obtain all the benefits you are entitled to.

Hiring Family Caregivers

If you decide to hire a relative to provide care, you should prepare a family caregiver agreement. For some families, if funds are available, it's important to compensate family members for the significant amount of time, effort, and money they spend providing care— especially if the caregiver has to stop working or reduce hours to provide care.

Sally, a full-time caregiver for her husband, has a family caregiving agreement with her daughter, who frequently steps in as a backup when Sally must be out of town for work. Instead of having to worry about finding either respite care at a community that has an available room or an agency that can provide an aide sporadically, she knows that she can depend on someone her husband knows and who knows his routine and care needs. This arrangement benefits everyone in the family without having to pay for outside care.

Some long-term care insurance policies may pay benefits to compensate family caregivers if there is a formal, reasonable contract. To be sure that the family caregivers will be able to take advantage of the benefit, the agreement should be in writing, set out the specific services the caregiver will provide, pay "reasonable" compensation, and be signed. Medicaid also requires that any agreement to pay a family member be in writing, pay a reasonable fair market value rate, and be for actual services provided. Otherwise, Medicaid will consider the payment as a gift that will delay when you qualify for Medicaid benefits. (You'll find more on long-term care insurance, Medicare, and Medicaid in Chapter 13.)

You'll probably want to involve other family members in any discussions of whether and how to compensate a family member. Consulting with them and having the agreement in writing can help avoid possible resentment or concern that the family caregiver is taking advantage of you or getting a larger share of your estate.

To determine the reasonable rate, as required by long-term care insurance and Medicaid, you'll want to research the going rate a home health care agency charges to provide similar services. The U.S. Administration on Aging has an elder care locator that can lead you to local agencies at https://eldercare.acl.gov. Genworth Financial tracks actual costs for care services across the country at www.genworth.com/corporate/about-genworth/industry-expertise /cost-of-care.html. The family caregiver may be willing to receive less than the average, but the amount paid should be comparable to what you would have to pay a third party. The agreement must be for future services; it can't cover services that have already been provided.

The Family Caregiver Agreement checklist in this chapter identifies some of the terms that should be considered in creating an agreement:

- what services are to be given in as much detail as possible
- when, how, and how much the caregiver will be paid
- what expenses will be reimbursed
- when the payment for care is to begin
- when the agreement will be reviewed and changed if necessary

It's a good idea to review the agreement every six months to make sure everyone is happy with the arrangements. Keep in mind that your circumstances or those of your family caregiver may change, making the agreement unworkable. If you do change the agreement, be sure that the changes are in writing.

There are tax considerations for both you and your paid family caregiver, depending on whether the IRS considers the family caregiver an "employee" or an "independent contractor." The IRS uses several factors to distinguish between employees and independent contractors, such as whether the person who hires them sets hours and responsibilities, determines the particulars of the job, and directs the activities of the care provider. The more specific the control, the more likely the worker is deemed to be an employee.

In contrast, the worker you hire through a third party, such as an employment agency or private-duty service provider, is typically an independent contractor. The tax withholding and reporting requirements are simple for independent contractors. You, as the care recipient, don't need to withhold, report, or pay taxes on wages paid to an independent contractor; those are the responsibilities of the individual or employing agency.

But if your caregiver is an employee, you have significant obligations. As an employer, you must withhold Social Security (FICA); withhold unemployment, state, and federal income taxes; file a W-2; provide a Form 1099; apply for an employer ID; report wages on Schedule H; pay unemployment taxes (FUTA); and pay at least the minimum wage. Whether your family member is an employee or independent contractor, your family caregiver must report all wages as income and pay federal and state income taxes, Social Security and Medicaid taxes, and possibly applicable state and local taxes or a business tax. There are some exclusions for "domestic workers in the private home" of the employer, so check with a tax advisor for details. You may be able to deduct as a medical expense what you pay your family caregiver if your total medical expenses are over 10 percent of your adjusted gross income. You should consult with a tax attorney if you have any questions about whether your caregiver—a family member or not—is an employee or an independent contractor.

You don't need to have a lawyer draft the agreement, but if you are using the family caregiving contract for Medicaid planning purposes or intend to seek long-term care insurance compensation, you should consult with one. Contact your local bar association's lawyer referral service or the National Academy of Elder Law Attorneys (www.naela.org) to locate a lawyer knowledgeable about Medicaid rules in your state. You may also want to involve an outside professional to avoid family friction over how your assets are being used. Having everything set out clearly and accurately as a true contractor or employer-employer relationship can minimize complications with Medicaid eligibility and reduce misunderstandings or disagreements among family members about who has responsibility to provide care and how it is to be compensated.

The following checklists are in Chapter 5:

- ❑ *Assistance I Need at Home*
- ❑ *Transportation Services Available to Me*
- ❑ *Food Delivery*
- ❑ *Home Care Provider Interviews*
- ❑ *Home Care Contracts*
- ❑ *Home Health Care Agency Interviews*
- ❑ *Home Health Care Agency Contracts*
- ❑ *Family Caregiver Agreement*

Assistance I Need at Home

Personal care

- ❑ Carry out the directions of the care plan
- ❑ Implement exercise regime
- ❑ Assist with mobility; safely use a walker, cane, or wheelchair
- ❑ Transfer in and out of bed and chairs
- ❑ Assist with toileting
- ❑ Assist with grooming, hair care, foot care, shaving
- ❑ Assist with dental hygiene
- ❑ Assist with showering/bathing
- ❑ Assist with dressing
- ❑ Shop for clothing, toiletries, or personal care items
- ❑ Other: _____

Household services

- ❑ Laundry
- ❑ Bed changing
- ❑ Housekeeping
- ❑ Other: _____

Social

- ❑ Provide companionship and assist as needed
- ❑ Arrange for social services
- ❑ Plan social engagements and activities
- ❑ Assist with exercise routine
- ❑ Go for a walk or assist with other physical exercise
- ❑ Transport to social events and shopping
- ❑ Other: _____

Nutrition

- ❑ Prepare nutritious meals and snacks
- ❑ Monitor nutritional needs compliance with dietary restrictions
- ❑ Track weight gain/loss
- ❑ Accompany to restaurants
- ❑ Shop for groceries and supplies
- ❑ Other: _____

Health

- ❑ Monitor physical and mental condition
- ❑ Arrange for medical assessment, services, and treatment
- ❑ Ensure medications taken on time with correct dosage
- ❑ Administer medications on time with correct dosage
- ❑ Manage prescription refills
- ❑ Note any drug reactions
- ❑ Schedule medical appointments
- ❑ Transport to medical appointments
- ❑ Administer injections
- ❑ Care for catheter
- ❑ Dress wounds
- ❑ Care for IV
- ❑ Care for ventilator
- ❑ Other: _____

Therapy

- ❑ Physical
- ❑ Speech
- ❑ Occupational
- ❑ Music
- ❑ Recreation

Recordkeeping

- ❑ Daily log of vital signs
- ❑ Daily log of activities
- ❑ Physical condition
- ❑ Behavior changes
- ❑ Patient progress updates
- ❑ Other: _____

Transportation

- ❑ Use client's car
- ❑ Use caregiver's car that is insured and registered
  - • Policy has a liability limit of $_____ for bodily injury.
  - • Policy has a liability limit of $_____ for property damage.
  - • Vehicle license #: _____
- ❑ Transport to medical appointments
- ❑ Transport for errands, shopping, and social engagements
- ❑ Other: _____

Transportation Services Available to Me

	Yes	No
Public bus, train, or subway		
Prepaid card	❏	❏
Discount for seniors	❏	❏
Doors lowered to make getting on and off easier	❏	❏
Wheelchair accessible	❏	❏
Bike rack	❏	❏
Convenient public transport stop	❏	❏
Covered bus stop	❏	❏
Lighted bus stop	❏	❏
Courteous drivers	❏	❏
Useful route	❏	❏
On time	❏	❏
Frequent runs	❏	❏
Schedule posted at bus stop	❏	❏
Posted alerts for delays	❏	❏

Phone number: _____

Website for information: _____

	Yes	No
Paratransit/Non-emergency medical transport (NEMT)		
Medicaid required	❏	❏
Voucher available	❏	❏
To any health care provider	❏	❏
To any hospital	❏	❏
To physical, speech, occupational therapy	❏	❏
I am in the service area	❏	❏
Round trip with waiting	❏	❏
One-way fee	❏	❏
Wheelchair accessible	❏	❏

Phone number to call to request ride: _____

Website for information: _____

Taxi

Name of company: _____

Phone number to call to request ride: _____

Discounts available	❑ Yes	❑ No
Prepaid card available	❑ Yes	❑ No
Wheelchair accessible	❑ Yes	❑ No
Driver will assist getting from house to cab	❑ Yes	❑ No

Name of company: _____

Phone number to call to request ride: _____

Discounts available	❑ Yes	❑ No
Prepaid card available	❑ Yes	❑ No
Wheelchair accessible	❑ Yes	❑ No
Driver will assist getting from house to cab	❑ Yes	❑ No

Ridesharing

Uber/Lyft	❑ Yes	❑ No
GoGoGrandparent	❑ Yes	❑ No
Community transportation services	❑ Yes	❑ No
Faith-based volunteers	❑ Yes	❑ No

Area Agency on Aging phone number for information: _____

Volunteer services	❑ Yes	❑ No

Phone number to call for information or ride: _____

Faith-based transportation	❑ Yes	❑ No

Phone number to call for information or ride: _____

Free or low-cost public circulator	❑ Yes	❑ No

Friends and family I can rely on for rides

Name: _____

Phone number to call: _____

Name: _____

Phone number to call: _____

Name: _____

Phone number to call: _____

Name: _____

Phone number to call: _____

Name: _____

Phone number to call: _____

Food Delivery

Favorite restaurants that deliver

Name: _____

Telephone: _____

Website: _____

Name: _____

Telephone: _____

Website: _____

Name: _____

Telephone: _____

Website: _____

Name: _____

Telephone: _____

Website: _____

Grocery delivery

Store website: _____

Home delivery ❑ Yes ❑ No

At-store pickup ❑ Yes ❑ No

Time between order and deliver: _____

Minimum dollar order: _____

Manufacturer coupons accepted ❑ Yes ❑ No

In-store sale prices available ❑ Yes ❑ No

Fresh produce available ❑ Yes ❑ No

Frozen foods available ❑ Yes ❑ No

Delivery cost: _____

Store website: _____

Home delivery ❑ Yes ❑ No

At-store pickup ❑ Yes ❑ No

Time between order and deliver: _____

Minimum order: _____

Manufacturer coupons accepted ❑ Yes ❑ No

In-store sale prices available ❑ Yes ❑ No

Fresh produce available ❑ Yes ❑ No

Frozen foods available ❑ Yes ❑ No

Delivery cost: _____

Meal kits

Provider website: _____

Fresh	❑ Yes	❑ No
Frozen	❑ Yes	❑ No
Variety of offerings	❑ Yes	❑ No
Foods I like to eat	❑ Yes	❑ No
Balanced nutrition	❑ Yes	❑ No
All ingredients included in kit	❑ Yes	❑ No
Calorie count provided	❑ Yes	❑ No
Tailored to dietary preferences/restrictions (gluten free, vegan/vegetarian, low salt, etc.)	❑ Yes	❑ No

Price range: _____

Minimum order: _____

Shipping costs: _____

Delivery time: _____

Provider website: _____

Fresh	❑ Yes	❑ No
Frozen	❑ Yes	❑ No
Variety of offerings	❑ Yes	❑ No
Foods I like to eat	❑ Yes	❑ No
Balanced nutrition	❑ Yes	❑ No
All ingredients included in kit	❑ Yes	❑ No
Calorie count provided	❑ Yes	❑ No
Tailored to dietary preferences/restrictions (gluten free, vegan/vegetarian, low salt, etc.)	❑ Yes	❑ No

Price range: _____

Minimum order: _____

Shipping costs: _____

Delivery time: _____

Home Care Provider Interviews

The following home care providers have been interviewed:

Provider interviewed: _____

Phone: _____ E-mail: _____

Address: _____

Criminal background check   ❏ Yes   ❏ No

Care license verified   ❏ Yes   ❏ No

Driver's license verified   ❏ Yes   ❏ No

Vehicle insurance verified   ❏ Yes   ❏ No

Qualifications: _____

Skills: _____

Availability: _____

Reference #1: _____

Phone: _____ E-mail: _____

Address: _____

Reference comments: _____

Punctuality: _____

Compatibility: _____

Other notable qualities: _____

Reference #2: _____

Phone: _____ E-mail: _____

Address: _____

Reference comments: _____

Punctuality: _____

Compatibility: _____

Other notable qualities: _____

Reference #3: _____

Phone: _____ E-mail: _____

Address: _____

Reference comments: _____

Punctuality: _____

Compatibility: _____

Other notable qualities: _____

Provider interviewed: _____

Phone: _____ E-mail: _____

Address: _____

Criminal background check   ❏ Yes   ❏ No

Care license verified   ❏ Yes   ❏ No

Driver's license verified   ❏ Yes   ❏ No

Vehicle insurance verified   ❏ Yes   ❏ No

Qualifications: _____

Skills: _____

Availability: _____

Reference #1: _____

Phone: _____ E-mail: _____

Address: _____

Reference comments: _____

Qualifications: _____

Skills: _____

Punctuality: _____

Compatibility: _____

Other notable qualities: _____

Reference #2: _____

Phone: _____ E-mail: _____

Address: _____

Reference comments: _____

Qualifications: _____

Skills: _____

Punctuality: _____

Compatibility: _____

Other notable qualities: _____

Reference #3: _____

Phone: _____ E-mail: _____

Address: _____

Reference comments: _____

Qualifications: _____

Skills: _____

Punctuality: _____

Compatibility: _____

Other notable qualities: _____

Home Care Contracts

The contract has been reviewed by the following lawyer:

Name: _____

Phone: _____ E-mail: _____

Address: _____

Lawyer's comments or suggestions: _____

Contracted services include the following:

Personal service

❑ Assist with bathing

❑ Assist with toileting

❑ Assist with grooming, hair care, foot care, shaving

❑ Other: _____

Personal care

❑ Carry out the directions of the care plan

❑ Implement exercise regime

❑ Assist with mobility and transfers

❑ Other: _____

Medication assistance

❑ Ensure medications taken on time with correct dosage

❑ Administer

❑ Manage refill schedule

❑ Note any drug reactions

❑ Other: _____

Household services

❑ Laundry

❑ Change bed linen

❑ Housekeeping

❑ Other: _____

Nutrition

❑ Feeding

❑ Meal preparation

❑ Grocery shopping

❑ Accompany to restaurants

❑ Other: _____

Recordkeeping

❑ Daily log on vital signs

❑ Physical condition

❑ Behavior changes

❑ Patient progress updates

❑ Other: _____

Transportation

❑ Use client's car

❑ Use caregiver's car that is insured and registered

- Policy has liability limit of $_____ for bodily injury.

- Policy has liability limit of $_____ for property damage.

- Vehicle tag #: _____

❑ Transport to medical appointments

❑ Transport for errands, shopping, and social engagements

❑ Other: _____

Medical care

❑ Injections

❑ Catheter care

❑ Wound dressing

❑ IV care

❑ Ventilator care

❑ Other: _____

Therapy

❑ Physical

❑ Speech

❑ Occupational

❑ Music

❑ Recreation

Care provider will maintain a daily written log of observations and care provided.

Care provider will report _____ (frequency) to _____.

Care provider will report emergencies to _____.

Care provider will work:

❑ Days: _____

❑ Hours: _____

❑ The schedule can be changed if _____.

❑ Backup plan if care provider is sick or otherwise unable to report on time: ___

_____

_____

_____

❑ Care services will begin: _____

❑ Probationary period will end: _____

Care provider will be paid:

❑ $_____ per hour

❑ Mileage when transporting client at $_____ per mile

Client will provide:

❑ Social Security (FICA) withholding

❑ Medicare withholding

❑ Federal tax withholding

❑ State tax withholding

❑ Worker's compensation

❑ Paid vacation

❑ Health insurance

Household expenses will be paid:

❑ Out of household account

❑ Approved credit/debit card

❑ Reimbursed with receipts for approved expenditures

❑ Other: _____

The contract can be terminated:

❑ With _____ days' notice

❑ Other: _____

Home Health Care Agency Interviews

The following home health care agencies have been interviewed:

Agency name: _____

Contact person: _____

Phone: _____E-mail: _____

Address: _____

Referred by: _____

Letters of recommendation: _____

_____

Recommended by (e.g., doctor, hospital discharge planner, social worker):

_____

State license verified	❏ Yes	❏ No
Checked www.medicare.gov/homehealthcompare	❏ Yes	❏ No
Medicare certified	❏ Yes	❏ No
Medicaid certified	❏ Yes	❏ No
Staffing available		
Companion care	❏ Yes	❏ No
Personal care	❏ Yes	❏ No
Skilled care	❏ Yes	❏ No
Physical therapy	❏ Yes	❏ No

Times available

    Daytime: _____

    Nighttime: _____

    Weekends/holidays: _____

    Intermittent respite: _____

Services can begin: _____

Services unable to provide: _____

Schedule of costs: _____

_____

Agency name: _____

_____

Contact person: _____

Phone: _____ E-mail:_____

Address: _____

Referred by: _____

Letters of recommendation: _____

_____

Recommended by (e.g., doctor, hospital discharge planner, social worker):

_____

State license verified: _____

Checked www.medicare.gov/homehealthcompare	❑ Yes	❑ No
Medicare certified	❑ Yes	❑ No
Medicaid certified	❑ Yes	❑ No
Staffing available		
Companion care	❑ Yes	❑ No
Personal care	❑ Yes	❑ No
Skilled care	❑ Yes	❑ No
Physical therapy	❑ Yes	❑ No
Times available		
Daytime	❑ Yes	❑ No
Nighttime	❑ Yes	❑ No
Weekends/holidays	❑ Yes	❑ No
Intermittent respite	❑ Yes	❑ No

Services can begin: _____

Services unable to provide: _____

Schedule of costs: _____

_____

Home Health Care Agency Contracts

The agency contract has been reviewed by the following lawyer:

Name: _____

Phone: _____ E-mail: _____

Address: _____

The agency contract was signed by _____.

The agency contract was signed by _____

on behalf of the care recipient as (guardian, agent with financial powers of attorney)
on _____.

The person responsible for payment: _____

Date the contract begins: _____

Services the agency will provide:

Personal service
- ❏ Assist with bathing
- ❏ Assist with toileting
- ❏ Assist with grooming
- ❏ Other: _____

Personal care
- ❏ Carry out the directions of the care plan
- ❏ Implement exercise regime
- ❏ Assist with mobility and transfers
- ❏ Other: _____

Medication assistance
- ❏ Ensure medications taken on time with correct dosage
- ❏ Manage refill schedule
- ❏ Note any drug reactions
- ❏ Other: _____

Household services
- ❏ Laundry
- ❏ Change bed linens
- ❏ Housekeeping
- ❏ Other: _____

Nutrition

- ❑ Feeding
- ❑ Meal preparation
- ❑ Grocery shopping
- ❑ Accompany to restaurants
- ❑ Other: _____

Recordkeeping

- ❑ Daily log on vital signs
- ❑ Physical condition
- ❑ Behavior changes
- ❑ Patient progress updates
- ❑ Other: _____

Transportation

- ❑ Use client's car
- ❑ Use agency's or worker's car that is insured and registered
  - • Policy has liability limits of $_____ for bodily injury.
  - • Policy has liability limits of $_____ for property damage.
  - • Vehicle tag #: _____
- ❑ Transport to medical appointments
- ❑ Transport on errands and to shopping and social engagements
- ❑ Other: _____

Medical care

- ❑ Injections
- ❑ Catheter care
- ❑ Wound dressing
- ❑ IV care
- ❑ Ventilator care

Agency will conduct functional assessment on: _____

Care provider will report emergencies to: _____

Agency will provide care services as follows:

- ❑ Days: _____
- ❑ Hours: _____
- ❑ The schedule can be changed if: _____
- ❑ Care services will begin: _____
- ❑ Probationary period will end: _____

Agency fees are:

- ❑ $_____ per hour
- ❑ Mileage when transporting client at $_____ per mile

Agency will provide:

- ❑ Social Security (FICA) withholding
- ❑ Federal tax withholding
- ❑ State tax withholding
- ❑ Worker's compensation
- ❑ Unemployment withholding
- ❑ Paid vacation
- ❑ Health insurance
- ❑ Insurance billing
- ❑ Medicare billing
- ❑ Medicaid billing

The contract can be terminated:

- ❑ With _____ days' notice
- ❑ Other: _____

Family Caregiver Agreement

The family caregiver agreement was signed by the caregiver on _____

The family caregiver agreement was signed by the care recipient on _____

The family caregiver agreement was signed by _____

on behalf of the care recipient as (guardian, agent with financial power of attorney)

on _____

The terms of the family caregiver agreement were discussed with other family members on _____

The lawyer assisting in the drafting of the family caregiver agreement is _____

_____

The start date for the agreement is _____

The agreement will be reviewed if there is significant change in the
health of the care recipient or caregiver or the ability of the caregiver
to perform the services.   ❑ Yes   ❑ No

The end date for the agreement is _____

The agreement can be terminated if _____

The family caregiver agreement covers the following services:

Personal service
❑   Assist with bathing
❑   Assist with toileting
❑   Assist with grooming
❑   Other: _____

Personal care
❑   Carry out the directions of the care plan
❑   Implement exercise regime
❑   Assist with mobility and transfers
❑   Other: _____

Medication assistance
❑   Ensure medications taken on time with correct dosage
❑   Manage refill schedule
❑   Note any drug reactions
❑   Other: _____

Household services
❑   Laundry
❑   Change bed linens
❑   Housekeeping
❑   Other: _____

Nutrition

❑ Feeding

❑ Meal preparation

❑ Grocery shopping

❑ Accompany to restaurants

❑ Other: _____

Recordkeeping

❑ Daily log on vital signs

❑ Physical condition

❑ Behavior changes

❑ Progress updates

❑ Coordinate household bills

❑ Other: _____

Transportation

❑ Use client's car

❑ Use caregiver's car that is insured and registered

   • Policy has liability limits of $_____ for bodily injury.

   • Policy has liability limits of $_____ for property damage.

   • Vehicle license #: _____

❑ Transport to medical appointments

❑ Transport on errands and to shopping and social engagements

❑ Other: _____

Medical care

❑ Injections

❑ Catheter care

❑ Wound dressing

❑ IV care

❑ Ventilator care

Coordination

❑ Interact with health care agent, health professionals, long-term care administrators, social service personnel, insurance companies, government workers

❑ Communicate with other family members

❑ Follow the directions of any financial or medical agent

❑ Other: _____

The family caregiver agrees to provide _____ hours of care each week.

The family caregiver's schedule is as follows: _____

_____

_____

_____

The family caregiver is:

❑ An employee

❑ An independent contractor

The care recipient agrees to pay the caregiver as follows:

❑ _____ per hour

❑ Lump sum calculated as follows: _____

_____

The family has discussed the tax and Medicaid implications of a lump sum payment with the following attorney: _____

The median hourly compensation for caregivers in the area is _____

The caregiver will be paid ___ weekly ___ biweekly ___ monthly

The caregiver's mileage will be reimbursed at the rate of $_____

The following out-of-pocket expenses will be reimbursed with receipts:

❑ Cell phone

❑ Restaurant meals with the care recipient

❑ Groceries for care recipient

❑ Personal care items for care recipient

❑ Clothing for care recipient

❑ Other: _____

Payment for services and reimbursement of expenses will be made on behalf of the care recipient by _____

The caregiver agrees to keep a daily log of services provided and receipts for all expenses.   ❑ Yes ❑ No

The care recipient agrees to withhold the following taxes and file all necessary forms or reports:

❑ Social Security (FICA)

❑ Federal unemployment

❑ Federal income

❑ State income

❑ State unemployment

❑ Worker's compensation

The caregiver understands the responsibility to pay federal and state income taxes and the appropriate share of Social Security and Medicare payments. ❏ Yes ❏ No

The care recipient agrees to provide health insurance for the caregiver as follows:

_____

The care recipient agrees to pay the caregiver for _____ days of respite or paid vacation.

Backup plan for when the caregiver is not available: _____

_____

_____

_____

CHAPTER 6

HAPPY TOGETHER: LIVING WITH OTHERS

Whether you're single and want company, have children boomeranging back home, want extra money to cover expenses, or need some extra help, you have many options for living with your family or others.

This chapter covers an option that has been around for centuries: sharing the family home. We explore the nuances of bringing family members or others under one roof. Living together has many rewards as well as emotional entanglements and legal complications to consider to make a home harmonious.

If you don't have enough space to accommodate more people, adding on to your home may be a solution. Innovative modular construction can convert a garage, add on to the home, or build a separate structure in the backyard. An accessory dwelling unit (ADU)—an apartment in the home or garage, or small unit that's located on the same lot as a larger single-family home—offers private space with companionship or caregiving not far away.

In this chapter we also discuss cohousing communities, which bring together folks who may be strangers as a way to age in place with a new, intentional "family." In these communities, residents live independently in their own homes and pitch in to maintain the common areas and help each other with life's challenges. Most cohousing developments strive to be diverse and multigenerational, but some are intended for residents over age 55.

Living with Family

Living with extended family members is becoming more popular, although the idea is as old as human history. Families living in multigenerational households grew from just 12 percent of the U.S. population in 1980 to 20 percent in 2016, according to the Pew Research Center. The draw? Pooling incomes to cover housing costs, enjoying companionship, and caring for the youngest or oldest members of the family.

Adding to the swell of two or more generations living under the same roof are the numbers of young adults who return to their parents' home while they seek employment and get established. For adults ages 18 to 34, living with parents is now a very common arrangement—for the first time in more than 130 years.

Others who are moving in with family are the suddenly single, who because of divorce or death of a spouse seek emotional and financial support. Grandparents or other family members can share childcare and living expenses. And the homeowners who face financial pressure may appreciate the extra income and assistance around the house.

Whatever the mix of generations and the reasons for multigenerational living, more and more families are finding it the right thing to do. For many, it just makes good sense. It can be a wise money-saving decision, particularly with today's high costs for housing, childcare, and elder care. Whether you move in with your relatives, or they move in with you, living together provides a safety network among the generations with benefits going both ways.

Sally, who moved in with her daughter, son-in-law, and two grandchildren for a time, knows that two or three generations living together takes some work, with lots of communication and much respect. She recommends talking in advance about how the details will work. All family members need to be able to express what they want, what they are willing to do, and what they won't do. Flexibility and compromise are part of the mix. Families who live together must balance issues of control and decision making. Is the owner of the home expecting to have more say-so over how the household is going to be run? How is caregiving for an older parent or younger children going to fit into the family routine? Who is going to pay for what?

Making Space

One of the first considerations is how to allocate space among the generations. Everyone in the family is going to need room for independence and privacy, as well as a place to keep personal items. Babies, children, teenagers, young adults, parents, and grandparents all have different needs. Infants need crib space for quiet naps, for instance, while toddlers need room to play. Teenagers want a place to entertain friends and be connected to their electronics. Grandparents may want to be able to get away from the hubbub.

Some families may be able to reconfigure the use of space in their homes. The young adult may be able to take over the basement; the dining room that gets occasional use can be converted into a bedroom or a playroom. If your house is going to become a multigenerational family house, look around. How can you accommodate everyone? Even if you don't have lots of extra space, try to find a place where the generations each have their own area. It might be just a corner in the living room reserved for the grandparent's chair next to a shelf for books and personal things.

Due to the rise in demand, developers are designing homes specifically for multiple families under one roof. Instead of the typical master bedroom and smaller bedrooms tailored for the nuclear family of two parents and minor children, some homes incorporate two master suites on the first floor; separate entrances into wings with common areas in the middle; or a home with a kitchenette, bath, sitting room, and bedroom within a home. For an example of a home within a home, check out the Lennar "NextGen" design at www.aarp.org/livable-com munities/housing/info-2016/a-home-within-a-home.html. Other options include adding on an in-law suite, converting a garage or floor above a garage into an apartment, or constructing an ADU on the property. We have more on ADUs on the next page.

Peace in the Family

The use of the kitchen is often a point of conflict in multigenerational homes, according to one AARP staff member. She confided to Sally how frustrated she was because her mother, who had recently moved in, could not stop telling her how to make the sandwiches she packed for her children's lunches. "It's driving me crazy!" she complained. She realized she needed to set down some ground rules on who cooks what meals—and how sand-wiches are made.

Sharing bathrooms when multiple people are getting ready for school and work can mean long waits and create conflicts. When Sally and Art moved in with their daughter's family, they expanded a half-bath on the first floor to add a walk-in shower. Now, not only did the oldest generation have a fully accessible full bathroom, but also, as it turns out, it came in handy when both grandkids were getting ready for school at the same time. It's also a super place to wash the dogs and muddy boots.

Sally's family found it essential to have some mutually agreed-upon rules about who does the laundry, dishes, housecleaning, cooking, and shopping. They had to work out in advance the roles and responsibilities of each member of the household. Who will take out the trash or go to the public dump? Does each family unit do their own laundry? If so, when? How much TV time at what volume? Hint: Earphones or wireless headsets can be very helpful. When are bedtimes, naptimes, study times, or other quiet times for everyone in the house? How much childcare or elder care is expected? Sally knew that if they didn't resolve these issues, the family harmony could easily turn to family strife.

Be sure you work out how you are going to resolve issues when you disagree. Frequent face-to-face communication is essential. You may want to schedule periodic family meet-ings so little annoyances don't fester. Toys in the hallway to the bathroom, shoes under the table, and lights left on in empty rooms were some of the things Sally worked on in her three-generation home. If the home sharing is intended to be temporary, what is the exit strategy? Sally's foray into home sharing lasted only six months, until she and her husband sold their old house and moved into a new one. You may want to set a deadline for the daughter who has moved in with you to find a job and move out on her own.

The biggest issue to resolve is household finances. Money can cause problems any time two or more people live together. Have clear-cut expectations of who is going to pay for what. You need to agree on how all living expenses are shared. While a formal agreement may not be necessary, getting the details in writing will help avoid problems down the road. Teenage grandsons eat a lot more than Grandpa. Does that need to be factored into the grocery budget? When you go out to eat as a family, does one person always pick up the check? If you have a family plan for your cell phones, work out how you are going to divide the data and who pays for any overage. You may be willing to be the family chauffeur, but should the others help pay for the gas? Without a good budget, you run the risk of someone feeling put upon or being taken advantage of. Look over the Living Together Budget checklist at the end of this chapter and decide which expenses should be shared among household members.

Discuss if one member of the family is going to provide services instead of contributing financially. One way is to calculate, for instance, how much a grandfather's services in providing after-school childcare five days a week saves the family in out-of-pocket expense and use that amount as his contribution toward the week's groceries. A more formal financial arrangement may be appropriate if a family member provides substantial caregiving. There's more about how to create a family caregiving agreement in Chapter 5.

Innovative Small Houses

Sidekick, *granny flat*, *backyard bungalow*, and *alley flat* are the fun names for some of the innovative places you can live very close to family. The technical name is *accessory dwelling units* (ADUs). The unifying idea is that they are self-contained living units with sleeping spaces, a kitchen or kitchenette, and a bathroom. ADUs share a single-family lot, either in, attached to, or detached from the main house. An ADU is a way for a parent or young adult to have her or his own space and privacy yet still be close to the main house.

Some cities see ADU construction as a solution to the shortage of affordable housing for millennials and older adults. Communities are increasingly developing housing codes or zoning laws to permit ADUs, usually with some restrictions on minimum or maximum size or who is permitted to live there. For example, a Fairfax City, Virginia, ordinance allows for one ADU at a single-family house that is owner occupied. At least one occupant of the ADU must be over 55 years old or have a physical or mental impairment. A Nashville, Tennessee, ordinance limits an ADU's living space to no more than 700 square feet. It can only be placed behind the principal dwelling and must be proportional in mass, size, and height and similar in style, design, and material color. You can find links to some of the municipal regulations governing ADUs at https://accessorydwellings.org. In any event, if you are considering building an ADU, even if it is just converting a garage into an apartment, you will need to go through the local permitting process and comply with building codes and zoning laws.

Accessory dwellings are not necessarily cheap. Most are custom designed, or you can purchase modular or prefabricated kits running from $65,000 to $100,000. ADUs are generally financed through some combination of savings, second mortgages, home equity lines of credit, and funds from family members—perhaps those who end up living in them. Check out the ABCs of ADUs at www.aarp.org/ADU.

Specialized Units and Communities

An innovative adaptation of ADUs is mini, modular medical units. Equipped like personal nursing home rooms, these modular units can either be freestanding or attached to the host house. For example, a PALS (Practical Assisted Living Solution) home, designed to be attached to the main home, is fully ADA compliant to accommodate a wheelchair user with

wide doorways and a roll-in shower. You can see how the modular unit is installed at www
.palsbuilt.org. A MED Cottage, designed by N2Care along with Virginia Tech University,
has rubber floors to cushion falls and technology that provides medication reminders,
monitors vital signs, and sends alerts if the resident falls. There are also kits and plans to
redo a garage, or you can lease a pod designed for short-term rehabilitation that comes on
an RV platform. Check out www.medcottage.com. Nationwide Homes also produces modular Little Care Cottages, which are designed for wheelchair users.

Bill Thomas, M.D., a gerontologist and an innovator of solutions to aging issues (see
Chapter 10), has introduced the Minka, a compact home of 640 square feet full of technology to help persons with dementia or physical disabilities live independently. Developed
in collaboration with the University of Southern Indiana and supported by AARP, the prefabricated design can be constructed in a week. Thomas is using the Minka—Japanese
for "house of the people"—to create pocket neighborhoods or entire villages with a blend
of student and elder housing. These Multi-Ability, Multi-Generation Inclusive Communities (MAGIC)—under way in Clearfield, Pennsylvania; Loveland, Colorado; and Victoria,
Texas—demonstrate how age-friendly communities can be built using advanced manufac-
turing technology and universal design accessibility.

The Clearfield MAGIC project, for example, is building a 60-home community for
families living with dementia. Along with one- and two-story Minka modules, a closed
elementary school will be converted into a community center with a mix of retail, health
services, and creative arts. Clearfield County Area Agency on Aging CEO Kathleen Gilles-
pie explained, "We're partnering with Dr. Thomas to build the Minka Village of Hope to
give families hope that people living with dementia can participate and enjoy life when
they live in a community that welcomes and includes them."

Cohousing

Another trend in community living is cohousing. Also called an intentional community,
cohousing is typically a group of private homes or units clustered around shared space
that the homeowners collaboratively design and manage. A key feature of a cohousing
development is the common house used by all the residents as an extension of their private
homes. A common house may have a large kitchen and dining room for regularly shared
evening meals or potluck parties, a living room with a reading nook or library, a children's
playroom, laundry facilities, an exercise room, a media room, and an art studio, plus guest
rooms. A typical cohousing project has lots of green space: play areas for adults, kids, and
pets; pathways and bike trails for exercise; and patios, porches, and plazas for neighborly
conversation. Cars are discreetly parked out of sight in a common parking lot.

Because the common house offers extra space for gatherings, the homeowners' units
can be comfortably smaller, or as one resident explained, "right-sized." The complex may
be two facing rows of townhomes with a shared common area or pods of homes intercon-
nected with walkways. While most cohousing developments are new construction of one-
to two-bedroom, single-story units or connected townhomes with several levels and more
bedrooms, one of Sally's college friends is working on repurposing into cohousing the

buildings on the grounds of a vacated convent. Another example is the development called the Railroad Cottages, named for the street they're on in Falls Church, Virginia, which has a common house and ten cottages available to those age 55 and older. It uses geothermal and solar energy and has a battery backup system in the common house so residents can shelter in place together during a major storm or power outage. Residents have privacy in their own home but are expected to commit to being part of the community and looking out for each other. As one resident said, "It's like an old-fashioned neighborhood of the future." The shared grounds and common spaces are intentionally designed to build opportunities for neighbors to get to know neighbors and encourage social connections. Shared resources may include the community lawnmower and garden tools, a single Internet or cable provider, pooled childcare, gardens for vegetables and herbs, and collective recycling and composting.

One of the unique features of cohousing is how it is managed. The legal organization is like a condominium: the homeowners individually own their units and jointly own the common space. (Learn more about condos in Chapter 7.) Residents purchase their unit, pay property taxes on it, and pay a monthly homeowners' association fee that covers upkeep on the common areas. Instead of a board of directors setting rules and regulations, the cohousing homeowners manage by consensus. All owners are expected to participate in monthly management meetings and serve on working groups that take care of the community property. Depending on how the community operates, participants may be expected to contribute their services according to their talents and ability. For example, residents may help cook a communal meal or weed the flower garden in the common plaza. Working groups may oversee groundskeeping, systems maintenance, bookkeeping, or social event planning. A resale committee may oversee identifying prospective homeowners or renters who appreciate the cohousing community concept. Sharing resources saves them money and helps build the spirit of community. "It's cheaper to maintain a yard, garden, library, and fitness center when you're sharing in the costs with your friends," explains a cohousing resident.

According to Cohousing USA (www.cohousing.org), there are over 170 cohousing projects in the United States, with more in the planning process. Most projects are intentionally intergenerational, like Takoma Village in the Washington, D.C., metro area (www .takomavillage.org). It has a mix of youngsters and adults, from infants to octogenarians. Residents with illnesses, injuries, or disabilities find that neighbors are quick to help with meals, rides to medical care, and more. On a larger level, there's always someone to socialize with. Like many other cohousing projects, Takoma Village emphasizes environmental sensitivity. In addition to a solar array and geothermal heating/cooling, all lumber and flooring for the buildings were chosen for sustainability and the walls were built with extra insulation. Light pipes (similar to skylights) brighten the upper floors. Pesticide use is minimized, and food waste is composted. Communal ownership of everything from treadmills to outdoor grills means less consumption. Many residents get by with one car or no car at all because of the nearby bus and train system, taxis, bikeshare station, and carshare options. Recycling bins are everywhere, including for unwanted mail. One owner collects batteries for recycling.

About 15 other projects are designed for residents age 55 and older, including Elderspirit in Abington, Virginia (elderspirit.net), and Oakcreek Cohousing Community in Stillwater, Oklahoma (www.oakcreekstillwater.com). As Oakcreek's website states, its members "recognize that interdependence of 'community' enables people to live independently much longer."

Check out the directory at www.cohousing.org maintained by the Fellowship for Intentional Communities. There you'll find links to cohousing developments with descriptions and photos.

The following checklists are in Chapter 6:

❑ *Who Does What: Splitting Home-Sharing Responsibilities*
❑ *Living Together Budget*
❑ *Making Space*
❑ *Cohousing Communities*

Who Does What: Splitting Home-Sharing Responsibilities

	Name	Name	Name	Name
Meals				
Fix communal breakfast:	_____	_____	_____	_____
Pack lunches:	_____	_____	_____	_____
Cook lunch:	_____	_____	_____	_____
Make dinner:	_____	_____	_____	_____
Wash the dishes:	_____	_____	_____	_____
Load/unload the dishwasher:	_____	_____	_____	_____
Housekeeping				
Laundry:	_____	_____	_____	_____
Sweep, mop, vacuum:	_____	_____	_____	_____
Change bed linens and towels:	_____	_____	_____	_____
Clean bathrooms:	_____	_____	_____	_____
Take out trash:	_____	_____	_____	_____
Take out recycling:	_____	_____	_____	_____
Minor household repairs:	_____	_____	_____	_____
Shopping				
Shop for groceries:	_____	_____	_____	_____
Shop for household supplies:	_____	_____	_____	_____
Transportation				
Drive kids to school:	_____	_____	_____	_____
Drive to activities, meetings, appointments:	_____	_____	_____	_____
Keep gas in the car:	_____	_____	_____	_____
Do or arrange for car repairs:	_____	_____	_____	_____
Change the oil:	_____	_____	_____	_____
Get car inspected:	_____	_____	_____	_____
Outside work				
Mow lawn/rake leaves:	_____	_____	_____	_____
Shovel snow:	_____	_____	_____	_____
Maintain garden:	_____	_____	_____	_____
Put up holiday decorations:	_____	_____	_____	_____

	Name	Name	Name	Name
Health				
Make medical appointments:	_____	_____	_____	_____
Transport to medical appointments:	_____	_____	_____	_____
Keep prescriptions refilled:	_____	_____	_____	_____
Monitor medications:	_____	_____	_____	_____
Pets				
Walk the dog:	_____	_____	_____	_____
Feed pets:	_____	_____	_____	_____
Monitor pets' health needs:	_____	_____	_____	_____
Take to veterinarian:	_____	_____	_____	_____
Pay for veterinarian:	_____	_____	_____	_____
Caregiving				
Get kids to bus stop:	_____	_____	_____	_____
Babysit:	_____	_____	_____	_____
Help members with activities of daily living:	_____	_____	_____	_____
Visit those who can't get around:	_____	_____	_____	_____
Accompany residents to doctors' appointments:	_____	_____	_____	_____

Living Together Budget

The people I am living with agree to share household expenses as follows:

Item	Total amount	Person #1	Person #2	Person #3
Rent:	_____	_____	_____	_____
Mortgage:	_____	_____	_____	_____
Home equity loan:	_____	_____	_____	_____
Property taxes:	_____	_____	_____	_____
Homeowners' insurance:	_____	_____	_____	_____
Electricity:	_____	_____	_____	_____
Water/sewer:	_____	_____	_____	_____
Cable service:	_____	_____	_____	_____
Landline phone:	_____	_____	_____	_____
Cell phones:	_____	_____	_____	_____
Lawn service:	_____	_____	_____	_____
Heating:	_____	_____	_____	_____
Minor maintenance:	_____	_____	_____	_____
Major repairs:	_____	_____	_____	_____
Remodel expense:	_____	_____	_____	_____
Groceries:	_____	_____	_____	_____
Meals out:	_____	_____	_____	_____
Gasoline:	_____	_____	_____	_____
Car loan:	_____	_____	_____	_____
Car repair:	_____	_____	_____	_____

Making Space

To make space for other people in your home, consider these options:

- ❑ Convert basement
- ❑ Convert attic
- ❑ Remodel garage
- ❑ Build addition attached to house
- ❑ Attach modular unit to house
- ❑ Locate modular unit on property

For each option, include:

- ❑ Living space
- ❑ Sleeping space
- ❑ Bath/half-bath
- ❑ Kitchen/kitchenette
- ❑ Lighting
- ❑ HVAC
- ❑ Closet/storage
- ❑ Personal entrance

I have planned for:

- ❑ Mobility needs of resident
- ❑ Adequate plumbing
- ❑ Adequate electrical wiring
- ❑ Safety egress
- ❑ Fire code regulations

I have complied with:

- ❑ Zoning ordinances
- ❑ Building codes
- ❑ Building setback
- ❑ Municipal ordinances
- ❑ Homeowners' association
- ❑ Deed restrictions
- ❑ Parking restrictions
- ❑ Property survey
- ❑ Neighbors' concerns

Cohousing Communities

Name of community: _____

Point of contact: _____

Website: _____

Membership committee contact information: _____

Copy of community vision or philosophy   ❏ Yes   ❏ No

Copy of bylaws   ❏ Yes   ❏ No

Copy of decision-making process   ❏ Yes   ❏ No

Expected level of participation in the community: _____

Frequency of community meetings: _____

Frequency of community meals: _____

Opportunities for community interaction: _____

Monthly HOA fee: _____

Includes:

	Yes	No
Water	❏	❏
Sewer	❏	❏
Trash	❏	❏
Insurance	❏	❏
Snow removal	❏	❏
Landscaping	❏	❏
External maintenance of units	❏	❏
Maintenance of common house	❏	❏

Other: _____

Type of housing:

Single-family dwelling	❏	❏
Duplex	❏	❏
Connected units	❏	❏

Price range: _____

Other: _____

Common house amenities:

Kitchen	❏	❏
Entertainment supplies	❏	❏
Dining hall	❏	❏
Game room	❏	❏
Children's play area	❏	❏
Computers	❏	❏
Laundry	❏	❏
Library	❏	❏
Personal storage units	❏	❏
Guest rooms	❏	❏

Other:_____

Shared resources:

Internet access	❏	❏
Cable	❏	❏
Geothermal power	❏	❏
Solar power	❏	❏
Emergency generator	❏	❏
Parking lot, carport, garage	❏	❏
Landscaping/gardening equipment	❏	❏
Security systems	❏	❏
Mail and package delivery	❏	❏
Trash collection	❏	❏
Composting	❏	❏
Recycling	❏	❏

Other: _____

CHAPTER 7
LIVE ON YOUR OWN SOMEWHERE ELSE

After 32 years in their single-family house, Larry and Ellen moved to a cooperative apartment. No more house to maintain. No more stairs to climb. No more snow to shovel. They couldn't be happier. It was the right choice.

Maybe you, like Larry and Ellen, have decided the single-family house that was the best choice when you were younger is no longer a good fit. Perhaps you'd like something smaller or with less expense and maintenance, or a place that has better weather or is closer to your children. You have changed, and so have your housing preferences.

Once you've made that big decision to look for something else, the obvious next step is to figure out what your next place will be. You have plenty of options, but which is best for you? Fortunately, for most of us, there isn't just one right answer. Many different housing options may meet our needs. But there may be one option that best meets both our needs and our wants. In other chapters, we address living with family and others (Chapter 6), age-specific communities (Chapter 8), and places where you can get some help (Chapters 9, 10, and 11). In this chapter, we focus on rental apartments and houses, condominiums, cooperatives, and mobile and other manufactured homes.

In addition to the social and financial considerations, there are also the legal differences to consider. So along with the decision-making process, we walk you through the legalese.

If you have reservations about moving out of a home you've lived in for many years, you're not alone. We personally have had those same feelings, as have many of our friends who have made similar moves. We've wondered what it would be like to move from a house into an apartment, with less space. Or to move to a new neighborhood, near family but away from friends. We have adjusted—sometimes taking a short time, sometimes longer. We hope our experiences help you with those adjustments, too.

Renting an Apartment or House

Selling a home and renting an apartment or a house—usually smaller—is a common move. Some people move into a rental thinking it will be their last move. Or maybe they know that in a few years they will be moving into independent living or assisted living. Either way, they don't want to invest in real estate. They just want to rent.

Others rent temporarily while looking around for a new house or condominium. They may have moved to a new town and don't want to buy until they are more familiar with the community's neighborhoods. Or maybe they know where they want to relocate but decide to rent until the right house or condominium comes on the market. Moving twice is expensive and time-consuming, but that may be the best option for you. You could even put your furniture in storage and rent a furnished apartment by the month.

Sally had friends who knew they wanted to move from the East Coast to somewhere in the Pacific Northwest. They thought they might like Seattle but weren't yet sure that was the right spot for them. To try out their idea, they rented a small furnished apartment and spent time scoping out various neighborhoods. Did they want to live in the vibrant downtown with lots of cultural activities, where office buildings were being repurposed into condominiums? Or in an older, residential neighborhood where they could walk about the quiet streets? Living in a temporary apartment for a few months was a small price to pay for learning more about the area before they decided where to move more permanently.

Whatever the motivation, renting has the advantage that you are committed only for the length of the lease, usually one year. If, after you move in, you discover that you don't like the place—you find it is in the wrong location, too small or too expensive, or the neighbors are too noisy—you can leave at the end of the lease term.

While you are thinking about where to rent and how long you'll stay, you need to decide how big a home you want, both the number of rooms and square footage. Most couples and individuals want two bedrooms: one to sleep in and the other to function as an office, a guest room, or a room to watch television or read. Increasingly, couples prefer three bedrooms or even more. The more bedrooms, the higher the rent, obviously, and, for apartments, the fewer the choices.

To help you determine how much space you'll need, think about how you use your house now. If you have an attic, basement, or third floor, do you use it for anything other than storage? If so, especially when you move to an apartment, you can expect to have a lot less storage space. If you now have a hobby that take lots of space such as woodworking, a small apartment may not be right for you. But if, like most of us, you use the basement for storage or your children used it to play and hang out, giving it up may be no big loss.

Next, consider where you eat. Many houses have both an eat-in kitchen and a dining room or a space shared by the dining table and the living room. You may now need only a casual eating space and not a formal dining area that can seat eight or ten. "But what about holidays?" you may ask. Without a large table, the family won't be able to sit down together. Weigh the options. You could pay more for a larger place or you could take the relatives out to dinner when they visit, rent out a party room in the building, or arrange for someone else to host.

You can approach the number of bedrooms the same way. Do you want to pay for a guest room that is empty most of the time or for a hotel a few nights for your guests? Or perhaps that spare bedroom can double as an office and, with a sleeper sofa, a guest room.

Consider the overall size of the place. How big are the bedrooms, kitchen, dining room, and living room? Most people probably want two bathrooms, or one and a half. The house or apartment may have three bedrooms but only one bathroom. A two-bedroom may have two bathrooms including a large master bedroom with a large modern in-suite bathroom. Also look at closets and storage. How many closets do you need and how big must they be? Is there a locker or storage space, and how large is it?

When looking for a rental, keep in mind that you may give up some things you love but gain others. The new place may lack a separate dining room, but it may have a small washer and dryer built into a closet. No more hauling your laundry down the stairs to the basement. You may want an apartment so you can be around other people, share the common areas where you can intersect with your neighbors, and enjoy the complex's pool and recreational facilities. Having a reserved parking place, especially in a covered garage, can be a big plus: no more shoveling out the car and the driveway after a snowstorm. Someone else is mowing the grass.

What about your current furniture? How much of it will fit in your new place? When Larry moved to his co-op, he sold his large oak dining room table and sideboard. They were just too large. He bought a new, smaller dining room table that was a better fit. You might think of selling some of your present furniture and buying new pieces that better suit the apartment.

A final concern: pets. If you have pets, you'll want to find a rental that accepts them. If you don't have a pet, give some thought to whether you are willing to live in a community that permits pets, particularly dogs, which are cute unless they live next door and bark at passing cars. And not all dog owners are careful to walk their dog away from well-used common areas. If dogs are allowed, ask some current non-dog-owner residents about whether they are ever annoyed by resident dogs.

Condominiums

In the simplest terms, a condominium is a unit—an apartment, townhouse, or freestanding house—that you own, but unlike a single-family home that you buy, you don't individually own the exterior and shared spaces. You own the unit and all the permanent fixtures in it, such as the dishwasher, washer, dryer, and ceiling fans. The condominium owners jointly own the land on which the building stands and the common areas: the halls, roof, stairways, elevators, basement, parking area, supporting walls, land around the building, and any recreational areas, such as exercise rooms, swimming pools, or tennis courts. Property taxes are assessed against each individual living unit. In addition, the condominium owners are jointly liable for the property taxes on the common areas.

Condo owners not only own the property; they also decide how to run it. Every state has passed laws that permit condominium ownership and lay out general guidelines for governance. Although the laws differ in detail, all provide that the unit owners—condominium law language for apartment, townhouse, or single-house owners—belong to a homeowners' association (HOA). The unit owners elect the board of directors to manage the property, with each unit usually having one vote. If there are only a few owners, they may govern directly without a board of directors.

The bylaws of the association specify the size of the board and how often it is elected. The board's authority is determined by state law and by the document that organizes the condominium association, called the declaration of condominium ownership. If you are considering buying a condominium, ask for a copy of the declaration as well as the bylaws, which contain detailed rules about the limits on how the unit owners can use their property, such as whether pets are allowed.

The condominium association assesses each unit owner a monthly fee—commonly called the homeowners' association or HOA fee—to pay for repairs, maintenance, insurance, and taxes on the common areas of the condominium. The fee also usually covers water, sewage, trash removal, and the upkeep of the common areas. Such fees typically run from $200 to $700 a month. Unit owners usually pay for their own heat, electricity, and cable. A few condominiums have central heat and cooling included in the monthly fee. The older the building, the more likely that the association will provide the utilities and pass the cost on to the unit owners. Be sure to get a breakdown of the HOA fee. Particularly note the amount collected to pay the property taxes on the common areas. Like any property tax, it may well rise in the years to come.

The board of directors, or the association by a vote by all unit owners, has the power to levy an assessment on each unit to pay for extraordinary expenses. This is in addition to the normal HOA fee. For example, a high-rise condominium may need to replace an elevator at a cost of $250,000. Say there are 50 units. Each owner would be assessed a one-time fee of $5,000. Or the association may decide to rehabilitate an aging swimming pool. If so, every unit owner must pay the assessment, even those owners who never use the pool.

When exploring the purchase of a condominium, you'll want to find out about assessments for the past ten years or so, which may give you an estimate of how much you might be assessed in the next ten to 15 years. When you look at the annual association budget, check to see if a reserve fund is being built up to cover future major repairs. If there is no reserve fund, you can be pretty sure you will be assessed for some necessary repairs in the future. Keep in mind that a condominium with a high HOA may be accumulating a reserve that will lessen the need for future assessments. A unit that has been assessed often should have a lower HOA. Major repairs must be paid for somehow, either by accumulating a reserve fund or by periodic assessments.

You'll also want to check on the condo's furnace and central air conditioner and find out when they were last replaced or overhauled. If you are serious about buying the unit, it might pay to have them inspected.

If the condo is relatively new, say ten years or less, there may not have been any assessments. That does not mean that there won't be in the future. Larry knows of a condominium that is 23 years old. This last year, each resident was assessed nearly $35,000 to reinforce the balconies on the units. Apparently, when the condominium was built, the developer failed to use a more expensive, but necessary, form of steel. As a result, the balconies began to pull away from the building. Another building in his neighborhood, which originally sold units at close to $1 million each, assessed owners to pay for costly repairs to a leaky roof only 11 years after it was built.

It's not always easy to spot shoddy construction. You should ask current owners about any problems they know of. You might also try to locate someone who recently sold a unit in the building. They may be willing to give you an accurate answer. If the building plans are available, you might want to hire a construction engineer to look at them to assess the quality of the construction.

When comparing condos, consider common areas and recreational facilities and what you will realistically use. Swimming pools and tennis courts are nice but costly to maintain. Will you use them? Even if you think you may use them some, will that still be the case in five or ten years? That large atrium filled with plants in the center of a high-rise building is attractive. But if the irrigation system leaks in ten years, will you be comfortable with an assessment to fix it?

Ask about garage and parking spaces. Some condominiums assign one or two spaces to each unit. In others, the owners of units also own the parking space, which they can sell to the purchaser.

You might want to avoid a condo that can only be reached by stairs or that has stairs between floors. If as you age you develop problems with your knees or your stability, even a short set of stairs may become difficult for you to navigate.

Many people are attracted to a condominium in a gated community or a high-rise building with a security guard or receptionist in part because it seems safer, more secure. Be sure that assumption is a reality before you move. If the front door has a buzz-in system, watch it for a while. Do the residents let others in when they are coming or going? Larry has friends who live in high-rise buildings where the residents will absolutely not let anyone enter without being buzzed in—not the grandson, the worker waiting to repair a sink, or the pizza delivery person. That is the kind of building you want to live in if security is a major concern. Visit the condominium at night. See whether the lighting is adequate for you to walk safely and to alert you to anyone lurking about.

Read over the bylaws carefully. You may be surprised what you find. If you have been living in a single-family home, you take for granted that you can do almost anything you like to your house. Not so with a condominium. Don't rely on a seller who tells you that the association does not strictly enforce the rules. If there is a rule that you don't like, ask the chair of the board of directors whether there is any flexibility in bylaw enforcement. But keep in mind that if it's in writing, it can be enforced. Here are some typical restrictions to watch for:

- *Exterior.* Apartment condominiums may severely limit personalization of hall doors to protect the hallway aesthetics. You can expect restrictions on what color you paint your door, what you can hang on it, and even whether you can install a doorbell. You may or may not be allowed to hang holiday decorations. While you might be allowed to hang a special door knocker, you likely won't be allowed to change the style of the door numbers. You may not be allowed to put up holiday displays on the lawn or in other common areas. Your window blinds may have to be white. A townhouse condominium will likely limit the choice of paint on the outside trim. The idea behind all such restrictions is to protect the quality of life of all unit owners by ensuring that the appearance of the building is not compromised.

- *Balconies.* If your unit has a balcony, you can expect limitations on how you use it and what you store there. Perhaps no grills or bike storage are allowed. You may not be able to install a satellite dish on your balcony.

- *Flooring.* If you want to put down a wood floor in your unit, you may be required to install soundproofing.

- *Guests.* The condominium may have limits on overnight guests.

- *Tennis courts.* If there is a tennis court, is it first come, first use, or is there a reservation system?

- *Pools.* What are the hours? Are there lifeguards? Limits on using floats or toys?

- *Parking.* In a condominium community of freestanding homes or townhouses, if the community owns the streets, bylaws may prohibit overnight parking on the street. Vehicles may have to be in a garage overnight. If you own an RV, you should ask whether you can park it on your driveway long term. If not, is there a special parking lot for RVs?

- *Pets.* Pets are often a contentious issue for HOAs. Many condominiums bar dogs and cats, and some even do not permit birds. Others permit each unit owner to own one cat or one dog. Limits on the dog's breed and size are common. Some condominiums may have in the past permitted dogs and cats but changed the rule, letting owners who already had a dog or cat keep their pets until they died. It is also possible that the dog you saw in the lobby was a service animal. Even if the condominium bars animals, by law it must let a service dog live in the building.

Cooperatives (or Co-ops)

A cooperative, like Larry's, is similar to a condominium except that you do not own your apartment. You own shares in a corporation that gives you the right to occupy a specific unit. Like condominiums, cooperatives—or co-ops, as they are called—are creatures of state law. Although the laws vary, cooperatives and condominiums are usually organized and operated in similar ways.

Co-ops exist in almost all cases because they were built before the state had enacted a condominium law. Once states allowed condominiums, very few new co-ops were built. Most co-ops, therefore, are found in older buildings.

The unit occupiers or tenants each own shares in the co-op, which is governed by a declaration and bylaws adopted by the co-op governing board of directors, who are elected by the unit shareholders. Each unit has one vote. Some smaller co-ops may have chosen to have all the unit owners serve on the governing board. After purchasing the co-op, tenants pay a monthly maintenance charge that is determined each year by the co-op board. The charge is often based on the square feet of the unit. The larger the unit, the higher the fee. In addition, the governing board can levy an assessment on each unit to pay for unusual expenses.

The co-op association is liable for all property taxes and the costs of maintaining the common areas, such as elevators, halls, and parking areas. In addition, most co-ops provide all utilities, such as electricity, gas, heating, air conditioning, water, and sewage. Some even pay for the cost of cable television. Unlike with condos, the co-op may also be responsible for repairs inside the unit. As a result, co-op fees may be higher than fees for a similar-sized condominium, but the condominium owner is paying a monthly condo fee plus utilities and property taxes.

You should ask a resident on the co-op governing board just what costs are borne by the co-op and what the unit owner must pay. For example, if a sink clogs up, does the co-op or the unit tenant pay for the plumber? Ask about parking. The co-op may charge a monthly fee.

How you finance your co-op purchase may be complicated. A bank may be reluctant to lend to co-op purchasers because they have a co-op share rather than a clear and direct title to the unit. Residents who have sold their recent homes may be able to pay cash for the unit with the sale proceeds. Co-ops also can refuse to permit the sale of their shares, and therefore a unit, to anyone for any reason. Co-ops may deny a sale because the buyer is financially insecure, has a reputation for being a difficult tenant, or is famous and would bring unwanted notoriety to the co-op. Some co-ops will not even sell to lawyers. The co-op cannot, however, refuse to approve the sale of a unit for illegal discriminatory reasons such as gender, race, religion, national origin, or ancestry.

For federal income tax purposes, ownership of a cooperative unit or share is treated the same as being the owner of a traditional house or a condominium unit. Co-op owners are allocated a proportion of the property taxes paid by the cooperative association and may deduct those taxes on their federal income tax return. If the association has debt, perhaps used to pay for capital improvements, the interest paid on the debt is also allocated to the co-op owners and is deductible just like interest paid on a mortgage. The sale of the co-op unit qualifies for the IRS exception for the gain on the sale of a house. (See Chapter 4 for tax consequences.)

Before purchasing a condominium or a co-op, review closely the declaration and the rules and regulations adopted by the governing board. You may want to have an attorney look over the documents. Either way, use our Questions to Ask about Condominiums and Questions to Ask about Co-ops checklists to be sure you get answers to the pertinent questions.

Mobile and Other Manufactured Homes

Many people economize and downsize by selling their house and buying a manufactured house: a mobile home or other prefabricated house that is manufactured off site and erected on or moved to a permanent location. An estimated 20 percent of manufactured housing is occupied by residents age 70 and older. Manufactured housing costs much less per square foot than a traditionally built house, and the property taxes, utilities, and maintenance costs are often lower. Some people sell their traditional homes and buy a manufactured house at a much lower price, investing the savings to create more income.

Mobile home communities can feature prefabricated homes that are not really mobile and often look like small houses with very well-maintained yards. The community may be gated and will almost certainly have attractive common spaces where neighbors can gather. They can be very safe, with neighbors looking out for each other. Larger parks may have an on-site manager, which adds a sense of security and means a quick response to residents' needs. Some communities provide shuttle services to stores and doctors' appointments.

Most mobile home parks are owned by a developer who rents the lots to the mobile homeowner. If you want to move into a park, you can lease a vacant lot, buy a newly built or used mobile home, and move it onto the lot you have leased. More likely you will buy a mobile home already on site and lease the lot where it is located. Usually the park owner will allow a buyer to take over the seller's existing lease. When that lease ends, you sign a new lease, probably with a rent increase.

The lot rent may include water, sewer, trash pickup, common area maintenance, lawn mowing around the mobile homes, and a parking area for RVs and boats. The rent will also pay for any clubhouse, swimming pool, or other recreational facilities.

Before leasing a lot, ask about the rent increase history. Talk with current residents about how well the park is managed. If you are buying an existing mobile home, work with a local real estate agent who regularly assists in the purchase and sale of mobile homes.

The cost of a mobile home depends on the size and age of the home, how well it has been maintained, when it was updated, whether it comes with furnishings, where the park is located, and where in the park the home is located.

One drawback to mobile homes is the financing. Many financial institutions treat a mobile home located on rented property as personal property and offer only short-term loans at higher interest rates than a mortgage on a traditional house. You may need to finance it yourself with savings or, if you're selling your previous home, with the sale proceeds. Another drawback is insurance. Casualty insurance for fire and wind damage is usually 15 to 20 percent higher for manufactured homes than for traditional homes because manufactured homes are more susceptible to fire and storm damage.

Depending on state law, a mobile home is taxed either as real property or personal property. If it is taxed as real property, it is treated the same as any traditional house. If it is considered personal property, it will not be subject to the property tax, but it may be subject to other state or local taxes.

If you have a pet or want to get one, be sure to ask about any pet restrictions on the number, breed, or size of pets.

Many states have enacted mobile home laws that protect tenants against unscrupulous landlords who own the land on which the mobile home sits. These laws typically require the ground lease to be in writing, restrict the landlord's ability to evict tenants, and prohibit the landlord from trying to intimidate tenants to leave or to sell at below-market value. If a mobile homeowner is evicted, the owner must sell the home because the cost of moving these homes is prohibitive. Landlords are also barred from unreasonably refusing to rent the lots. A few states and localities have enacted rent-control laws that limit how much a landlord can raise the rent when it comes time to renew a ground lease.

The following checklists are in Chapter 7:

- ❑ *Picking a Rental, Condo, or Co-op*
- ❑ *Questions to Ask about Condominiums*
- ❑ *Questions to Ask about Co-ops*
- ❑ *Questions to Ask about Leasing a Mobile Home Lot*

Picking a Rental, Condo, or Co-op

Unit

Monthly cost (for rentals and condos): _____

Average cost of utilities: _____

Cost of parking: _____

Steps leading to and in the unit ❏ Yes ❏ No

Square footage: _____

Number of bedrooms: _____

Number of bathrooms: _____

Adequate condition of bathrooms ❏ Yes ❏ No

Adequate eating space ❏ Yes ❏ No

Adequate closet space ❏ Yes ❏ No

Adequate storage space ❏ Yes ❏ No

Adequate size of kitchen ❏ Yes ❏ No

Adequate kitchen appliances ❏ Yes ❏ No

Good view from unit ❏ Yes ❏ No

Direct sunlight ❏ Yes ❏ No

Balcony or outside patio ❏ Yes ❏ No

Building

Year of construction: _____

Number of units: _____

Common outdoor gathering areas, such as patio, roof garden,
or interior courtyard ❏ Yes ❏ No

Reserved parking spaces ❏ Yes ❏ No

Welcoming lobby ❏ Yes ❏ No

Receptionist ❏ Yes ❏ No

Exercise room ❏ Yes ❏ No

Party room ❏ Yes ❏ No

Other common indoor spaces available to tenants ❏ Yes ❏ No

On-site management or supervisor ❏ Yes ❏ No

Buzzer system for visitors ❏ Yes ❏ No

Dedicated mail room ❏ Yes ❏ No

Dedicated package room ❏ Yes ❏ No

Extra storage units ❏ Yes ❏ No

Pets permitted and if so, limits on breed, size, or quantity ❏ Yes ❏ No

Restrictions on renting unit through Airbnb or similar services ❏ Yes ❏ No

Safety

Building secure	❏ Yes	❏ No
24-hour receptionist	❏ Yes	❏ No
Parking secure and safe	❏ Yes	❏ No
Street and entryway well lit at night	❏ Yes	❏ No
Street and entryway safe at night	❏ Yes	❏ No
Neighborhood considered safe to walk around at night	❏ Yes	❏ No
Town or city served by local police, a county sheriff, or the state highway patrol	❏ Yes	❏ No
Neighborhood volunteer watch	❏ Yes	❏ No
Private security for the complex	❏ Yes	❏ No
Gated community	❏ Yes	❏ No

Neighborhood

Shopping

Big-box discount stores	❏ Yes	❏ No
Center city	❏ Yes	❏ No
Convenience store	❏ Yes	❏ No
Farmers market	❏ Yes	❏ No
Grocery store	❏ Yes	❏ No
Pharmacy	❏ Yes	❏ No
Shopping mall or shopping district	❏ Yes	❏ No

Dining

Coffee shop or deli	❏ Yes	❏ No
Favorite restaurants	❏ Yes	❏ No
Lower-cost or chain restaurants	❏ Yes	❏ No

Services nearby

Airport	❏ Yes	❏ No
Car repair services	❏ Yes	❏ No
Gas station	❏ Yes	❏ No
Library	❏ Yes	❏ No
Religious institution	❏ Yes	❏ No

Recreation

Biking paths	❏ Yes	❏ No
Golf course	❏ Yes	❏ No
Gym or exercise facility	❏ Yes	❏ No
Park	❏ Yes	❏ No

Pool	❏ Yes	❏ No
Tennis courts	❏ Yes	❏ No
Walking paths	❏ Yes	❏ No

Health
Health care providers	❏ Yes	❏ No
Hospital	❏ Yes	❏ No
Urgent care facility	❏ Yes	❏ No

Transportation
Bike lanes	❏ Yes	❏ No
Car services	❏ Yes	❏ No
Public transportation with convenient stops	❏ Yes	❏ No
Ridesharing	❏ Yes	❏ No
Taxis	❏ Yes	❏ No

Questions to Ask about Condominiums

Is the condominium governed directly by the shareholders or by an elected board of directors?   ❏ Yes   ❏ No

When voting for the board of directors or for changes in the rules or regulations, how many votes does each unit owner have? _____

What are the limits on rules or regulations that the governing board may adopt? ____

_____

What are the limits on rules or regulations that the association of unit owners may adopt? _____

Is there on-site management?   ❏ Yes   ❏ No

Are there any restrictions on in-unit modifications?   ❏ Yes   ❏ No

What is the current monthly fee? _____

How much did the monthly fee rise in each of the last three years? _____

How many special assessments have been made in the past ten years? _____

Who pays the utilities? _____

Who pays for cable and the Internet? _____

Who is the cable provider? _____

Are there limitations on who can be selected to provide Internet service?   ❏ Yes   ❏ No

Are there any additional fees for the use or maintenance of recreational facilities?   ❏ Yes   ❏ No

Are there any limits about the use of recreational areas?   ❏ Yes   ❏ No

If there is a swimming pool, when may it be used? _____

May guests use the recreational facilities?   ❏ Yes   ❏ No

Can minor guests use the recreational facilities?   ❏ Yes   ❏ No

Are there any limits on overnight guests?   ❏ Yes   ❏ No

Can the unit be leased or rented?   ❏ Yes   ❏ No

Can the unit be rented as an Airbnb or similar service?   ❏ Yes   ❏ No

Are there any restrictions on in-unit floor coverings or window treatments?   ❏ Yes   ❏ No

Are there any restrictions on the use or storage of items on balcony or patio?   ❏ Yes   ❏ No

Are television satellite dishes permitted? ☐ Yes ☐ No

Are there restrictions on screening or glassing in a balcony? ☐ Yes ☐ No

Are there restrictions on the design, color, or decoration of the
outside hall or front door of the unit? ☐ Yes ☐ No

Does the unit come with guaranteed parking with a
designated space? ☐ Yes ☐ No

Is it possible to have an additional parking space for an
additional fee? ☐ Yes ☐ No

Are there any limits on the size or type of vehicle that may use the
parking lot? ☐ Yes ☐ No

Which items, such as air conditioners, plumbing, and windows, are the responsibility
of the unit owner and which are the responsibility of the association? _____

_____

Does the unit come with a designated storage area or room? ☐ Yes ☐ No

Are there any restrictions on the sale of a unit? ☐ Yes ☐ No

Must a unit sale be approved by the board of directors or other unit
owners? ☐ Yes ☐ No

Is there any ongoing litigation against the association, the board
of directors, officers, or professional management? ☐ Yes ☐ No

If the condominium is newly constructed, what rights of governance has the developer retained and when are those rights terminated? _____

_____

Questions to Ask about Co-ops

Is the cooperative governed directly by the unit owners or an elected
board of directors? ❑ Yes ❑ No

What are the limits on rules or regulations that the governing board
may adopt? _____

What are the limits on rules or regulations that the shareholders may adopt? _____

_____

What are the restrictions on the sale of a share? _____

Must a share sale be approved by the governing board or other
shareholders? ❑ Yes ❑ No

Is there on-site management? ❑ Yes ❑ No

Are there any restrictions on in-unit modifications? ❑ Yes ❑ No

Must in-unit modifications be approved by the governing board
or other shareholders? ❑ Yes ❑ No

What is the current monthly fee? _____

How much did the monthly fee rise in each of the last three years? _____

How many special assessments have been made in the past ten years? _____

Who pays the utilities? _____

Who pays for cable and the Internet? _____

Who is the cable provider? _____

Are there limitations on who can be selected to provide
Internet service? ❑ Yes ❑ No

What recreational facilities are provided? _____

Are there any additional fees for the use or maintenance of
recreational facilities? ❑ Yes ❑ No

Are there any limits about the use of recreational areas? ❑ Yes ❑ No

If there is a swimming pool, when may it be used? _____

May guests use the recreational facilities? ❑ Yes ❑ No

Can minor guests use the recreational facilities? ❑ Yes ❑ No

Are there any limits on overnight guests? ❑ Yes ❑ No

Can the unit be leased or rented? ❑ Yes ❑ No

Can the unit be rented as an Airbnb or similar service? ❑ Yes ❑ No

Are there any restrictions on in-unit floor coverings or window treatments? ❑ Yes ❑ No

Are there any restrictions on the use or storage of items on balcony or patio? ❑ Yes ❑ No

Are television satellite dishes permitted? ❑ Yes ❑ No

Are there restrictions on screening or glassing in a balcony? ❑ Yes ❑ No

Are there restrictions on the design, color, or decoration of the outside hall or front door of the unit? ❑ Yes ❑ No

Does the unit come with guaranteed parking with a designated space? ❑ Yes ❑ No

Is it possible to have an additional parking space for an additional fee? ❑ Yes ❑ No

Are there any limits on the size or type of vehicle that may use the parking lot? ❑ Yes ❑ No

Is there valet parking 24/7? ❑ Yes ❑ No

Which items, such as air conditioners, plumbing, and windows, are the responsibility of the shareholder? _____

Does the unit come with a designated storage area or room? ❑ Yes ❑ No

Is any litigation ongoing against the cooperative? ❑ Yes ❑ No

Questions to Ask about Leasing a Mobile Home Lot

What are the tenants' rights to use common areas? _____

_____

What are the tenants' rights to store vehicles or other items on the rented property?

_____

Can tenants lease or rent their homes to others?   ❑ Yes   ❑ No

Can the home be given away or passed by will without terminating
the lease?   ❑ Yes   ❑ No

Mobile home unit

What are the limits as to the size, style, or building materials? _____

_____

What are the requirements about skirting, removal of wheels, or the use of a
foundation? _____

What are the limits on porches, overhangs, awnings, or outdoor grills? _____

_____

Common areas and recreational facilities

Does the landlord maintain common areas and recreational facilities? ❑ Yes   ❑ No

Do guests of the tenant have the right to use the common areas and
recreational facilities?   ❑ Yes   ❑ No

Park rules

Are all current rules attached to the lease?   ❑ Yes   ❑ No

Are any restrictions on overnight guests attached to the lease?   ❑ Yes   ❑ No

Are any restrictions on pets attached to the lease?   ❑ Yes   ❑ No

Are the rules applying to the use of the common areas and
recreational facilities attached to the lease?   ❑ Yes   ❑ No

Are the rules that mandate the upkeep of the homes and the property
lots attached to the lease?   ❑ Yes   ❑ No

Sale of the mobile home

Can the tenant sell the home to a third party or must it be sold to
the landlord?   ❑ Yes   ❑ No

Does the landlord have the right to veto any purchaser?   ❑ Yes   ❑ No

Is there a fee if the home is sold?   ❑ Yes   ❑ No

Is there any limit on a rental increase that applies to a new purchaser
of the home?   ❑ Yes   ❑ No

Eviction

What events give the landlord the right to evict the tenant? _____

_____

How late can a rental payment be made before the landlord has the right to evict?

_____

Does the tenant have a right to mediate any attempted eviction?   ❑ Yes ❑ No

If evicted, how much time does the tenant have to move or sell the mobile home?

_____

Sale of park

What happens to the tenant if the landlord sells the park? _____

_____

If the new owner wants to close the park, how much notice must be given? _____

_____

CHAPTER 8
LIVING IN AGE-SPECIFIC HOUSING

As we get older, many of us prefer to live among others who are about our same age. Fortunately, a variety of housing attracts or requires residents to be "of a certain age."

The residents in age-specific communities are in a similar place in life. They have often worked hard, raised a family, and retired, and they now seek the "good life" of personal fulfillment and good times with friends. Here you have like-minded people around you to work out in the gym or go for morning walks, take classes in ceramics or current affairs, join bridge or book clubs, plan local excursions and exotic trips of a lifetime, and engage in charitable activities. The atmosphere is more relaxed. No early morning commuters rushing off to work, no loud teenagers, no crying babies.

Of course, this type of housing doesn't appeal to everyone. "Too many old people," Larry's father, then 80, complained after visiting one of these communities. We've heard complaints that people feel that without a mix of ages, age-specific communities are too sterile an environment. Some folks like seeing small children playing, enjoy a backyard barbeque with families at all stages of life, and are even willing to put up with a teenager flying by on a skateboard.

But if this type of living appeals to you, read on. This chapter introduces you to different types of age-specific communities. You might find one right in your own neighborhood where you are already living. Throughout the country, you can find naturally occurring retirement communities (NORCs), Villages, active communities, age-restricted communities, and subsidized housing as well as apartment or condominium buildings, subdivisions, or even entire cities that attract older people or have age restrictions on who can live there. We acquaint you with the various options, laying out the distinctive features and the pros and cons to help you figure out what is the best fit for you.

Naturally Occurring Retirement Communities

Some people don't have to move to enjoy the benefits of living around others who are like them. That's because they're already living there. Over time, some neighborhoods, individual apartment buildings, or condominiums have attracted residents with similar interests who have stayed in place as they've grown older, which in turn draws other older residents. Artists and theater lovers, for example, may come together to live in a neighborhood full of galleries and theaters and stay as they age. In some cases, these neighborhoods developed when individuals chose to age in place and younger residents moved on. Or they evolved when older individuals gravitated to the area because they were attracted by the nearby services and the neighborliness of the community. There are no formal age restrictions; it's just that many older people independently chose to live there. Such communities or buildings are known as naturally occurring retirement communities, or NORCs.

NORCs are typically found in cities where the population density supports the services and features that residents want or need. Neighboring houses, townhouses, condominiums, and apartments gradually fill up with an older population. As their numbers increase, more of the services they want become available in the neighborhood. The local dry cleaner begins to pick up and deliver clothes. A restaurant that opens early for breakfast becomes a gathering place for locals who stretch a bagel and a cup of coffee into a long morning visit. A visiting nurse agency opens a branch office down the street. The takeout deli puts in a few tables and soon enjoys a booming business of leisurely lunches. Governmental and nonprofit social service agencies open an office where the neighborhood residents can find out about available services.

Larry lives in a high-rise co-op in which over 80 percent of the residents are age 65 or older. The building is not marketed toward retirees. Rather, they're attracted to the layout of the building and the services within walking distance. The building has valet indoor parking. There are elevators and, in the units, no stairs. Several restaurants, a deli, a dry cleaner, a large chain drug store, and several pizza parlors are within two or three blocks. The central public library is close by. City buses run frequently at the corner. A half-dozen churches and synagogues are within a mile, as are several doctors' offices and a hospital. In short, the surrounding neighborhood offers many of the services that make life better for the older residents.

Villages

In some cities, residents of neighborhoods with a high percentage of older residents have formed a special entity to help make their lives easier. Sometimes called a Village, it's a grassroots, self-governing community that serves older people living in a defined neighborhood. This new model for aging in place grew out of Baby Boomers' desire to expand the ways they could stay independent in their own familiar neighborhood with the support of their neighbors. Bettie Farrar, a Village advocate, explained, "We come together so we can support each other through the bumps in the road as we successfully age in our own community."

The Beacon Hill Village in Boston was the first to popularize the concept of bringing together neighbors to help each other age in place. A member-driven organization for local residents age 50 and older, it provides programs and services to its members, who pay an annual fee. The concept is that neighbors will age in place and still have an involved and vibrant life. The Beacon Hill Village negotiates discounts from various providers of goods and services such as meal deliverers, dog walkers, electricians, people to do odd jobs, and even computer and tax experts. Members have access to discounted gym memberships, personal trainers, home health care, and physical therapists. The Village organizes trips to concerts and lectures and brings members together who have common interests such as a love for bridge or travel.

The Beacon Hill prototype has grown into a national network of various neighborhood, city, community, and county Village programs. Today, more than 155 villages serve 25,000 older adults. About one-third are in urban areas, one-third are in suburban areas, and the other third are in rural or mixed areas. Membership fees range from $0 to $1,000, with an average cost of about $430 for an individual and $600 for a household. Three-fourths have discounted membership fees for neighbors with lower incomes. In the Villages surveyed by the Village to Village Network, a national organization that supports the growth of Villages, a third of the members were ages 65 to 74, another third were 75 to 87, and about a fifth were 85 or older.

Some Villages follow the Beacon Hill model. Others have been designed to respond to the unique needs of their community. Whatever the organizational structure, most offer social activities, educational programs, opportunities for companionship, transportation services, and various levels of support by paid staff, community volunteers, or member volunteers. Many have lists of preferred providers of home repair, home care, or computer assistance who may offer discounts to Village members. Collaboration with nearby social services agencies, hospitals, religious institutions, and colleges strengthens the support the Village can bring to its members. Carol Cronin, a co-leader of the Bay Ridge At Home near Annapolis, Maryland, told Sally that the primary goal of her Village is to build a good, old-fashioned sense of community by helping connect neighbors with similar interests and needs.

To locate a Village near you, go to the Village to Village network interactive map at www.vtvnetwork.org.

Active Adult Communities

Active adult communities are designed to appeal to potential residents who want a vibrant community, reduced home maintenance, and access to nearby recreational facilities, restaurants, and other community activities. Even if a community has no age restrictions, most residents tend to be older.

Active adult communities come in a variety of housing choices, including single-family houses, townhouses, and apartments. Some communities are clustered around a recreation center that features an indoor or outdoor swimming pool and perhaps a tennis court. Others feature houses along a golf course that has a community clubhouse. Then there are condominiums and apartment complexes, particularly in the Sunbelt states, that may not offer much in the way of services or recreation, but you can be sure that your next-door neighbors won't include a teenager who is learning to play the drums.

The homeowner is responsible for the maintenance and upkeep of the house, but the community will likely maintain the common areas—such as clubhouses, tennis courts, and swimming pools—including mowing lawns, shoveling snow, and removing the trash.

The community may also maintain the house exteriors, including painting, keeping gutters clear, and repairing the roofs. It may be gated to restrict entry. If so, even the streets will be owned by the community.

In many respects, owning a house in such a community is like owning a condominium unit (see Chapter 7). A monthly homeowners' association (HOA) fee covers the maintenance and services provided by the community. Residents typically have downsized into a smaller home that is easier to clean, lacks steps, and is located in a quiet neighborhood with other similar houses. There may be a café on the grounds but no communal dining, health care, or transportation.

Services can be extensive: gated entry, security patrols, and shuttle services around the community and to off-site stores and even restaurants. Recreational facilities can include swimming pools, fitness centers, aerobics and yoga centers, clubhouses, tennis courts, hobby rooms, social club meeting rooms, libraries, walking and bike trails, tennis courts, pickleball courts, lawn-bowling lawns, and shuffleboard courts. Many have an activities coordinator who plans trips, activities, classes, and on-site entertainment. Some are located adjacent to a golf course or a lake. If the community you're considering lacks your favorite activities, keep looking. The next complex you visit may have what you want.

Although many active adult communities are not age restricted, most residents are older or retired. New residents can expect to befriend others who, like themselves, want to enjoy an active, involved retirement. The community provides opportunities to socialize in the clubhouse, exercise on the community walking path, and make new friends with neighbors.

Regardless of the location or size of the community, these communities are generally run by an association of unit owners. Each unit is assessed a monthly fee. You'll want to find out the amount of the monthly fee and exactly what it covers, which will vary from community to community. Fees probably pay for the maintenance of the common areas, recreational facilities, a clubhouse, and classes that may be offered, although some entertainment may require an extra fee. The unit owners often own only the house and are not responsible for the maintenance of the yard. The fee will also likely pay for insurance, water, sewer, and trash pickup. While unit owners will likely be responsible for any property taxes on their unit, the association fee will pay for property taxes on the association-owned property. Utilities provided by the association, such as an HVAC system that provides heat and air to all the units, will be covered by the monthly fee. The unit owner may have to pay for electricity and water and will most likely pay for cable, Internet, and phone.

Age-Restricted Communities

Age-restricted housing offers many of the same services and activities as active adult communities, but you have to be at least a certain age to live there. Throughout the country, you'll find age-restricted communities of various sizes. Some of the largest age-restricted communities are Sun City in Arizona, with nearly 40,000 residents, and Leisure World in Orange County, California, with 9,000 residents.

If you are thinking of moving to age-restricted housing and choose one with an age 62 requirement, you can be sure that all your neighbors will be at least age 62. Of course, they have the right to have younger guests who may stay overnight or longer, unless that's prevented by the community rules. If, however, you select housing limited to those age 55 and older, up to 20 percent of the others who live there may be younger than age 55. (See the box that follows.) You may find that your 70-year-old neighbors have invited their 35-year-old daughter to move in with her 10-year-old son while she finalizes her divorce. She can do that unless the community prohibits anyone under age 18 living there. Or younger people can move in, so long as that 80–20 balance is maintained.

Whether the age restriction is age 55 or 62, be sure to find out whether overnight guests are permitted and whether those guests can be younger than the restriction of either age 55 or 62. If guests are permitted, is there a limit on how long they can visit? Can they use the swimming pool or golf course? Even if the answer is yes, ask some residents about how guests are treated if seen in the swimming pool or lounging about the clubhouse. In some communities, residents may make guests feel uncomfortable even though they have a right to be there.

Yes, Age-Restricted Housing Is Legal

If you sell a home or rent out an apartment, you can't discriminate on the basis of race, sex, religion, and a number of other factors, including whether a resident has children. But under certain circumstances, a community, neighborhood, or building can legally discriminate on the basis of age:

- Housing can be restricted to those solely age 62 or older, no exceptions. If you're 62 but your partner is 60, you can't move in together. Both must be 62 or older. Residents cannot rent or sublease to anyone under age 62.

- Housing can be intended and operated for those age 55 and older as long as 80 percent of the residents are 55 or older. If you're 56 but your partner is 50, you might be able to move in as long as at least 80 percent of all the residents are age 55 and older. You might even be able to move in with, say, your 35-year-old daughter, and even your 10-year-old grandchild. If, however, your moving in would reduce the percentage of age 55 and older residents to below 80 percent, you cannot move in. When you're considering such a community, ask for a breakdown of the residents by age: the number of people under age 55 and the median age of the residents. Also ask if there's a minimum requirement for residents, such as age 18.

Age 55 or 62 Limit?

One advantage to living in an age 55 and older community is that as a resident, you have some flexibility in whom you may live with, assuming the community permits occupancy by some who are under age 55. That could be a spouse or a partner, but it might also be an adult child or grandchild who needs a temporary residence. Just be sure that the community permits you to add someone under age 55 to your household without approval from the community association. Some age 55 communities do not allow anyone under the age of

55 to live there even though the law permits them to. This lets the community sell or rent to a larger number of potential residents including couples where one spouse is over age 62 but the other is at least age 55 but not 62.

If the community has an age 62 restriction, you know that no one under that age will live there. You are assured of living with only mature adults. When you visit the community, ask the average age and look around as you tour the community. Some age-restricted housing may trend older. The average age is what is important. If, for example, the average age is 70, then at least 50 percent of the residents are younger than 70. If you are age 68, this might be a very good fit. If the average age is 80, then you know that 50 percent of the residents are older than 80.

The average age of residents is often in part a function of the age of the community. Residents often move in when they are in their 60s and age in place. If the community is new and still attracting new residents, the average age will probably be younger than in a long-established community. The new, founding residents will tend to be younger, but as the years pass, they age. If you are looking at a community that is over 20 years old, be sure to ask about the average age of the residents. Also ask about the average age of those who buy into the community. Whatever the answer, you probably want to move where you are about the same age as others who are moving in.

Enforcement of Age Restrictions

Residents of age-restricted housing have a right to expect the homeowners' association, property manager, or condo board to enforce the age requirements. If they're not enforced, you can file a complaint with the local office of the federal Housing and Urban Department asking that the underage resident be evicted. The state where you live may also have laws that permit age-restricted housing. If you suspect a violation, you can complain to the appropriate state office.

If you are buying a house in an age-restricted development, inspect the deed to make sure it contains a covenant that bars sale to anyone who does not meet the age restriction. This covenant passes on to any new owner and cannot be removed unless all the property owners in the development agree. If even one property owner objects, the age restriction cannot be removed from any of the deeds and must be enforced.

When buying a condominium, look at the condominium declaration and bylaws for assurance that the unit is in fact subject to an age restriction. The governing documents should grant the governing association the right to approve all purchases and ensure that prospective buyers meet the age requirements. Depending on state law and the condominium declaration, it is possible that some percentage of the unit owners can agree to remove the age restriction. Before purchasing a condominium, you'll want to know if that is a possibility. Some owners might want to remove the restriction so they can sell to younger buyers and lower the average age of the community. If that happens, you might find that when you reach age 80, you no longer fit in with the younger residents.

Whether an age 62 or age 55 restricted community, the governing association must show its intent to operate age-restricted housing by having procedures in place to verify the age of prospective residents, follow those procedures, and enforce its rules. If the rules and procedures are not in writing, you may find that the age restriction is not uniformly enforced. In that case, the association might not be legally permitted to enforce the restriction if a younger person wants to buy into the community. For example, in an age 55 community, the governing association should have a process by which it determines whether a sale to someone younger than 55 will be allowed based on the percentage of units that are occupied by someone age 55 or older. The association should regularly check each housing unit to verify that at least 80 percent of the units are occupied by someone age 55 and older. An age 62 or older community should require new residents to provide proof of their age and check to see that no one younger than age 62 moves into a unit.

If you rent an apartment or house in an age-restricted community, be aware that after your lease is up, you have no guarantee that the community will continue to be age restricted. For example, say your lease is for 12 months. When the lease ends a year later, you may find that the community or building will no longer be age restricted as soon as the last of the existing leases expires. Of course, if you don't want to live in a community with people of all ages, you can move. You have no legal right to make the community continue to operate as an age-restricted property after your lease has ended.

Buying or Renting

When you are considering an active or age-restricted community, think about whether you want to rent or buy, if both are an option. Renting, of course, has the advantage of being less of a commitment. If you move in and later decide that this house is not for you, just move out when your lease expires. You can rent with the idea of testing whether age-restricted housing is a good fit. Take a year's lease and see what it's like. You may quickly make friends with your neighbors, or you may find their interests are not compatible with yours. You may like sharing an exercise room, taking classes, and enjoying entertainment with others about your age. Or you may find that you miss being around younger folks. You may discover that while the community is restricted to those age 62 or older, the average age is much older than you are.

If you decide to rent, be sure that the lease guarantees that the recreational and other services that attracted you will be maintained for the period of your lease. Do not rely on oral promises. They are not enforceable. Of course, you'd be correct to assume that the current swimming pool is not going to be drained next summer, but you might want more assurances that the tennis court will be kept in service or that a party room will not be converted to some other use. If you can't get assurances that the services and facilities you want will be continued during the term of your lease, you may want to negotiate for the right to terminate the lease under specified conditions. For example, if you are an avid swimmer and the indoor pool closes, you would have the option to terminate your lease without any penalty.

Renting may be a good alternative if you want to live as a snowbird. For example, you might live in a cottage on a lake in Minnesota or a small home in a town near the mountains in Montana for four months and spend the rest of the year in an age-restricted community in the Sunbelt. In short, you enjoy the best of both worlds.

If you like the concept of age-restricted housing but don't want to be cut off from younger folks, consider an age-restricted subdivision. You'll live in a homogeneous population next to more diverse neighborhoods. You will still have the advantages of age-restricted housing, such as a shared tennis court or pickleball court, and you will be secure and safe, particularly if you are living in a gated community. But you can walk, bike, or drive out of your subdivision to mingle with younger folks.

Lower-Cost Age-Restricted Housing

If age-restricted housing appeals to you and you're on a limited budget, don't despair. There are age-restricted housing options that you should be able to afford. If you are flexible as to where you live, investigate your options across the country. Like houses everywhere, the selling price of a house depends on its age, location, number of square feet, number of bedrooms, and number of bathrooms. If you buy a less expensive house or unit, you still will have access to the many shared community facilities, such as swimming pools, clubhouses, and walking trails. Just like those who own the most expensive houses, you will scoot around town on your modified golf cart, enjoy the same early bird specials at the restaurants, and check out books and CDs at the community library.

In the lower-cost condominiums with lower HOA monthly fees, your unit may be smaller with fewer amenities, such as perhaps no granite counters in the kitchen. The complex may not have a pool, but you may not care for swimming anyway or you could use the local YMCA pool and gym. Regardless of your finances, you should be able to find a condominium that both fits your budget and meets your housing needs. It is the same with age-restricted rental apartments. Just keep looking until you find a place that you can afford and that feels right. And keep in mind that if you later come to regret your rental choice, you can always move.

Another option for those on a tighter budget is manufactured housing, which we discuss in Chapter 7.

HUD-Subsidized Housing for People 62 and Older

If you have a relatively low income, you may qualify for federally subsidized public housing that is restricted to those age 62 or older. Federal programs operated by the U.S. Department of Housing and Urban Development (HUD) help pay for affordable housing for seniors with low incomes by paying the landlord part of the rent. Potential residents must meet HUD age and income requirements to be eligible. You can locate HUD-subsidized housing in your area on the HUD website, www.hud.gov/program_offices /housing/mfh/hto/inventorysurvey. To meet the HUD age requirement for senior housing, the head of the household needs to be age 62 or older. Many senior housing communities also rent a percentage of the units to younger persons with disabilities. You apply with the program manager of the senior housing where you wish to live. The manager will determine if you meet the eligibility requirements.

HUD's federally subsidized housing for people 62 and older, called Section 202, is the only federal housing program that is exclusively for older Americans. It provides loans to private, nonprofit organizations to build or adapt current housing for low-income seniors and to provide rent subsidies to those with very low incomes. If you are 62 or older and you meet the income-level requirements, you are eligible to live in Section 202 housing. Your rent is based on your income, usually no more than 30 percent of your monthly income. The housing typically consists of one-bedroom apartments with special design features, such as grab bars and ramps. Some services, such as transportation, may be provided, but the available supportive services vary from housing community to community. Some communities have an on-site service coordinator who helps residents get necessary services to be able to continue to live in the community. Be warned, however, that you will likely be put on a wait list. A wait of one or two years is typical.

The following checklists are in Chapter 8:

❏ *What to Look for in Active Adult or Age-Restricted Communities*
❏ *Active Adult or Age-Restricted Communities Contracts*

What to Look for in Active Adult or Age-Restricted Communities

Community

Is it restricted to those aged 55+?	❑ Yes ❑ No
Is it restricted to those aged 65+?	❑ Yes ❑ No
Can the age restriction be changed in the future?	❑ Yes ❑ No

What is the average age of the current residents? _____

Is the community the right size for you, not too big, not too small?	❑ Yes ❑ No
Does the community provide the services or facilities you want?	❑ Yes ❑ No
Does the community recommend service providers?	❑ Yes ❑ No
Does the community arrange for discounts for goods and services in the area?	❑ Yes ❑ No

When was it constructed or last had a major
renovation? _____

Is it a gated community or have other restricted access?	❑ Yes ❑ No
Does it have adequate security?	❑ Yes ❑ No
Are new housing units being added?	❑ Yes ❑ No

   If so, how many and what type? _____

Appearance

Are the grounds well maintained?	❑ Yes ❑ No
Are the common areas clean and well furnished?	❑ Yes ❑ No

Unit

What types of housing does it offer? _____

Does the living unit have adequate closets and storage?	❑ Yes ❑ No
Is there a separate storage area?	❑ Yes ❑ No
Are there limits on the use of a patio or balcony (such as no grilling, no bicycle storage)?	❑ Yes ❑ No
Are there restrictions on decorating the interior or exterior of the units?	❑ Yes ❑ No

Costs

If a rental, what is the history of rent increases? _____

What is the sales history for the individual units? _____

What is the monthly HOA fee? _____

What is the history of annual increases? _____

Has the community levied an assessment on the homeowners in the past?	❑ Yes	❑ No
Can it do so in the future?	❑ Yes	❑ No
Are rent subsidies available?	❑ Yes	❑ No

Neighborhood

Do you like the neighborhood?	❑ Yes	❑ No
Does it feel safe?	❑ Yes	❑ No
Are neighborhood services such as banks, libraries, the post office, social services, grocery stores, and convenience stores close by?	❑ Yes	❑ No
Are there nearby hotels for family and friends visiting?	❑ Yes	❑ No
Is it near quality health care?	❑ Yes	❑ No

Parking and transportation

Are there adequate and secure parking places, either outdoors or in a garage?	❑ Yes	❑ No
Is there an extra fee for parking?	❑ Yes	❑ No
Is there parking for guests?	❑ Yes	❑ No
Can a unit owner park an RV or trailer overnight either by the unit or nearby?	❑ Yes	❑ No
Does the community provide transportation?	❑ Yes	❑ No
Is public transportation nearby and accessible?	❑ Yes	❑ No
Are taxis and ridesharing services available?	❑ Yes	❑ No
Is the neighborhood walkable?	❑ Yes	❑ No
Are there bike paths?	❑ Yes	❑ No

Recreation and entertainment

Are there recreational facilities, clubs, and social activities that interest you?	❑ Yes	❑ No
Is there a clubhouse or community-gathering facility?	❑ Yes	❑ No
Are there charges for the recreational facilities?	❑ Yes	❑ No
Are there limits on the use of the recreation or social meeting facilities?	❑ Yes	❑ No

What are the opportunities to meet and engage with neighbors? _____

_____

What activities are offered?		
Book clubs	❑ Yes	❑ No
On-site entertainment such as music, movies, and guest entertainers	❑ Yes	❑ No

Lectures and classes	❏ Yes	❏ No
Walking groups	❏ Yes	❏ No
Trips to stores and libraries	❏ Yes	❏ No
Trips to theaters, museums, and other events	❏ Yes	❏ No
Is there an exercise room?	❏ Yes	❏ No
Does it have group or individual training?	❏ Yes	❏ No
Is there a swimming pool?	❏ Yes	❏ No
Does it have organized classes?	❏ Yes	❏ No
Are there tennis courts?	❏ Yes	❏ No
Are there other outdoor recreational facilities such as a shuffleboard court or putting green?	❏ Yes	❏ No
Is there an indoor walking track?	❏ Yes	❏ No
Is there an outdoor walking path?	❏ Yes	❏ No
Is there a community garden or individual garden plots?	❏ Yes	❏ No
Is there a library with books, magazines, newspapers, and computers?	❏ Yes	❏ No
Are religious services and celebrations available on site?	❏ Yes	❏ No
Are there volunteer activities within the community?	❏ Yes	❏ No

Guests

Are overnight guests permitted?	❏ Yes	❏ No
Are there age limits for overnight guests?	❏ Yes	❏ No
Is there a limit on the duration of a visit?	❏ Yes	❏ No
Can guests use the recreational facilities?	❏ Yes	❏ No
Is there a rental guest room or living unit?	❏ Yes	❏ No
Is parking for guests convenient?	❏ Yes	❏ No

Other

Are pets permitted?	❏ Yes	❏ No
If so, are there any restrictions?	❏ Yes	❏ No
Do you have a copy of the unit owners' association rules and regulations?	❏ Yes	❏ No

Active Adult or Age-Restricted Communities Contracts

Purchase contract

What is the minimum age requirement? _____

How frequently does the community verify the age of its residents? _____

Who owns the common areas of the community: the unit owners or a separate
entity? _____

Who owns the community's recreational facilities? _____

What restrictions are in the deed on the use of the unit? _____

What restrictions are in the deed on the external use or appearance of the
unit? _____

What are the provisions for purchasing housekeeping from the community? _____

_____

If you own a condominium, how is the community governed? _____

If you own a condominium, what restrictions on the use of your unit are in the condominium bylaws? _____

What are the restrictions on renting your unit as an Airbnb or similar short-term
rental? _____

If the common areas or recreational facilities are owned by a separate entity, who is
that and what is its relation to the unit owners? _____

What are unit owners assessed to pay for the upkeep of the community property?

_____

Are there any limitations on the frequency or amount of assessments?	❏ Yes	❏ No
Are there any limits or restrictions other than the age of a purchaser on the sale of a unit?	❏ Yes	❏ No
Must a sale of a unit be approved by the community?	❏ Yes	❏ No
Can the owner of a unit rent it to someone who meets the community's age requirement?	❏ Yes	❏ No
Is parking part of the purchase of the unit?	❏ Yes	❏ No
If not, can a parking space be purchased?	❏ Yes	❏ No
If parking must be leased, is parking guaranteed?	❏ Yes	❏ No

Lease agreement

What is the term of the lease? _____

What utilities are covered by the rent? _____

What utilities must the resident pay? _____

How much has the rent on the unit been raised annually in the last five
years? _____

What furnishings are supplied? _____

Can the resident request different furnishings?   ❑ Yes   ❑ No

Is housekeeping included in the lease?   ❑ Yes   ❑ No

If not, can it be purchased from the community?   ❑ Yes   ❑ No

Are there additional payments for the use of any common areas
or recreational facilities?   ❑ Yes   ❑ No

Are additional payments mandatory or voluntary?   ❑ Yes   ❑ No

Are there any limits on the use of the rental unit?   ❑ Yes   ❑ No

Are pets allowed?   ❑ Yes   ❑ No

What kind of pets and what limitations on size and number? _____

_____

Can the resident have overnight guests?   ❑ Yes   ❑ No

Can the resident sublet so long as the community's age
restrictions are followed?   ❑ Yes   ❑ No

What is the penalty if the resident voluntarily breaks the lease and
leaves? _____

_____

What happens if the resident must terminate the lease for health
reasons? _____

_____

What happens if the resident dies during the term of the lease? _____

_____

CHAPTER 9
WHEN YOU NEED A LITTLE MORE HELP: ASSISTED LIVING

We know many people who have gotten to the point when they're done driving, cooking, and cleaning. They may feel less steady on their feet and don't always remember to take their medications. They want some day-to-day help. In Chapter 5, we discussed how to get services you need to live independently in your own home. At some point, though, you may want to consider moving to where you can have more companionship, get more support, and feel safe while retaining as much independence as possible. Let someone else cook, clean, and do your laundry.

This chapter covers three types of housing that supply that support: congregant housing, assisted living communities, and board and care homes. Different names are used to describe supportive housing. Very similar providers may go by different names in different states. For example, what is called a "board and care home" in one place may be called a "personal care home" in another place. Don't let the name confuse you. What is important are the types of services that are provided.

You've probably seen ads for these types of supported housing that boast hotel-type amenities—lovely meals and grounds, staff who will take care of your every need. That may be what you want. You'll want a place where you're treated with respect and dignity, where your opinions count, and where you're encouraged to flourish. Jill Vitale-Aussem, author of AARP's book *Disrupting the Status Quo of Senior Living: A Mindshift* and CEO of The Eden Alternative (see Chapter 11), encourages us to seek out places that help us continue to grow, be independent, and find purpose.

The Right Fit

Whether you're looking at congregate living, board and care homes, or assisted living communities, you'll want to match your capabilities, both physical and mental, with the range of services offered. Keep in mind that every supportive housing community must comply with regulations on whom it can admit. Most supportive housing discussed in this chapter is regulated by the states. Every state has its own set of laws and regulations governing how these supported housing options operate. A community may not be able to accept you because state regulations limit the types of services it can offer. If, for example, the community is not licensed to administer daily medications, it will not be permitted to admit residents who need that type of help. Another may not be set up to take care of people who have memory problems, dementia, or certain physical limitations or illnesses.

Your local area agency on aging (AAA) is your go-to resource to find supportive housing in your area. It should have a directory that includes the type, size, licensing status, eligibility requirements, cost range, services, and amenities offered. For covering some of the costs of supportive housing, see Chapter 13.

Personal Touch

More important than the bricks and mortar is the quality of the staff: the administrators, care staff, activities coordinators, receptionists, nutritionists, dining room aides, and groundskeepers. This is going to be your new home, so you'll want to be welcomed and treated with grace and dignity. Even the most elaborately furnished housing can become a disappointment if staff is aloof or unfriendly. During your visits, observe how the staff treat the residents and each other. Are they respectful? Do they let residents make their own decisions? Or are they patronizing, dismissive, or distracted?

And ask questions. What is the overall philosophy of care? The philosophy of care in supportive housing is changing. Although initiated to reform the philosophy of care in nursing homes, The Eden Alternative's focus on person-centered care has appropriately spread to other types of supported housing. We discuss The Eden Alternative in detail in Chapter 11.

The community's personality and personnel are crucial to the success of your stay. Is the focus on the well-being of each resident? What training and experience do the administrators have? How frequently do all staff receive continuing training? What is the ratio of staff to residents? What is the staff turnover the last few years?

Congregate Housing

Designed for healthy individuals and couples, congregate housing—sometimes called independent living, for instance when it's part of a complex with assisted living—provides a noninstitutional setting for independent living with limited supportive services. These group-living communities are designed for those who need a little help with their day-to-day activities but want to live in a group setting. Some are administered by nonprofit organizations that receive some federal or state funding. If so, the cost may be on a sliding scale based on the resident's income.

What can you expect in congregate housing? You must be able to live relatively independently and be mentally alert. You'll live in an apartment building in your own one-bedroom or studio apartment. You'll probably eat at least some meals in the common dining room. If the complex offers only an evening meal, as is sometimes the case, your unit will have a small kitchenette with a refrigerator and stove. The community will also have several common rooms that provide spaces for residents to socialize and enjoy organized activities. Of course, residents are free to come and go, but if they prefer not to, they can spend their time with other residents and participate in the available activities. As a result, congregate housing appeals to those who may feel socially isolated, who prefer that others prepare their meals and provide housekeeping services, or who have mild physical impairments and don't want to depend on driving to get around town.

If you move into congregate housing, you will find a community you can join right outside your apartment door. Some have a minimum age requirement, such as age 62. Others sell condominium units to residents, but most lease apartments on a monthly basis, so residents avoid the hassle of homeownership.

Congregate living facilities vary in what they provide, but most will offer most, if not all, of the following:

- some meals
- light housekeeping including linen service
- controlled entry
- 24-hour on-site security
- 24-hour emergency response system
- exercise classes
- social activities
- a computer center
- recreation rooms, such as a card room
- a library or reading room
- regular wellness services, such as blood pressure checks
- a hair salon
- a laundry room
- transportation
- utilities (except cable TV)

Congregate living facilities often are not licensed to provide health care, but they do provide some personal care. If you require more assistance, you may be allowed to hire outside help, such as visits from an in-home care agency. It may be part of a larger community that also includes assisted living and skilled nursing. At these campus-like communities, congregate housing residents who later need more personal assistance and health care can move on site to more appropriate housing. To locate congregate living options in your area, contact your local AAA.

Assisted Living

Assisted living communities (or assisted living, as it is usually referred to) provide a place to live for people who do not need significant assistance with health care but who want companionship and need help with what are called "activities of daily living" (ADLs) or "instrumental activities of daily living" (IADLs). ADLS and IADLs are sets of skills that are used by health care professionals to get a general idea of a person's ability to live independently and to gauge what help might be necessary to keep the person safe.

ADLs are basic self-care tasks needed to take care of physical needs:

- transfer in and out of a chair or bed and move from one place to another
- shower or bathe without assistance
- maintain continence and toilet without assistance
- get dressed and select appropriate clothes
- eat without assistance

IADLs are slightly more complex skills. These activities are not indispensable to survival and fundamental functioning, but they do let you live independently and function well as a self-reliant individual:

- manage finances
- handle transportation
- shop for and prepare meals
- use the telephone or other communication devices
- manage medications, including taking accurate dosages at the appropriate times and managing refills
- perform housework such as doing laundry, washing dishes, vacuuming, and maintaining a reasonably clean residence
- do basic home maintenance

Individuals who have difficulty with ADLs or IADLs may decide to move into assisted living to be relieved of having to deal with activities they have trouble with. For example, if you do not feel up to shopping and preparing meals, living where you can have all your meals prepared for you may be very appealing.

Assisted living communities do just as their name suggests: assist individuals by providing personal care and assistance with ADLs and IADLs. Staff can help residents who need assistance getting in and out of bed, bathing or showering, selecting clothes and dressing, and eating. If the resident is incontinent, staff will assist with toileting as needed.

Assisted living has become very popular. Nearly 1 million residents live in more than 28,000 assisted living communities, according to the National Center on Assisted Living. Over half the residents are age 85 or older. On average they are home to 60 to 70 residents, although larger ones are becoming more common.

Assisted living is not cheap. The average annual cost is about $50,000—over $4,000 a month. Still, compared to nursing homes, which cost on average over $90,000 a year, assisted living is an attractive alternative for those who need personal assistance but not the level of skilled medical care that is provided in a nursing home. (See Chapter 11.)

Services

Typically, assisted living provides these services:

- meals
- housekeeping
- laundry
- 24-hour help available from staff on duty
- assistance with bathing, dressing, toileting, and getting in and out of bed and to common areas
- on-site activities
- assistance with medications
- off-site transportation to medical appointments
- on-site medical care

If you are considering assisted living, get a written list of the services provided to residents. The assisted living place where Sally's mother was staying had tiered levels of assistance. As her health declined over time and she needed more staff time to help with bathing and dressing, she moved up to the next level of care. Of course, the higher level of care came at a greater cost.

Physical Layout

Assisted living communities try to create a homelike atmosphere. Residents usually have a one-bedroom unit, although some offer shared rooms or two rooms sharing a bathroom at a lower cost. The rooms may come with basic furniture, although residents may like to furnish their own space or add familiar items to the furnishings provided. Many encourage residents to hang a personal item on the outer apartment door, such as special wreath, to help them identify their apartment.

Because residents do not need to prepare meals, the unit may not have a kitchen, although some states require small kitchens in every unit. If you do have a kitchen, it will often have a microwave oven, sink, and small refrigerator. A personal coffee maker may or may not be permitted. When you enter assisted living, a receptionist will probably greet you. For security, the receptionist monitors both visitors and the residents. The healthier residents come and go as they please. But if a mildly forgetful resident heads for the street entrance to get some air, the receptionist may remind her to walk in the building's inner courtyard or call a staffer to accompany her for a short walk outside.

Beyond the reception area, you will usually find a large common room furnished very much like a living room, where residents congregate and watch TV. If you don't see many residents sitting there, they are probably in the other common rooms, such as an activities room where more is going on. The community will almost certainly have a room dedicated to rehabilitation and exercise, and maybe even an indoor pool and spa.

Many have an outdoor area, such as an enclosed courtyard and large porch with chairs, where residents can sit, socialize, and walk.

The largest room will probably be the dining room. Here, residents take their meals, although those who need help eating, such as people with advanced dementia, may use a separate dining room. When you enter the dining room, you may be impressed by the quality of the furnishings. Many, especially in higher-end communities, feature multiple chandeliers above tables that sit six to eight, like a fancy restaurant.

While there are many stand-alone assisted living communities, increasingly they are part of a larger complex that also includes skilled nursing. This way residents can move from assisted living to nursing care if their needs change.

Meals

Typically, meals are served to the residents by wait staff, although for residents who can carry their trays, a buffet line may be used for breakfast or lunch. The quality of the meals is very important to the happiness of the residents. Residents may choose from a menu of entrees and side dishes or substitute a sandwich for the meal of the day. Make sure the kitchen can accommodate any special dietary needs you may have, such as vegetarian, vegan, gluten-free, lactose-free, halal, or kosher. Some assisted living communities cater to a particular religion or at least advertise that they are sensitive to the dietary preferences and personal care needs of people of a particular faith.

Ask if residents can have an occasional meal delivered to their rooms—perhaps because they are ill or just want to be alone—and if there is a fee charged. Also ask the policy and fee for guests joining residents for occasional meals.

Before moving in, ask to have a meal there. This is your opportunity to sample the food and talk with the residents about how they like living there.

Activities

Assisted living residents should be able to pick from a robust selection of activities, sometimes coordinated by an activities director. Bingo, word games, craft activities, and sing-alongs are common. Residents and staff may plan community service projects, bring in lecturers, or arrange visits with service pets. Local adult and youth performers may give concerts. There may be a designated activities room, fitness center, and small reading room or library with computers so residents can send e-mails, use social media, or surf the web.

Ask how the community involves all the residents in its operations. Is there a residents' council that regularly meets with the staff and management? How is that council selected? Do residents volunteer? Are they elected? How long can they serve? What kind of issues does management bring to that council? Are there resident committees to plan social functions, recreation, on-site entertainment, lectures, and off-site travels? Do residents have a say about the menus? Residents aren't just long-term guests. It is their home, and they should have input in how it is run.

Health Care and Medications

The amount of health care provided often depends on the state licensing regulations. When Sally's mother first moved into assisted living after a hospital stay, she needed someone to help with catheter care. The staff wasn't licensed to provide that level of care, so Sally hired a private-duty nurse to come once a day for a few weeks. Be sure you know whether you can hire a personal care or health care provider if the staff can't meet your needs.

A key benefit that residents reap from assisted living is help with medications. On average, older people take five or more daily prescription medications. Taking these prescriptions as directed literally can have life-or-death consequences. Although assisted living communities are limited in the degree of medical care they can provide, they are permitted to remind residents when to take their medications, dispense medications, help residents take medications, and manage refills. Whether the residence can administer medications, such as injecting them, depends on whether state law allows it to do so. Find out before you move in the level of assistance you can get with your medications.

Also ask about procedures to ensure that the residents properly take their medications and where prescriptions are filled. Some residences have a pharmacy on site or a specific pharmacy that fills all prescriptions. Provide a list of the medications you take and ask the cost for refills. If the price is higher than what you currently pay, you may want to look into other options, such as using mail order or a different pharmacy. Or you might, for convenience, just use the on-site services.

In addition to providing personal care, the residence may have 24-hour nursing assistance. When visiting, ask about on-site medical assistance in case of an illness, injury, or emergency. Ideally it has medical supplies, equipment, and trained personnel to be able to respond immediately to residents' acute medical needs. The more it operates along a medical model by employing medical staff and providing regular visits by physicians and other health care providers, the longer it will be able to accommodate you if your need for medical care increases. Assisted living is not skilled nursing care or a hospital, however, and so it can deal with only immediate medical needs. More severe incidents may require a call to emergency medical services, a move to a nursing home, or a visit to the hospital.

Because of licensing restrictions, a community may be required to discharge residents if it can no longer meet their evolving health needs. For example, in most states an assisted living community cannot continue to care for you if you become bedridden. You'd need to move to a skilled nursing home. In some states, however, you could stay so long as a physician certifies you don't need the level of care that is provided in a skilled nursing home.

The residence may also have to discharge residents whose behavior puts themselves or others at risk. For example, a resident with dementia who becomes physically abusive to the staff and other residents may be asked to leave. Ask about the process for difficult residents and the number of residents involuntarily discharged in the last year due to disruptive or dangerous behavior. If the number is more than a handful, ask why.

Dementia

Dementia often creates the need for personal care. Almost all assisted living communities can care for individuals with mild dementia, but some are not prepared to take care of individuals with severe dementia, who require more care and supervision.

Today, many assisted living communities have a dedicated dementia wing or floor—sometimes called a memory care unit—for residents with moderate to severe dementia. Residents may enter assisted living with mild dementia and live with the general population. Later, when the dementia has progressed, they may move to memory care. Even if you don't now have signs of dementia, ask how the community handles residents who develop severe dementia but are otherwise physically healthy. Ask how residents with dementia are integrated into the community.

For more on memory care, turn to Chapter 10.

Fees and Payment

Paying for assisted living is difficult for many families because it is so expensive. The average cost of assisted living as of 2018 was more than $4,000 a month, nearly $50,000 a year, with the cost varying greatly across the country, according to Genworth's Cost of Care Survey. Some assisted living communities have a variable monthly rate. The more help you need, the higher the monthly fee. In addition to the monthly fee, you may have to put down a security deposit or entrance or community fee, which may be nonrefundable. You may also have the right to voluntarily pay for more extensive care, such as a personal assistant.

Most assisted living residents—or their families—pay for the cost of care. (By contrast, Medicaid covers most of the cost of skilled nursing care. See Chapter 13 for details on paying for care services.)

Medicaid may cover some of your assisted living costs if you meet the state's income and resource eligibility standards. Medicaid, a joint federal and state program, pays for both skilled nursing care as well as custodial nursing care—the term used for taking care of someone's personal, nonmedical needs, which are the services provided in assisted living. Even so, it was only a few years ago that Medicaid in some states began to pay for some residents of assisted living.

Federal law sets out the general guidelines for how states run their Medicaid programs. One federal requirement is that states cannot pay for the room-and-board portions of assisted living care. Some states will pay for the costs of care over and above room and board. Others use state funds to help pay the room-and-board costs for eligible residents. To find out what your state might pay toward the cost of assisted living, go to www.paying forseniorcare.com/medicaid-waivers/assisted-living.html#title2.

Medicaid eligibility qualifications vary from state to state and are quite complex. It's a good idea to talk with an elder law attorney familiar with Medicaid regulations in your state about eligibility requirements.

Some residents of assisted living have long-term care insurance policies that help pay for their cost of care. If you have a long-term care insurance policy, read it closely. A few older policies pay for care only in skilled nursing homes. But most policies purchased in the last few years pay benefits for assisted living as well. A long-term care insurance policy generally pays a daily benefit rate for insured care for a set period, typically three, four, or five years. Chapter 13 goes into much greater detail on the ins and outs of long-term care insurance.

If you do not have a long-term care insurance policy and own your home, you may be able to pay for assisted living by selling your house. If you can sell your house for $200,000, for example, you have enough money to pay for about four years of assisted living.

Termination

If the resident dies while in assisted living, the contract should state how much time the family has to clear out the apartment of any personal belongings and what happens to the resident's remaining personal effects. Any final charges, such as cleaning the apartment, and a prorated refund for the remaining days of the month should be addressed.

The contract should also say what happens if the resident must temporarily leave to receive medical care in a hospital. Ideally, the resident will return to the same unit and pay a reduced fee for the days he or she was gone if it was for more than a set number of days, such as seven.

Some residents voluntarily leave, whether to return home, move in with relatives, or go to a skilled nursing home. Sometimes staff will approach residents and explain that it can no longer support their needs and suggest they move to a skilled nursing home. Usually residents agree and move out. If not, the community may go to court for an eviction order. If a resident's medical needs exceed the care the community can provide under its state license, the court will approve the eviction.

Some residents run out of money and can no longer afford the monthly fee. If that happens, the management will work with residents to see if they are eligible for Medicaid or some other state program that helps pay for assisted living. If that is not possible, the residents will need to find a new place to live—perhaps a skilled nursing home, where Medicaid may be available to help pay.

Contract

Residents sign an admission contract. You should examine that contract carefully and perhaps have an elder law attorney review it. There is no standard contract. Still, the contract should, and likely will, contain the following items:

- *Monthly fee and date due.* The monthly fee, penalty for late payment, and conditions of notice of any fee change.
- *Security deposit.* The amount and under what conditions it will be returned.

- *Health requirements at the time of entry*. A physician's form attesting that you meet a minimum level of health. If you don't move in for some period of time after you apply, you may have to pass another physical examination.

- *Date of occupancy*. The date you can move in. Ideally you will have some flexibility so that you can move in earlier by a few days or later if something, like your health, prevents you from moving in on the exact date. You will likely need to pay starting the day you move in.

- *Identification of your unit*. The specific unit you will occupy, or its style and size.

- *Furnishings*. The furnishings provided and whether you can bring in your own, either to replace or supplement what's there. If you don't like what is provided, ask for changes before you move in.

- *Possible modification of your unit*. For example, you might want to enlarge a closet or replace the carpet. If so, be sure the contract clearly states your right to do so and who will pay for the modification. The contract should also state whether, upon leaving, you must return the unit to its original condition.

- *Services*. The services you will get for the monthly fee and any additional services that a resident can purchase and the cost.

- *Right of privacy*. When and for what reasons staff can enter your apartment. In particular, the contract should state when staff can enter if you are in your unit but you do not give permission or do not open the door.

- *Liability*. The contract will probably try to limit the facility's liability and may require the resident to agree to mandatory, binding arbitration of any disagreement, such as whether it is providing the services it promised. Under current federal regulations, communities can ask you to agree to arbitration, but the facility cannot require it as a condition of admission.

- *Residents' rights*. Your rights should anything go wrong. You want to know who to complain to if you are unsatisfied with your care. Before you sign a contract, ask if there is a residents' council that meets with management to deal with resident complaints or proposed operational changes.

- *Required action or documents*. Residents eligible for Medicaid or Medicare may be required to apply for these benefits. You may also be required to have a power of attorney naming someone to manage your financial affairs and also have a health care power of attorney that appoints someone to make health care decisions for you in case you are unable to do so. Make sure these documents are part of your medical records.

- *Termination*. The conditions for termination prior to the end of the contract, usually because the resident voluntarily leaves or dies, or because the resident is evicted.

Use the Supported Housing Contracts checklist in this chapter to make sure the essential information is included. If the contract doesn't cover all these points, ask for an explanation.

Board and Care Homes

Like assisted living, a board and care home is an option for older people who are reasonably healthy but need some degree of care and services, although not medical care. The distinguishing factor between assisted living and board and care homes is size. The section on assisted living in this chapter applies to board and care homes as well.

Board and care homes—also called "personal care homes," "domiciliary care," and "sheltered housing"—predate congregate housing and assisted living facilities. Some house only one gender. They charge a monthly fee that may be more affordable than congregate living or assisted living. Some states subsidize the monthly fee for lower-income residents. When considering a board and care home, ask what is covered in the monthly fee.

Many board and care homes are operated by families or individuals, perhaps in a large, older home converted to house a limited number of older individuals. Often the people who operate the home live on site or nearby. For this reason, many board and care homes are small, housing only eight to 20 residents.

As with assisted living, residents get room and board, and a staff member is on call 24/7. You have your own bedroom, may share a bathroom. and eat your meals in the dining room. Usually you are provided housekeeping, linen service, laundry, some modest personal assistance, and some activities and recreation.

The board and care home you are considering should be licensed by the state and meet state-imposed standards on the services they can provide to residents. If it's not licensed, ask why it's not and whether it is operating legally.

The following checklists are in Chapter 9:

❑ *What to Look for in Supported Housing*
❑ *Supported Housing Contracts*

What to Look for in Supported Housing

Appearance

Are the grounds well maintained and easy to navigate?	❑ Yes	❑ No
Is the reception area clean?	❑ Yes	❑ No
Are the halls clean?	❑ Yes	❑ No
Are nursing stations clean, well organized, and staffed?	❑ Yes	❑ No
Is the administrative office well organized and adequately staffed?	❑ Yes	❑ No
Are the common areas clean, well furnished, and free of odor?	❑ Yes	❑ No
Are the hallways light and clutter free?	❑ Yes	❑ No
Is there space dedicated to resident therapy?	❑ Yes	❑ No
Are the physical therapy rooms clean, and is the equipment in order?	❑ Yes	❑ No
Is the dining area clean?	❑ Yes	❑ No
Is the kitchen area clean?	❑ Yes	❑ No
Are the lawn and parking lot free of litter and debris?	❑ Yes	❑ No
Is there a dedicated dementia floor or wing?	❑ Yes	❑ No

Individual living spaces

Do the individual units seem comfortable?	❑ Yes	❑ No
Are the resident rooms clean and free of odor?	❑ Yes	❑ No
Is the space large enough?	❑ Yes	❑ No
Is there natural lighting? (Visit both in the morning and in the afternoon.)	❑ Yes	❑ No
Is there adequate storage space and closets?	❑ Yes	❑ No
Is there a separate storage area?	❑ Yes	❑ No
Are the rooms pleasantly furnished?	❑ Yes	❑ No
Can residents choose furnishings or, if they choose, bring their own?	❑ Yes	❑ No
Can residents personalize their doors?	❑ Yes	❑ No
Can residents personalize their units, such as with pictures, bedspreads, and mementos?	❑ Yes	❑ No
Is the kitchen or kitchenette adequate?	❑ Yes	❑ No
If rooms are shared, do residents have any choice of roommates?	❑ Yes	❑ No
Can they change roommates?	❑ Yes	❑ No
Do residents have access to an emergency pull cord system?	❑ Yes	❑ No

Common areas

Are the common areas clean, pleasantly furnished, and free of odors?	❑ Yes	❑ No
Are they large enough to accommodate several residents at once?	❑ Yes	❑ No
Do they have natural light?	❑ Yes	❑ No
Are there common spaces dedicated to activities?	❑ Yes	❑ No
Are family and friends visiting residents?	❑ Yes	❑ No
Are there common outside areas for residents to use?	❑ Yes	❑ No

Dining area

Is the dining area attractive and the atmosphere pleasant?	❑ Yes	❑ No
Does it have natural light, or is it well lit?	❑ Yes	❑ No
Does the food look appealing and fresh?	❑ Yes	❑ No
Are meals nutritious, with fruits and vegetables?	❑ Yes	❑ No
Is the menu varied?	❑ Yes	❑ No
Do residents have menu choices at every meal?	❑ Yes	❑ No
Do residents have access to between-meal snacks?	❑ Yes	❑ No
Is there sufficient space for the residents to be comfortably seated?	❑ Yes	❑ No
Are residents encouraged to eat in the dining area?	❑ Yes	❑ No
Are meals served in residents' rooms upon request or when necessary?	❑ Yes	❑ No

What is the cost, if any, for meals served in a resident's unit? _____

Does the community accommodate special dietary needs and preferences?	❑ Yes	❑ No

What are the mealtimes? _____

Are they flexible?	❑ Yes	❑ No
If you attended a meal, were you satisfied that the residents were given proper attention?	❑ Yes	❑ No
Does the staff assist residents with eating as necessary?	❑ Yes	❑ No
Does the staff monitor adequate nutrition?	❑ Yes	❑ No

Activities

How much control do residents have over their daily routine? _____

How many and what kinds of activity rooms are available? _____

What activities are offered?

• Book clubs	❑ Yes	❑ No
• On-site entertainment such as music, movies, and guest entertainers	❑ Yes	❑ No
• Lectures	❑ Yes	❑ No

- Walking groups   ❑ Yes   ❑ No
- Trips to shopping and libraries   ❑ Yes   ❑ No
- Trips to theaters, museums, and other events   ❑ Yes   ❑ No

Is there an exercise room?   ❑ Yes   ❑ No

Does it have group or individual training?   ❑ Yes   ❑ No

Is there a swimming pool?   ❑ Yes   ❑ No

Does it have organized classes?   ❑ Yes   ❑ No

Is there an indoor walking track or area?   ❑ Yes   ❑ No

Is there a safe and accessible outdoor area?   ❑ Yes   ❑ No

Does the area have seating?   ❑ Yes   ❑ No

Does the area have walking paths?   ❑ Yes   ❑ No

Is there a community garden or individual garden plots?   ❑ Yes   ❑ No

Is there a library with books, magazines, newspapers, and computers?   ❑ Yes   ❑ No

Are there quiet spaces for residents where there is no television?   ❑ Yes   ❑ No

Are there on-site services, such as a hair and nail salon?   ❑ Yes   ❑ No

Are there unattended residents in wheelchairs in the hall?   ❑ Yes   ❑ No

Are residents moving about on foot or with walkers?   ❑ Yes   ❑ No

Are residents in a common room engaged, or are they sitting in front of a television apparently unattended?   ❑ Yes   ❑ No

Did you see family and friends visiting residents?   ❑ Yes   ❑ No

Are residents who are in bed alert, reading, watching television, or using a handheld electronic device?   ❑ Yes   ❑ No

Are religious services and celebrations available?   ❑ Yes   ❑ No

Are there common rooms on every floor?   ❑ Yes   ❑ No

What services are on site? Bank? Small store? Hair salon? Barber shop? _____

Care and safety

Is there a proper balance between supervision and personal autonomy?   ❑ Yes   ❑ No

How often and when does staff check on residents in their rooms? _____

What is the privacy policy for staff access to the individual units? _____

What are the procedures in case a resident has a medical incident or emergency? _____

How are medical emergencies handled? _____

To what hospital are residents sent? _____

What are the emergency evacuation procedures?_____

Are there backup generators in case of power outages? ❑ Yes ❑ No

Is there a controlled entry system? ❑ Yes ❑ No

Residents

What is the average age of residents? _____

What is the average length of residency? _____

What percentage of residents have moderate or severe dementia? _____

Who decides whether a resident should be placed in a dementia unit? _____
_____

What is your sense of the care and concern for residents with significant dementia? _____

Medical and personal care

Can residents have a personal physician not affiliated with the community? ❑ Yes ❑ No

Are residents required to use the community pharmacy to fill prescriptions? ❑ Yes ❑ No

Is non-emergency transportation for routine medical appointments provided? ❑ Yes ❑ No

How often and when does staff check on residents in their rooms? _____
_____

How frequently are care plans reviewed? _____

Are family members encouraged to participate in care plan review? ❑ Yes ❑ No

Does the staff respond quickly when residents push their call button? ❑ Yes ❑ No

How often are residents provided therapies, such as physical therapy, when needed? _____

Are therapies provided by staff, by outside providers, or by both? _____

Is there a room dedicated to physical or other types of therapy? ❑ Yes ❑ No

How is a resident's dietary plan created? How often is it reviewed? _____

Who are the on-staff or consulting physicians? What is their training and background? _____

Does the community employ or contract with geriatric social workers or geriatric psychiatrists to meet with the residents? ❑ Yes ❑ No

What medical care is provided on site? Podiatrists? Neurologists? Psychologists or psychiatrists? _____

What is the staff-to-resident ratio during the day? _____

What is the staff-to-resident ratio at night? _____

How is the staff instructed to respond to a resident having a medical incident or emergency? _____

Does the staff seem to care for and treat residents with respect and dignity? ❑ Yes ❑ No

Does the staff engage with residents and recognize residents as unique individuals? ❑ Yes ❑ No

How does the staff manage residents who wander?_____

What is the policy for managing hostile or physically aggressive residents? _____

Is there a dedicated dementia floor or wing? ❑ Yes ❑ No

Family involvement

Is it close enough so your family can visit frequently? ❑ Yes ❑ No

Are there limits on visiting hours? ❑ Yes ❑ No

Are families encouraged to participate in the resident's care planning? ❑ Yes ❑ No

How are families informed of changes in the resident's condition and care needs? _____

What supportive services are offered to the family? _____

Are guest rooms available for visitors? ❑ Yes ❑ No

Can the family share meals with the residents? ❑ Yes ❑ No

If so, is there a fee? ❑ Yes ❑ No

Is there a family visiting area or dining area? ❑ Yes ❑ No

Location

Is the neighborhood safe? ❑ Yes ❑ No

Is it near shopping? Convenience stores? Coffee shops? ❑ Yes ❑ No

Is it independently operated? ❑ Yes ❑ No

Is it associated with a larger institution? ❑ Yes ❑ No

Are the premises secure? ❑ Yes ❑ No

Can you hear traffic and street noise inside? ❑ Yes ❑ No

Are there nearby hotels for visiting family and friends? ❑ Yes ❑ No

Transportation and parking

Are there adequate parking places? ❑ Yes ❑ No

Is there a fee for parking? ❑ Yes ❑ No

Is there parking for guests? ❑ Yes ❑ No

Is outdoor parking safe and convenient? ❑ Yes ❑ No

Is there a secure parking garage?   ❑ Yes   ❑ No

Does the community provide transportation?   ❑ Yes   ❑ No

Is public transportation available?   ❑ Yes   ❑ No

Are taxis and ridesharing services available?   ❑ Yes   ❑ No

Is the neighborhood walkable?   ❑ Yes   ❑ No

Are there bike paths?   ❑ Yes   ❑ No

Staff and management

Does the staff seem friendly?   ❑ Yes   ❑ No

Does the staff seem caring?   ❑ Yes   ❑ No

Does the staff seem knowledgeable?   ❑ Yes   ❑ No

Does the staff seem professional?   ❑ Yes   ❑ No

What is your perception of the staff and their interaction with residents? _____

_____

What is the rate of staff turnover? _____

What was your impression of the chief administrator? _____

_____

Did the director of activities seem knowledgeable about
individual residents?   ❑ Yes   ❑ No

Are social workers either on site or regularly available?   ❑ Yes   ❑ No

Are nurses available 24/7?   ❑ Yes   ❑ No

What kind of and how many professionals such as nurses are employed there? _____

_____

How many certified nursing assistants (CNAs) are on duty during the day and at
night? _____

What is the ratio of aides to residents? _____

What are the qualifications for staff, including aides? _____

What background checks are performed on staff? _____

What are the ongoing training requirements for aides and other staff? _____

Does the staff receive special abuse prevention training?   ❑ Yes   ❑ No

Are the staff fluent in the language the resident speaks?   ❑ Yes   ❑ No

What are the procedures for keeping families informed about the resident? _____

_____

How are medical emergencies handled? To what hospital are residents sent? _____

_____

Who makes the decision to send a resident to a hospital for emergency care? _____

_____

Administration

Who are the owners? _____

Is it for-profit or nonprofit? _____

What is the community's philosophy? _____

Other

Is there a residents' council?   ❏ Yes   ❏ No

Is there a family council?   ❏ Yes   ❏ No

Are pets allowed? If so, are there restrictions on kind, breed, and size? _____

_____

Is smoking or vaping allowed?   ❏ Yes   ❏ No

What is the average age of the residents? _____

How many rooms are there? How many residents? How many couples? _____

_____

What is the average duration of stay? _____

What were the opinions of the residents and their families that you talked with? ____

_____

Supported Housing Contracts

Lawyer who reviewed the contract: _____

Date resident signed the contract: _____

Person who signed the contract on behalf of the resident: _____

in the legal role of _____

(agent with power of attorney, guardian)

Person liable for payment of fees: _____

Term (length) of the contract: _____

Contract can be reviewed/renewed on _____

Intent to terminate requires _____ days' notice

Conditions for termination by resident: _____

Conditions for termination by management: _____

Levels of care licensed to provide: _____

Additional fees for each level of care: _____

Procedure for change in level of care: _____

Additional fees for extra services provided: _____

Level of care needed at application: _____

Physical examination needed before acceptance   ❑ Yes   ❑ No

Immunizations required: _____

Tuberculous test required   ❑ Yes   ❑ No

Initial or application fee: _____

- Refundable   ❑ Yes   ❑ No

- Conditions for refund: _____

Security deposit fee: $_____

- Refundable   ❑ Yes   ❑ No

- Conditions for refund: _____

Monthly fee: $_____

  ❑ Meals

  ❑ Room

  ❑ Personal care

  ❑ Housekeeping

  ❑ Linens

  ❑ Other: _____

Due date: _____

Late penalty: _____

Move-in date: _____

Assigned room number: _____

Furnishings provided: _____

Cost for furnishings, if any: _____

Furnishings provided by resident: _____

Modifications to be made to unit: _____

Responsibility for lost or damaged personal property: _____

_____

Renter's insurance required	❑ Yes	❑ No
Private room	❑ Yes	❑ No
Shared room	❑ Yes	❑ No
Private bath	❑ Yes	❑ No
Shared bath	❑ Yes	❑ No

Maximum number to share a room: _____

Maximum number to share a bathroom: _____

Procedure for selecting or changing rooms or roommates: _____

_____

Overnight guest policy: _____

Guest meal policy: _____

Visitation policy: _____

Grievance procedure: _____

Residents' council	❑ Yes	❑ No
Statement of residents' rights provided	❑ Yes	❑ No
Privacy right to personal unit	❑ Yes	❑ No
Limits on liability for resident's injury	❑ Yes	❑ No
Is arbitration required	❑ Yes	❑ No
Requirement to have advance directive	❑ Yes	❑ No
Requirement to have power of attorney	❑ Yes	❑ No
Requirement to have Do No Resuscitate Order	❑ Yes	❑ No

Procedure for change in ownership or management: _____

CHAPTER 10
WHEN YOU NEED MEMORY CARE

Dementia, including Alzheimer's disease, can be debilitating, destroying memory, eroding thinking skills and judgment, and taking away the ability to carry out even the simplest tasks. But that doesn't mean the person can't retain a good quality of life. Caring for a loved one with dementia can be time consuming and emotionally draining. That's why many people with dementia live in a community with professionals specially trained to help them.

Nursing homes or assisted living communities may have wings or floors dedicated to caring for people with dementia, or those residents may be integrated into the community. You can now also find specialized dementia care facilities, often called memory care.

Wherever it is located, quality memory care has staff who are extensively trained in caring for those with dementia with the goal of providing them with the best quality of life possible. Programming is tailored to residents' specific needs and abilities. One colleague tells how her stepmother placed her father, with worsening Alzheimer's disease, in a memory care unit. At first, our colleague adamantly opposed the move, thinking he'd do best with a 24-hour aide at home, in familiar surroundings with familiar people. But her father thrived under the daily structure and stimulation and the consistent, gentle, and patient treatment he received in memory care. He would not have gotten that quality of care at home.

This chapter looks at memory care units and how to pick the best one for your circumstances.

Rise of Specialized Dementia Care

The number of memory care units is growing every year in response to the growth in the number of individuals with dementia. The Alzheimer's Association reports that 5.8 million Americans have Alzheimer's disease. Many others suffer from other forms of dementia or related brain diseases, such as Parkinson's disease or frontotemporal degeneration. It is estimated that nearly 15 percent of people over the age of 65 have some form of dementia. More startling is that up to half of those 85 and older will develop Alzheimer's or some other form of dementia.

Dementias are brain diseases that cause gradual decreases in an individual's ability to remember and think. As the disease progresses, it eventually interferes with the individual's ability to function. Often those with dementia develop mood swings, become confused and uncertain of where they are, and have difficulty finding the right words. At later stages, everyday activities such as walking, eating, swallowing, going to the bathroom, and talking can become harder. Individuals may be prone to wandering, leaving the house without supervision and often getting lost. In some cases, the individual becomes physically aggressive, putting the safety of caregivers at risk.

Scientists are searching but have yet to find a cure for Alzheimer's disease or the other dementias. Nor is there any proven way to slow down dementia's progression. Some medicines can help alleviate the symptoms for some individuals, but only for a time. Research presented at the Alzheimer's Association's International Conference 2019 suggests that healthy lifestyle choices—including eating right, exercising, not smoking, and engaging in cognitively stimulating activities—may reduce the risk of developing dementia, even among people with a genetic predisposition to the disease. For current advances on maintaining and improving brain health, consult the Global Council on Brain Health (www.aarp.org/gcbh), an independent collaborative of scientists, scholars, health professionals, and policy experts from around the world convened by AARP.

Faced with the reality of this progressive disease, many families seek care tailored to the needs of the individual with dementia. They admit that they cannot provide round-the-clock care. In response, the family looks for a community that will provide the best possible environment for their loved one, with relevant stimulating activities, safe and reassuring routines, and engaged, trained, and caring staff. So, they turn to memory care.

Who Needs Memory Care?

How do you determine if the dementia has progressed enough to need memory care? Close family members may not recognize or may overlook the early signs of dementia in a loved one. It is sometimes difficult to distinguish the symptoms of dementia and those signs of a poor memory associated with age, fatigue, medications, or confusion and frustration with the modern world and its gizmos and speed.

Larry first realized that his father, then age 85 and whom he hadn't seen for five months, might be developing dementia when the two of them had lunch at a restaurant buffet that featured tacos. You walked down a counter with a variety of ingredients that you selected to build a customized taco. Larry led the way. He selected a hard taco shell and proceeded to put on his favorite ingredients: pork, lettuce, sour cream, guacamole, and hot sauce. He returned to his table. His father came back to the table with a plate that contained a spoonful of salsa. He explained that he didn't know what to do with the ingredients because he had never eaten a taco before. Larry accepted that explanation and made a taco for his father. Only later that day did it occur to Larry that his father had eaten tacos before. That he had forgotten how to make one was a sign that something was wrong.

Over the next few days, Larry closely watched his father. Unfortunately, his fear that his father was developing dementia seemed confirmed. Larry noticed that his father had a substantial amount of money in an interest-free checking account. Having experienced the Great Depression in the 1930s, his father had always kept a minimum amount of money in his checking account, routinely investing any extra funds in U.S. Treasury bonds. When Larry asked about the money in the checking account, his father said that he just "wasn't sure what to do with it." Finally, Larry found a biography of Abraham Lincoln given to his father for his recent birthday. When asked if had enjoyed the book, his father admitted that he had stopped reading about halfway through because, he said, "I couldn't remember what I had read the day before."

What Larry was looking for were the subtle changes in behavior that may signify the onset of dementia. Those include losing interest in hobbies or activities. Perhaps your mother did the newspaper crossword puzzle every day, but she no longer does it. When you ask, she says she has lost interest in it or the newspaper has made the puzzle too hard. Or your father no longer plays cards with his buddies. When asked why not, he has no real answer.

One colleague's father forgot how to set the microwave; he also forgot how to start the car—while he was in a Target parking lot. Others may have trouble following a familiar recipe, keeping track of monthly bills, or remembering the rules to a favorite game. They may sleep a lot during the day and roam about at night. Disorientation is common. The police found Sally's father-in-law wandering around the small town where he had lived for 50 years looking for his car. He couldn't remember where he parked it and didn't know his way back to the house.

As we age, we all may lose our keys more often or strain to remember a name, but if your father has forgotten that he sold his car and no longer drives, it may be a sign of dementia. When Larry's mother was age 96, she was residing in assisted living. One night she had chest pains, and she went to the hospital by ambulance. She stayed overnight and returned the next day. A month later when Larry was in town visiting her, he asked her about that incident, but she had no memory of it. Her response was emphatic: "I was never in the hospital. If I had been in the hospital, I would remember that." Her reaction confirmed Larry's suspicion that she was developing dementia.

Sally's friend knew her husband had dementia when he couldn't remember if they had been to church one Sunday. They had, but he repeatedly asked her if they had gone. Requesting the same information over and over is a typical pattern of behavior for those with dementia. Another friend had to intervene when his mother began to repeatedly buy items being sold on television. So many packages were delivered that she stopped opening them. Soon the closet in the guest room overflowed with boxes.

A common symptom of dementia is the person's tendency to roam, responding to a need to get somewhere, such as to a former office or previous home. A resident who walks away from home or a care community can be at great risk. To prevent what's called "elopement," the door of a memory care unit may require a special key, combination, or fob that prevents residents from leaving unattended. Some communities use monitoring bracelets that trigger an alarm if an unattended resident leaves the area.

Poor judgment, difficulty in recognizing personal risk, and neglecting personal hygiene are some of the indicators of behavioral variant frontotemporal dementia (bvFTD). It differs from Alzheimer's in that it's caused by nerve cell loss in the front part of the brain that controls conduct, judgment, empathy, and foresight.

Parkinson's disease, another form of brain disease, often starts with a tremor in one hand. It can cause slow movement, stiffness, loss of balance, trouble sleeping, and a change in voice, as well as other symptoms. As it progresses, confusion and difficulty in thinking and understanding may develop.

Signs of Dementia

Dementia is a progressive disease. In the beginning it is difficult to detect because the early signs, such as short-term memory loss, don't seem that important or are considered a normal sign of aging. As the disease progresses and the signs become more apparent, it is important that the individual be examined by a physician, neurologist, geriatrician, or geriatric psychiatrist. Getting a probable diagnosis is complicated because dementia takes many forms and no single test pinpoints the source or cause of the disease. If some form of dementia is confirmed, family members must begin to make plans on how they can assist the individual.

Alzheimer's disease is a form of dementia. Here are the Alzheimer's Association's ten warning signs and symptoms, along with typical age-related changes that are not a necessarily a sign of dementia:

1. *Memory loss that disrupts daily life.* One of the most common signs of Alzheimer's disease, especially in the early stage, is forgetting recently learned information. Other signs include forgetting important dates or events, asking the same question over and over again, or increasingly needing to rely on memory aids (such as reminder notes or electronic devices) or family members for things the person used to handle on his or her own.

   A typical age-related change? Sometimes forgetting names or appointments but remembering them later.

2. *Challenges in planning or solving problems.* Some people living with dementia may experience changes in their ability to develop and follow a plan or work with numbers. They may have trouble following a familiar recipe or keeping track of monthly bills. They may have difficulty concentrating and take much longer to do things than they did before.

   A typical age-related change? Making occasional errors when managing finances or household bills.

3. *Difficulty completing familiar tasks*. People living with Alzheimer's disease often find it hard to complete routine tasks. Sometimes they may have trouble driving to a familiar location, organizing a grocery list, or remembering the rules of a favorite game.

   A typical age-related change? Occasionally needing help to use microwave settings or to record a TV show.

4. *Confusion with time or place*. People living with Alzheimer's can lose track of dates, seasons, and the passage of time. They may have trouble understanding something if it is not happening immediately. Sometimes they may forget where they are or how they got there.

   A typical age-related change? Getting confused about the day of the week, but figuring it out later.

5. *Trouble understanding visual images and spatial relationships*. For some people, vision problems are a sign of Alzheimer's. They may also have problems judging distance and determining color or contrast, causing issues with driving.

   A typical age-related change? Vision changes related to cataracts.

6. *New problems with words in speaking or writing*. People living with Alzheimer's may have trouble following or joining a conversation. They may stop in the middle of a conversation and have no idea how to continue or repeat themselves. They may struggle with vocabulary, have trouble naming a familiar object, or use the wrong name.

   A typical age-related change? Sometimes having trouble finding the right word.

7. *Misplacing things and losing the ability to retrace steps*. People living with Alzheimer's may put things in unusual places. They may lose things and be unable to go back over their steps to find them again. They may accuse others of stealing, especially as the disease progresses.

   A typical age-related change? Misplacing things from time to time and retracing steps to find them.

8. *Decreased or poor judgment*. Individuals may experience changes in judgment or decision making. For example, they may use poor judgment when dealing with money, or pay less attention to grooming or keeping themselves clean.

   A typical age-related change? Making a bad decision once in a while, like neglecting to change the oil in the car.

9. *Withdrawal from work or social activities*. People living with Alzheimer's may experience changes in the ability to hold or follow a conversation. As a result, they may withdraw from hobbies, social activities, or other engagements. They may have trouble keeping up with a favorite team or activity.

A typical age-related change? Sometimes feeling uninterested in family or social obligations.

10. *Changes in mood and personality.* Individuals living with Alzheimer's may experience mood and personality changes. They may be easily upset at home, at work, with friends or when out of their comfort zone.

    A typical age-related change? Developing very specific ways of doing things and becoming irritable when a routine is disrupted.

For a detailed description of the types, early signs, and stages of dementia and Alzheimer's disease, go to www.nia.nih.gov/health/what-dementia-symptoms-types-and-diagnosis.

Decision to Move

The level of care an individual needs depends on the stage of dementia and how fast it is progressing. In the mild stage, individuals may stay at home with a spouse or family, having others drive them and accompany them when they leave the house. Doctors generally recommend patients with dementia stop driving. If the disease progresses to the moderate stage, you might need more in-home help or consider a memory care unit.

The entire family—including the person living with dementia, to the extent possible, if it's not too disturbing and distressing—should be included in conversations about where to live, engage in online research of communities, and tour possible places to live. If you are a relative or caregiver, keep in mind that people with dementia may not understand or may simply not want to accept that they should move to a memory care unit. Don't be surprised if after a tour, they state very strongly that they have no intention of ever moving there. A dementia diagnosis is a frightening thing. Just be patient and respectful. You may want to bring a non-family member into the conversation, perhaps a close friend or professional, to help reduce conflict and tension. Having the decision to move come from a medical expert may help.

Be sure that the whole family is on board with the decisions on the placement. Be prepared for a family member to insist that there's no need to move, that Mom or Dad is okay. If that happens, a medical expert's recommendation could help the family face the reality of the diagnosis and the need for professional care.

A Closer Look at Memory Care

A memory care unit, or special care unit, is a residential community that specializes in providing care to individuals with dementia. It may be physically located as part of a larger residential care community such as assisted living, nursing home, or continuing care retirement community, or it may stand alone. Although memory care units accept individuals in the early stages of dementia, most residents move in when the disease has progressed to the moderate or severe stage. They may move to a memory care unit from living alone or with a spouse or family, or from assisted living or other supportive housing such as a board and care home.

The key to quality memory care is professional staff who understand how best to respond to the medical, social, and behavioral effects of the disease. Staff should know each resident's unique life story, abilities, and interests and create an atmosphere that is meaningful, caring, and supportive. Residents should feel a sense of belonging and dignity and have as much independence as is consistent with their personal safety.

Ideally the staff undergo extensive and ongoing training. Ask about the qualifications of staff and the extent of their training. If you have any doubts about the staff qualifications, especially those who interact daily with the residents, keep looking. You want the best care possible, not just a nice-looking building that does little more than keep residents from wandering out the door.

When considering a residence, you should visit more than once and when you're not expected. Ask to watch staff interacting with the residents. See if the community will put you in contact with some family members of residents so you can get their perspective. What you are looking for is a community that creates a personalized care plan that adapts to residents' changing needs and abilities. You want a homelike environment that avoids depersonalization and a sense of coldness.

Ask about the use of psychotropic drugs that affect a person's mind, emotions, and behavior. Certainly, some individuals with dementia may benefit from carefully prescribed and monitored prescription drugs, but some communities use psychotropic drugs to manage the residents for the convenience of the staff. This can happen despite efforts by the Centers for Medicare and Medicaid (CMS) to reduce the use of these chemical restraints. The drugs, if misused, can create zombie-like residents who are easily controlled. In short, be sure any psychotropic drugs are used for the benefit of the residents, not the staff.

Individuals with dementia can have physical symptoms that memory care should be well-qualified to address. Some of these symptoms or behaviors are apathy, aggression, loss of inhibition, an inability to sleep through the night, agitation, and depression. Although the underlying dementia may not be treatable, many of the symptoms can be reduced by an individualized care plan and, where appropriate, the carefully monitored use of prescription drugs.

You want memory care that has daily structured activities for each resident, such as performing small tasks, participating in planned outings, or being entertained. It should encourage interaction between the residents and staff, such as talking about the resident's life or singing together. Ask how the staff meets the residents' spiritual, creative, physical, and intellectual needs.. Look at the daily schedule.

At a minimum, activities should include these:

- gross motor activities through exercise or dancing
- promotion of self-care, such as dressing and personal hygiene
- social activities, including music and games
- remembrance promotion by looking at photographs and picture books
- sensory enhancement, such as stimulating the senses and touching and handling objects

The number of staff and the extent of their training depend on state licensing law. For memory care units in nursing homes, federal law requires 24-hour licensed nursing care, typically by registered nurses (RNs) or licensed practical nurses (LPNs), and an RN to be on duty eight hours a day, seven days a week. Those requirements, however, don't take into account how many residents are being caring for and the extent of their needs. Some states have mandatory staff-to-resident ratios, but many facilities struggle with staff turnover. Use Medicare's Nursing Home Compare, at www.medicare.gov/NursingHomeCompare/Data/Staffing.html, to find data on staffing ratios at the residences you are considering.

The nursing staff should be experienced in how to best respond to often challenging behavioral problems. They should understand the value of therapeutic activities and know how to employ those activities. Some staff members should be certified in or trained to monitor and administer medications.

Administrators and staff must also be aware of the important role that the family plays in the resident's well-being. Staff should frequently communicate with the family about the resident's condition and how the family can help the individual. Family members should feel they are an important and welcomed part of the team.

If the resident has a dog or cat, find out if pets are allowed. If so, ask who takes care of them. Hopefully residents will be engaged in caring for their pets for as long as possible. The community may have a resident cat or dog, or both, or periodically bring in a therapeutic pet. If so, the animal was selected because of its calm and friendly temperament. One of the more famous therapy cats is Oscar, who lives at Steere House in Providence, Rhode Island. Oscar is the subject of geriatrician David Dosa's book *Making Rounds with Oscar: The Extraordinary Gift of an Ordinary Cat*. Residents will be encouraged to engage with the community pet, and perhaps even walk or feed it. Just be sure that staff keep pets away from a resident who is allergic to them or just doesn't like being around them.

The best test of a memory care unit is your overall reaction. Does it "feel" right? Does it treat each resident with respect and dignity? Do residents appear to be engaged and feel a sense of belonging? Does it create activities that appeal to and engage the individual's interests? For instance, are paints and paintbrushes provided to residents who like to paint? Is there a residents' chorus for those who like to sing? What you want is the best possible life at each stage of the disease in a homelike setting that respects the dignity and individuality of each resident.

Admission

Memory care units are licensed by the state, which regulates who they can admit. In addition, the unit will have its own admission requirements. Prior to admission, it will assess the prospective resident to see if the unit has the ability to meet the individual's care needs. For example, a memory care unit may decide not to admit an individual who is easily upset and becomes agitated and even physically aggressive, or someone who has a serious ongoing medical condition in addition to the dementia. It is probably not permitted to admit a new resident who is not ambulatory, although it may be able to keep residents whose disease progresses to the point that they are bedridden.

To be admitted, the individual must have a physician's diagnosis of dementia and a recent general physical health examination. The individual must have a tuberculosis test and current immunizations, such as a flu shot and pneumonia vaccine. The prospective resident or the family will be required to demonstrate the financial ability to pay the monthly fee for an extended time. Finally, the prospective resident will be assessed by staff members.

Upon admission, staff will create a written care plan based on the assessment of the individual's needs that took place before admission. Depending on state law, the care plan will be updated at least annually and when there is a change in the resident's condition and care needs. State law may require the memory care unit to provide activities that are appropriate to the needs of each resident and adapt those activities as necessary. The state may also require daily therapeutic activities. Even if not required by state law, the community should do so on its own initiative.

Costs and Contracts

Memory care is typically more expensive than assisted living but less expensive than nursing homes. Instead of costly drugs and treatments for heart and cancer patients, the primary expense for those with dementia is the trained staff to provide 24-hour supervised care. The cost depends greatly on the level of services provided, staff-to-resident ratio, and whether the unit is free-standing or combined with assisted living, nursing home, or continuing care retirement community. Residents who meet the Medicaid income and asset eligibility requirements often choose nursing homes for memory care because Medicaid may help cover the costs. (Medicaid is explained in Chapter 13.)

The contract for a memory care unit will be a standard agreement that in some states is approved by state regulators. Use the Memory Care Contracts checklist in this chapter for the important provisions: entry fee, monthly fee, services covered by those fees, termination rights by both the resident and the community, and the property rights of the resident who furnishes his or her room. The contract should state what happens if the resident must be hospitalized for any period of time. Usually, the community will hold the resident's room as long as the resident continues to pay the monthly fee.

The memory care unit may publish a resident handbook, which will probably contain general information, such as these:

- emergency procedures
- meals
- pet policies
- how to handle complaints
- contact information for the family
- policies regarding gifts or tips to staff members

The following checklists are in Chapter 10:

❑ *What to Look for in Memory Care*
❑ *Memory Care Contracts*

What to Look for in Memory Care

Appearance

Are the grounds well maintained and easy to navigate?	❑ Yes	❑ No
Is the community clean?	❑ Yes	❑ No
Is it kept up to date?	❑ Yes	❑ No
Is it easy to navigate?	❑ Yes	❑ No
Are the hallways well lit and clutter free?	❑ Yes	❑ No
Are common areas clean and well furnished?	❑ Yes	❑ No

Individual living spaces

Do the individual units seem comfortable?	❑ Yes	❑ No
Are resident rooms clean and free of odor?	❑ Yes	❑ No
Is the space large enough for you?	❑ Yes	❑ No
Is there natural lighting? (Visit in both the morning and the afternoon.)	❑ Yes	❑ No
Are there adequate storage spaces and closets?	❑ Yes	❑ No
Are the rooms pleasantly furnished?	❑ Yes	❑ No
Can residents personalize their units (e.g., with pictures, bedspreads, and mementos)?	❑ Yes	❑ No
Are the entrances to bedrooms decorated in an individual manner so that residents can identify their own room?	❑ Yes	❑ No
If rooms are shared, do residents have any choice of roommates?	❑ Yes	❑ No
Can they change roommates?	❑ Yes	❑ No
Do residents have access to an emergency pull cord system?	❑ Yes	❑ No

Common areas

Are the common areas clean, pleasantly furnished, and free of odors?	❑ Yes	❑ No
Are they large enough to accommodate several residents at once?	❑ Yes	❑ No
Do they have natural light?	❑ Yes	❑ No
Are there common spaces dedicated to activities?	❑ Yes	❑ No
Did you observe family and friends visiting residents?	❑ Yes	❑ No
Are there common outside areas for residents to use?	❑ Yes	❑ No
Are there unattended residents in the hall in wheelchairs?	❑ Yes	❑ No

Dining area

Is the dining area attractive and the atmosphere pleasant?	❑ Yes	❑ No
Is the area sunlit?	❑ Yes	❑ No
Does the food look appealing and fresh?	❑ Yes	❑ No

Are meals nutritious, with fruits and vegetables?	❏ Yes	❏ No
Is the menu varied?	❏ Yes	❏ No
Do residents have menu choices at every meal?	❏ Yes	❏ No
Do residents have access to between-meal snacks?	❏ Yes	❏ No
Is there sufficient space for the residents to be comfortably seated?	❏ Yes	❏ No
Are residents encouraged to eat in the dining area?	❏ Yes	❏ No
Are meals served in residents' rooms upon request or when necessary?	❏ Yes	❏ No

What is the cost, if any, for meals served in a resident's unit? _____

Does the community accommodate special dietary needs and preferences?	❏ Yes	❏ No

What are mealtimes, and are they flexible? _____

Do residents have menu choices at every meal?	❏ Yes	❏ No
If you attended a meal, were you satisfied that the residents were given proper attention?	❏ Yes	❏ No
Does the staff assist residents with eating as necessary?	❏ Yes	❏ No
Does the staff monitor adequate nutrition?	❏ Yes	❏ No

What is the policy on hand feeding residents who can no longer feed themselves? (Are family members allowed to hand feed? May the family refuse to approve hand feeding for a resident?) _____

_____

Activities

How much control do residents have over their daily routine? _____

_____

How many and what kind of activity rooms are available? _____

_____

Are activities individualized to meet the residents' interests and abilities?	❏ Yes	❏ No

What specific activities are offered, and how often? _____

_____

• Book clubs	❏ Yes	❏ No
• On-site entertainment such as music, movies, and guest entertainers	❏ Yes	❏ No
• Lectures	❏ Yes	❏ No
• Walking groups	❏ Yes	❏ No
• Trips to shopping and libraries	❏ Yes	❏ No
• Trips to theaters, museums, and other events	❏ Yes	❏ No

Is there an exercise room?	❑ Yes	❑ No
Does it have group or individual training?	❑ Yes	❑ No
Is there a swimming pool?	❑ Yes	❑ No
Does it have organized classes?	❑ Yes	❑ No
Is there an indoor walking area or track?	❑ Yes	❑ No
Is there a safe, accessible, and well-monitored outdoor area with seating and walking paths?	❑ Yes	❑ No
Is there a community garden or are there individual garden plots?	❑ Yes	❑ No
Is there a library with books, magazines, newspapers, and computers?	❑ Yes	❑ No
Are there quiet spaces for residents where there is no television?	❑ Yes	❑ No
Are an-site religious services and celebrations available?	❑ Yes	❑ No
Are there unattended residents in the hall in wheelchairs?	❑ Yes	❑ No
Are residents moving about on foot or with walkers?	❑ Yes	❑ No
Are residents in a common room engaged?	❑ Yes	❑ No
Are residents who are in bed alert, reading, watching television, or using a handheld electronic device?	❑ Yes	❑ No
Are there common rooms on every floor?	❑ Yes	❑ No

What services are on site? Bank? Small store? Hair salon? Barber shop? _____

_____

Does the unit frequently bring in speakers and entertainment for the residents?	❑ Yes	❑ No
Are activities available mornings and afternoons as well as evenings and weekends?	❑ Yes	❑ No
Do the residents seem to respond to and enjoy the activities?	❑ Yes	❑ No
Do residents have a flexible schedule on when to wake up and go to sleep?	❑ Yes	❑ No
Is personal care, such as bathing, done with respect and dignity?	❑ Yes	❑ No
Is transportation available to medical appointments?	❑ Yes	❑ No

Care and safety

Is there a proper balance between supervision and personal autonomy?	❑ Yes	❑ No

How often does the staff check on residents in their rooms? _____

_____

What is the privacy policy for staff access to the individual units? _____

_____

What are the procedures in case a resident has a medical incident or emergency? ___

_____

How are medical emergencies handled? _____

_____

To what hospital are residents sent? _____

What are the emergency evacuation procedures? _____

_____

Are there backup generators in case of power outages?   ❑ Yes   ❑ No

Is there a controlled entry system?   ❑ Yes   ❑ No

How are residents prevented from wandering away? _____

_____

Is medical care provided?   ❑ Yes   ❑ No

Is adequate personal care and assistance provided?   ❑ Yes   ❑ No

What training do the staff get in how to interact with and assist
individuals with dementia? _____

How often does staff receive training? _____

Does the unit have registered nurses trained in dealing with
individuals with dementia?   ❑ Yes   ❑ No

Is a registered nurse on site at all times?   ❑ Yes   ❑ No

Who are the on-staff or consulting physicians? _____

What is their training and background? _____

Does the unit employ or contract with geriatric social workers or
geriatric psychiatrists to regularly meet with the residents?   ❑ Yes   ❑ No

What medical care is provided on site? Podiatrists? Neurologists?
Psychologists or psychiatrists? _____

What is the staff-to-resident ratio during the day?
(State law often requires a 1:5 ratio.) _____

What is the staff-to-resident ratio at night? _____

How is the staff instructed to respond to a resident having a medical emergency? ___

_____

Does the staff seem to care for and treat residents with respect
and dignity?   ❑ Yes   ❑ No

Does the staff engage with residents and recognize residents as
unique individuals?   ❑ Yes   ❑ No

Is staff experienced with the care needs of residents with
non-Alzheimer's forms of dementia?   ❑ Yes   ❑ No

Are you satisfied with the proposed care plan?   ❑ Yes   ❑ No

Are physical, occupational, speech, and recreational therapies
available on site?   ❑ Yes   ❑ No

Residents

What is the average resident age? _____

What is the average length of residency? _____

What percentage of residents are bedridden? _____

What percentage of residents have moderate or severe dementia? _____

What is your sense of the care and concern for residents with significant dementia?

_____

Family involvement

Is the unit close enough so that family can visit frequently?   ❏ Yes   ❏ No

Are there limits on visiting hours?   ❏ Yes   ❏ No

Are families encouraged to participate in care planning?   ❏ Yes   ❏ No

How are families informed of changes in the resident's condition
and care needs? _____

What supportive services are offered to families? _____

_____

Are guest rooms available for visitors?   ❏ Yes   ❏ No

Can families share meals with the residents?   ❏ Yes   ❏ No

What is the charge for guest meals?_____

Is there a family visiting area or dining area?   ❏ Yes   ❏ No

Location

Is the neighborhood safe?   ❏ Yes   ❏ No

Did you feel comfortable there?   ❏ Yes   ❏ No

Is it near public transportation? Shopping? Convenience stores?
Coffee shops?   ❏ Yes   ❏ No

Is it secure?   ❏ Yes   ❏ No

Can you hear traffic and street noise inside?   ❏ Yes   ❏ No

Are there nearby hotels for family and friends visiting?   ❏ Yes   ❏ No

Staff and management

Does the staff seem friendly?   ❏ Yes   ❏ No

Does the staff seem caring?   ❏ Yes   ❏ No

Does the staff seem knowledgeable?   ❏ Yes   ❏ No

Does the staff seem professional?   ❏ Yes   ❏ No

What is your perception of the staff and their interaction with residents? _____

_____

What is the rate of staff turnover? _____

What were your impressions of the chief administrator? _____
_____

Did the director of activities seem knowledgeable about individual
residents?   ❑ Yes   ❑ No

Are social workers either on site or regularly available?   ❑ Yes   ❑ No

Do volunteers visit?   ❑ Yes   ❑ No

How many registered nurses (RNs) are on duty during the day and at night? _____
_____

How many certified nursing assistants (CNAs) are on duty during the day and at
night? _____

What is the ratio of aides to residents? _____

What are qualifications for staff, including aides? _____
_____

What background checks are performed on staff? _____
_____

What are the ongoing training requirements for aides and other staff? _____
_____

Does the staff receive special abuse prevention training?   ❑ Yes   ❑ No

Does the staff interact with and converse with residents and
know their names?   ❑ Yes   ❑ No

Are the staff fluent in the language the resident speaks?   ❑ Yes   ❑ No

Who makes the decision to send a resident to a hospital for emergency care? _____
_____

Administration

Who are the owners? _____

Is it for-profit or nonprofit? _____

What is its philosophy? _____
_____

Is it certified by Medicare and Medicaid?   ❑ Yes   ❑ No

Does it accept Medicaid reimbursement for residents?   ❑ Yes   ❑ No

Other

What is the policy on factors that would lead to discharge, such as a change in behavior or financial circumstances? _____

If restraints are used, how many residents are in restraints, and what type? _____
_____

What happens when residents wander? _____

_____

How does the staff react if a resident becomes aggressive to staff or other residents?

_____

What is the policy for responding to residents who become romantically or sexually attracted to one another? _____

What happens if a resident's dementia becomes severe? What if a resident becomes bedridden? _____

_____

Can the resident remain in the same room as the dementia
progresses?   ❑ Yes   ❑ No

Are palliative medical care or hospice care provided to residents
who are dying?   ❑ Yes   ❑ No

What were the opinions of the residents and their families that you talked with?_____

_____

Memory Care Contracts

Lawyer who reviewed contract: _____

Date resident signed contract: _____

Person who signed contract on behalf of the resident: _____

in the legal role of _____
(agent with power of attorney or guardian)

Person liable for payment of fees: _____

_____

Term (length) of the contract: _____

_____

Contract can be reviewed/renewed on _____

Move-in date: _____

Intent to terminate requires _____ days' notice.

Conditions for termination by resident: _____

_____

Conditions for termination by management:
- ❑ Necessary for the resident's welfare
- ❑ Skilled care is no longer required
- ❑ Health and safety of others is endangered
- ❑ Failure to pay for services
- ❑ Ceases to operate

Levels of care the facility is licensed to provide: _____

Medicare certified ❑ Yes ❑ No

Accepts Medicaid ❑ Yes ❑ No

Basic daily rate includes:
- ❑ Room
- ❑ Meals
- ❑ Housekeeping
- ❑ Linens
- ❑ General nursing care
- ❑ Medical records services
- ❑ Recreation
- ❑ Personal care
- ❑ Other: _____

Price list for extra services not included in the basic rate provided ❑ Yes ❑ No

187

Procedure for change in price lists: _____

_____

Application fee: $_____

Refundable   ❑ Yes   ❑ No

Conditions for refund: _____

Private room   ❑ Yes   ❑ No

Private bath   ❑ Yes   ❑ No

Maximum number to share a room: _____

Procedure for selecting or changing rooms or roommates: _____

_____

_____

Furnishings provided by management: _____

_____

Furnishings provided by resident: _____

_____

_____

Resident may decorate room and door   ❑ Yes   ❑ No

Responsibility for lost or damaged personal property: _____

_____

_____

Overnight guest policy:

_____

_____

Guest meal policy:

_____

_____

Visitation policy:

_____

_____

Grievance procedure: _____

_____

_____

Statement of residents' rights provided	❑ Yes	❑ No
Requirement of private pay	❑ Yes	❑ No
Right to apply for Medicare and/or Medicaid	❑ Yes	❑ No
Bed hold policy consistent with Medicare/Medicaid requirements	❑ Yes	❑ No
Limits on liability for resident's injury	❑ Yes	❑ No
Arbitration required	❑ Yes	❑ No
Requirement to have advance directive	❑ Yes	❑ No
Requirement to have a do not resuscitate order	❑ Yes	❑ No
Requirement to have a durable power of attorney	❑ Yes	❑ No

CHAPTER 11

NURSING HOMES

Nearly 1.5 million people currently get the personal and health care they need in a nursing home. They don't need to be in a hospital, but they do need the level of skilled nursing care that is provided in a nursing home.

Paying for round-the-clock care at home for months or years is simply not feasible for most families. A home care aide at $20 an hour would cost $480 a day. A nursing home, by contrast, is more affordable—in 2019 the cost on average was $275 a day for a private room; even a shared room will cost about $250 a day.

In the past, relatively healthy older people often moved to nursing homes because they needed custodial or personal care, not because of serious medical problems or dementia. Today those individuals are getting care at home or in assisted living or memory care. As a result, nursing homes find themselves filled with residents who have significant medical conditions or advanced dementia.

The dedicated staff in most nursing homes strive to make the residents' lives as comfortable as possible. Because of the complex needs of the residents, nursing homes must operate more like a hospital rather than an extended stay hotel—the model for most assisted living communities. Nursing homes must be ready to provide medical care to dozens or even hundreds of residents with diverse physical and mental needs.

When choosing a nursing home, look at ratings (more on that in the following sections) and make sure the it provides the specific care you need. Visit, preferably more than once, and do so when no one is expecting you. As with assisted living, the best places are those that treat their residents with dignity and respect and encourage independence, purpose, and growth, says Jill Vitale-Aussem, The Eden Alternative CEO and author of AARP's *Disrupting Senior Housing: A Mindshift*.

What Is a Skilled Nursing Facility?

Most of us refer to a nursing home as a nursing home. Today, the technical term is *skilled nursing facility* (SNF, pronounced "sniff") or *nursing facility* (NF). Federal regulations determine whether a nursing home qualifies as a SNF or NF and therefore is eligible for federal payments from Medicaid or Medicare for the residents who live there. Because nursing homes are so dependent on federal payments for their residents, almost all qualify as a SNF or NF or both. In Chapter 13, we explain Medicare and Medicaid reimbursements in greater detail.

A SNF is for residents who need skilled health care but not the level of acute care provided by a hospital. A SNF provides health and personal care services that typically include nursing care, 24-hour supervision, three meals a day, and assistance with the activities of daily living mentioned in Chapter 9, which include bathing, dressing, and moving around. Skilled nursing home residents often have severe illnesses, such as a respiratory condition or heart disease, or are recovering from a serious injury, such as a broken hip. SNFs provide both rehabilitative care and long-term skilled nursing care.

Because hospitals are so very expensive, many patients in a hospital for surgery, illness, or injury transfer to a SNF to recover, where there are trained nurses on duty to assist them. The cost savings are considerable. Each day in the hospital may cost $2,000, while a SNF may cost $300. If you have congestive heart failure, for instance, you may get immediate treatment in a hospital. Once you are stable, you may continue your recovery in a SNF because you still need medical attention for your ongoing heart condition. You could spend a few days or weeks in recovery. SNFs also provide shorter term rehabilitation services—such as physical and occupational therapy—for those who need nursing care while recovering from an injury or surgery.

Residents with dementia, such as Alzheimer's disease, or those who are too frail to live alone need personal attention more than they need nursing care. That difference is where nursing facilities—NFs—come in. They provide custodial care, not health care. Almost all nursing homes qualify as both SNFs and NFs, perhaps providing primarily nursing care in one wing and custodial care in another. Additionally, SNFs and NFs may also have special memory care units dedicated to caring for residents with dementia. We devote Chapter 10 to memory care.

Levels of Care

Most nursing homes provide a range of care services: custodial, skilled, subacute, and rehabilitative care. Be sure the nursing home you are considering provides the care you need.

Custodial Care

All nursing homes provide custodial care, which, as mentioned, is the term used for taking care of someone's personal, nonmedical needs. Staff help residents get in and out of bed, dress, bathe, toilet, get into a wheelchair, move from room to room, and eat; monitor (but not administer) medications and other medical therapies; and provide a safe environment. You might ask, after reading Chapter 9 on assisted living, isn't that the care you would expect to receive in an assisted living residence? To a degree, yes. Assisted living provides residential custodial care, and so do NFs and SNFs. But state licensing requirements limit the extent of medical care that an assisted living community can provide. Many individuals need assistance that, due to state and federal laws and regulations, can only be provided by NFs and SNFs. As we explain in this chapter, the source of payment may also determine where you can best be cared for.

Plan of Care

You don't just pick a nursing home and move in. There must be a match between what you need and what the nursing home can provide. For each new resident, the nursing home is required by law to make a comprehensive assessment of a potential resident's care needs and develop a written care plan that will meet those needs. Federal law also requires the nursing home to reassess each resident at least once a year, or more frequently if a resident's condition changes significantly, and update the care plan appropriately. The assessment evaluates the individual's social, emotional, mental, and medical condition. A care plan lays out how the community will respond to the individual's condition and care needs such as incontinence, special dietary needs, therapies, loss of vision, or dementia. The plan is supposed to maximize the individual's independence and enable the individual to function at the highest level possible. Be sure to review the plan of care. It should not read like it is just boilerplate but should be tailored to the individual's needs.

Skilled Nursing Care

Skilled nursing care is medical care. If you have a medical problem that requires ongoing medical care, the nursing home will provide it. Skilled nursing homes have registered nurses (RNs) who are available 24 hours a day to provide medical care. RNs help create a resident's care plan (see the "Plan of Care" box) and provide medical care that includes giving residents medicine and injections, providing tube feeding and wound care, monitoring vital signs, providing necessary medical equipment, and reacting to changes in the resident's condition. Nursing homes also have certified nursing assistants (CNAs) or licensed practical nurses (LPNs) who provide more basic nursing and custodial care and usually are supervised by an RN. Nursing homes can also assist with their residents' needs for rehabilitation and recovery from operations or medical events, such as a stroke. Nursing homes see that the residents get the physical, speech, and other therapies they may need. These therapies may be provided in an on-site rehabilitation center by the nursing home staff or by outside providers, as explained on the next page.

Subacute Care

Because of the high cost of care in a hospital, increasingly nursing homes provide subacute care, which is comprehensive care for someone suffering from an acute illness, an injury, or a flare up of a chronic condition. Subacute care is typically provided after a hospitalization. Once such individuals have been stabilized in the hospital, they may be moved to a much less expensive subacute care unit in a nursing home. As individuals recover, they may move to assisted living, to a rehabilitation center, or back home to continue their recovery. Nursing homes have opened these subacute care units because they can charge a much higher daily rate than they'd otherwise charge—often paid for by Medicare for a limited time—and because they may be unable to fill all their beds with residents who need only more basic care.

Rehabilitation Care

A nursing home with an inpatient rehabilitation center provides physical medicine and the physical, speech, and occupational therapies residents need to restore their abilities after an illness or injury. For inpatients, the centers work on helping them heal and reenter life. Nurses monitor them and assist with bathing, dressing, and grooming as well as seeing that individuals take their prescribed medicines. Therapy is provided on a regular schedule in specially designed rooms with appropriate equipment where the residents work with therapists to rebuild their strength, coordination, and balance. Some communities offer therapy in a dedicated water therapy pool.

Physical therapy is the most common form of therapy. Physical therapists help residents reduce pain, improve strength and balance, and in general recover their physical well-being. Speech therapists assist those who because of a stroke, a brain injury, or a progressive neurological disease have difficulty talking, comprehending speech, or swallowing.

Occupational therapy helps individuals to regain daily life skills such as dressing, getting up and lying down, taking a shower, and using a walker. Therapists can help residents regain the ability to perform the instrumental activities of daily living (discussed in Chapter 9), such as getting into and out of a car, shopping, and making phone calls. The goal is to help residents better meet their personal care needs. Once residents have sufficiently recovered the skills that allow them to return to their former daily lives, they may move back home or into supportive housing, such as into assisted living.

Some nursing homes only offer short-term rehabilitation stays; others offer long-term stays, and still others specialize in certain forms of therapies. The extent, duration, and type of therapy that is needed determines which option is best for an individual. Wherever the rehabilitation services are offered, the community must be licensed by the state to provide it. It's also important to know if Medicare or Medicaid will cover any of the costs of the rehabilitative care.

Choosing a Nursing Home

An online tool run by the Centers for Medicare & Medicaid Services (www.medicare .gov/nursinghomecompare) rates more than 15,000 nursing homes that are certified by that agency on a scale of one to five stars (the more stars, the better). Ratings are based on three categories: how the home fared on health inspections, whether it is staffed adequately, and how it rated on other quality measures (for example, how many residents reported bedsores or were physically restrained). Experts advise that you look behind the rating numbers. Although one or two stars usually signify problems, a five-star facility isn't necessarily great, but it is probably worth considering. Each report is packed with useful information; be sure to read inspection reports thoroughly.

But that's just the start. Now you'll want to visit the places. Visit more than once and when you're not expected. We have a checklist in this chapter to tell you what to look for. It will help you to focus on what is important, spot deficiencies, and even eliminate nursing homes that come up short. In the end, however, you must make a choice based on what feels right. Is this nursing home going to provide the best quality of life possible?

State licensing requirements dictate the look and operation of nursing homes. Facilities also must comply with the requirements of Medicare and Medicaid to be eligible for reimbursement from these federal programs (see Chapter 13). The result is that most nursing homes look similar. For example, the windows in residents' rooms must be a designated distance from the floor to discourage any resident from opening the window and falling out. To prevent falls, handrails line brightly lit hallways and rooms. Hospital-style layouts with long corridors interspersed with nursing stations are common. Two residents may share a room because Medicaid will only pay for a shared room. You will see a common dining room, usually one to a floor, and a common living room at the end of the corridor with a television set that is seemingly always on. The home may have a special floor or wing with secured doors for residents with advanced dementia.

When you're visiting, talk to residents and their families. If they were not available during your visit, ask staff if they can put you in touch with them. Their observations and opinions may be very revealing. Be sure to get several opinions.

Ask how the community involves residents in its operation. Is there a residents' council that regularly meets with the staff and management? If so, ask to talk to one of its members. Find out how effective the council is in suggesting changes. Does management bring important issues to that council? Is management responsive to the suggestions of council members? You are looking for a nursing home that recognizes that it is the residents' home. They should have input in how it is run.

In the end, you must rely on what you see. How well do the residents appear to be doing? How engaged are the residents in their own care? Is the staff competent and caring? Is the community clean? Does the decor seem warm and comfortable, or is there an institutional sense of coldness? If you are not sure if this community is the right one, keep looking. Try to make sure that this is the best choice, a place that can feel like home.

Person-Directed Care Based on The Eden Alternative

In 1991, William Thomas, a medical doctor and gerontologist, created The Eden Alternative, which he saw as a way to rid nursing homes of their sterile, unwelcoming, institutionalized environment.

The Eden Alternative partners with nursing homes and other supportive housing to help them change their environment so that residents are cared for in a less institutional setting. The aim is to turn the focus from just housing frail and sick residents to creating a warm, caring setting. The Eden Alternative addresses the physical layout and design of nursing homes but perhaps more importantly also trains the staff to provide person-directed care. The goal is to transform the experience for both residents—whom it calls "elders"—and staff through improved quality of care.

The Eden Alternative is based on ten principles, including these:

- Loneliness, helplessness, and boredom account for the bulk of suffering among our elders.

- Loving companionship is the antidote to loneliness.

- Opportunities to give as well as receive care are the antidote to helplessness.

- Daily life with variety and spontaneity by creating an environment in which unexpected and unpredictable interactions and happenings can take place is the antidote to boredom.

- Medical treatment should be the servant of genuine human caring, never its master.

To find an Eden Alternative home, go to www.edenalt.org/resources/find-a-registry-member/registry-member-map/.

The Eden Alternative offers staff training that has been adopted by some facilities, while others have incorporated similar values. There are, of course, homes that do little more than announce that the nursing home is resident centered. But others have taken the concept to heart and are trying to move from a culture of institutionalization that imposes a plan of care upon the residents to a genuine culture of respecting the individuality and needs of each resident. If you are considering nursing homes, ask if the staff has been enrolled in the Certified Eden Associate Training program or similar such training. If not, ask why not.

While The Eden Alternative tries to reform existing communities, the Green House Project, also founded by Thomas, features specially designed homes that create a comfortable setting for individuals who need nursing care.

The number of Green House Project homes is limited, but, like The Eden Alternative, they provide a model of what a better nursing home can be. Many nursing homes have tried to adopt at least some of the Green House Project concepts. When looking for a nursing home, see if there is a Green House–style nursing home near you. If so, check it out. You may be pleasantly surprised at what you see.

Green House homes are generally a cluster of small buildings that form a small community. The physical setup of the houses and the attitudes of the staff are designed to help residents feel more in control of their lives and to have a sense of autonomy. The furnishings and decor avoid the institutional feeling and feature warm and comforting colors and design. Lots of sunlight and houseplants bring the outside in.

Residents often have private rooms and baths and can participate in preparing their own meals. The small buildings with the private rooms will have a common living room and perhaps a small kitchen. There may even be sleeping quarters for visiting family members. Perhaps there is a small patio and even a bit of a garden. The idea is that the residents get to know and be friends with the other residents in their building, and that the staff develop personal relations with the residents. Volunteers from the surrounding community are encouraged to visit and interact with the residents.

Proponents of the Green House project claim that the houses significantly improve the quality of life for residents. Compared to a traditional nursing home, residents generally have more privacy, dignity, and autonomy and better relationships with the staff and other residents. Staff members, in turn, have a better sense of satisfaction. They are less stressed, feel more empowered, and spend more meaningful time with the residents. If you are looking for a nursing home, look for a Green House nursing home or a home with Green House features.

As of 2017, there were more than 250 Green House project nursing homes in 32 states with some 150 in the planning or construction stages. Reimbursement through Medicaid or Medicare is the same as with other nursing homes.

The following checklists are in Chapter 11:

- ❏ *What to Look for in a Nursing Home*
- ❏ *Nursing Home Contracts*

What to Look for in a Nursing Home

Appearance

Are the grounds well maintained and easy to navigate?	❏ Yes	❏ No
Is the reception area clean?	❏ Yes	❏ No
Are the hallways light and clutter free?	❏ Yes	❏ No
Is there natural light in the common areas?	❏ Yes	❏ No
Are nursing stations clean, well organized, and staffed?	❏ Yes	❏ No
Is the administrative office well organized and adequately staffed?	❏ Yes	❏ No
Are the common areas clean, well furnished, and free of odor?	❏ Yes	❏ No
Are the physical therapy rooms clean, and is the equipment in order?	❏ Yes	❏ No
Is the dining area clean?	❏ Yes	❏ No
Is the kitchen area clean?	❏ Yes	❏ No
Are the lawn and parking lot free of litter and debris?	❏ Yes	❏ No

Individual living spaces

Do the individual units seem comfortable?	❏ Yes	❏ No
Are the resident rooms clean and free of odor?	❏ Yes	❏ No
Is the space large enough for you?	❏ Yes	❏ No
Is there natural lighting? (Visit both in the morning and in the afternoon.)	❏ Yes	❏ No
Is there adequate storage space and closets?	❏ Yes	❏ No
Are the rooms pleasantly furnished?	❏ Yes	❏ No
Can residents choose furnishings or, if they choose, bring their own?	❏ Yes	❏ No
Can residents personalize their units (e.g., with pictures, bedspreads, and mementos)?	❏ Yes	❏ No
Can residents personalize their doors?	❏ Yes	❏ No
If rooms are shared, do residents have any choice of roommates?	❏ Yes	❏ No
Can they switch roommates?	❏ Yes	❏ No
Do residents have access to an emergency pull cord system?	❏ Yes	❏ No
How often does staff visit residents in their rooms? _____		

Common areas

Are the common areas clean, pleasantly furnished, and free of odors?	❏ Yes	❏ No
Are they large enough to accommodate several residents at once?	❏ Yes	❏ No
Do they have natural light?	❏ Yes	❏ No
Are there common spaces dedicated to activities?	❏ Yes	❏ No
Are family and friends visiting residents?	❏ Yes	❏ No
Are there common outside areas for residents to use?	❏ Yes	❏ No
Are there unattended residents in the hall in wheelchairs?	❏ Yes	❏ No

Dining area

Is the dining area attractive and the atmosphere pleasant?	❏ Yes	❏ No
Does the food look appealing and fresh?	❏ Yes	❏ No
Are meals nutritious, with fruits and vegetables?	❏ Yes	❏ No
Is the menu varied?	❏ Yes	❏ No
Do residents have menu choices at every meal?	❏ Yes	❏ No
Do residents have access to between-meal snacks?	❏ Yes	❏ No
Is there sufficient space for the residents to be comfortably seated?	❏ Yes	❏ No
Are residents encouraged to eat in the dining area?	❏ Yes	❏ No
Are meals served in residents' rooms upon request or when necessary?	❏ Yes	❏ No

What is the cost, if any, for meals served in a resident's unit? _____

Does it accommodate special dietary needs and preferences?	❏ Yes	❏ No

What are mealtimes? Are they flexible? _____

If you attended a meal, were you satisfied that the residents were given proper attention?	❏ Yes	❏ No
Does the staff assist residents with eating as necessary?	❏ Yes	❏ No
Does the staff monitor adequate nutrition?	❏ Yes	❏ No

What is the policy on hand feeding residents who can no longer feed themselves? (Are family members allowed to hand feed? May the family refuse to approve hand feeding for a resident?) _____

_____

Activities

How much control do residents have over their daily routine? _____

_____

Do residents have a flexible schedule on when to wake up and go to sleep?	❏ Yes	❏ No
Are activities individualized to meet the residents' interests and abilities?	❏ Yes	❏ No

How many and what kind of activity rooms are available? _____

_____

What activities are offered?

Book clubs	❏ Yes	❏ No
On-site entertainment such as music, movies, and guest entertainers	❏ Yes	❏ No
Lectures	❏ Yes	❏ No
Walking groups	❏ Yes	❏ No
Trips to shopping and libraries	❏ Yes	❏ No
Trips to theaters, museums, and other events	❏ Yes	❏ No

Is there exercise or an exercise room?	❑ Yes	❑ No
Does it have group or individual training?	❑ Yes	❑ No
Is there a swimming pool?	❑ Yes	❑ No
Does it have organized classes?	❑ Yes	❑ No
Is there an indoor walking track or area?	❑ Yes	❑ No
Is there a safe and accessible outdoor area?	❑ Yes	❑ No
Does it have walking paths with seating?	❑ Yes	❑ No
Is there a community garden or individual garden plots?	❑ Yes	❑ No
Is there a library with books, magazines, newspapers, and computers?	❑ Yes	❑ No
Are there quiet spaces for residents where there is no television?	❑ Yes	❑ No
Are residents moving about on foot or with walkers or wheelchairs?	❑ Yes	❑ No
Are residents in a common room engaged?	❑ Yes	❑ No
Are residents who are in bed alert, reading, watching television, or using an electronic device?	❑ Yes	❑ No
Are religious services and celebrations available?	❑ Yes	❑ No
Are there common rooms on every floor?	❑ Yes	❑ No

What services are on site? Bank? Small store? Hair salon? Barber shop? _____

_____

Care and safety

Is there a proper balance between supervision and personal autonomy?　　　　　　　　　　　❑ Yes　❑ No

How often and when does the staff check on residents in their rooms? _____

_____

What is the privacy policy about staff access to the individual units? _____

_____

What are the procedures in case a resident has a medical incident? _____

_____

How are medical emergencies handled? _____

_____

To what hospital are residents sent? _____

_____

What are the emergency evacuation procedures? _____

_____

Are there backup generators in case of power outages?	❑ Yes	❑ No
Is there a controlled entry system?	❑ Yes	❑ No

Residents

What is the average age of residents? _____

What is the average length of residency? _____

What percentage of residents are bedridden? _____

What percentage of residents have moderate or severe dementia? _____

Who decides whether a resident should be placed in a dementia unit? _____

_____

What is your sense of the care and concern for residents with significant dementia?

_____

How are residents with dementia prevented from wandering away? _____

_____

Medical and personal care

Can the resident have a personal physician not affiliated with
the community?   ❑ Yes   ❑ No

Are residents required to use the community pharmacy to fill
prescriptions?   ❑ Yes   ❑ No

Is nonemergency transportation for routine medical appointments
provided?   ❑ Yes   ❑ No

How does it meet the condition and care needs of individual residents? _____

_____

How frequently are care plans reviewed? _____

Does the staff respond quickly when residents push their call button? ❑ Yes ❑ No

How often are residents provided therapies, such as physical therapy,
when needed? _____

_____

Are therapies provided by staff, by outside providers, or by both? _____

_____

How is a resident's dietary plan created? _____

_____

How often is it reviewed? _____

Is a registered nurse on site at all times?   ❑ Yes   ❑ No

Who are the on-staff or consulting physicians? _____

_____

What is their training and background? _____

_____

Does it employ or contract with geriatric social workers
or geriatric psychiatrists to regularly meet with the residents?   ❑ Yes   ❑ No

What medical care is provided on site? Podiatrists? Neurologists? Psychologists or psychiatrists? _____

What is the staff-to-resident ratio during the day? (State law often requires a 1:5 ratio.) _____

What is the staff-to-resident ratio at night? _____

_____

How is the staff instructed to respond to a resident having a medical emergency?

_____

Does the staff seem to care for residents and treat them with respect and dignity?	❑ Yes	❑ No
Does the staff engage with residents and recognize residents as unique individuals?	❑ Yes	❑ No

What is the policy for use of physical or chemical restraints?_____

_____

If restraints are used, how many residents are in restraints, and what type? _____

_____

What are the procedures in case a resident has a medical incident or emergency? ___

_____

What is the policy for managing hostile or physically aggressive residents? _____

_____

Are palliative and hospice care available?	❑ Yes	❑ No
Is there a dedicated dementia floor or wing?	❑ Yes	❑ No
Is there a dedicated hospice unit or suite?	❑ Yes	❑ No

Family involvement

Is the location close enough so that family can visit frequently?	❑ Yes	❑ No
Are there limits on visiting hours?	❑ Yes	❑ No
Are families encouraged to participate in care planning?	❑ Yes	❑ No

How are families informed of changes in the resident's condition and care needs? _____

_____

What supportive services are offered to family? _____

_____

Are guest rooms available for visitors?	❑ Yes	❑ No
Can family share meals with the residents?	❑ Yes	❑ No
Is there a family visiting area or dining area?	❑ Yes	❑ No

Location

Is the neighborhood safe?	❏ Yes	❏ No
Did you feel comfortable there?	❏ Yes	❏ No
Is it near public transportation? Shopping? Convenience stores? Coffee shops?	❏ Yes	❏ No

Is it freestanding, or is it associated with other care providers? _____

_____

Is it secure?	❏ Yes	❏ No
Can you hear traffic and street noise inside?	❏ Yes	❏ No
Are there nearby hotels for family and friends visiting?	❏ Yes	❏ No

Staff and management

Does the staff seem friendly?	❏ Yes	❏ No
Does the staff seem caring?	❏ Yes	❏ No
Does the staff seem knowledgeable?	❏ Yes	❏ No
Does the staff seem professional?	❏ Yes	❏ No

What is your perception of the staff and their interaction with residents? _____

_____

Does the staff interact with and converse with residents and know their names?	❏ Yes	❏ No
Are the staff fluent in the language the resident speaks?	❏ Yes	❏ No

What is the rate of staff turnover? _____

What were your impressions of the chief administrator? _____

_____

What were your impressions of the director of nursing? _____

_____

Does the director of activities seem knowledgeable about individual residents and suitable activities and engaged?	❏ Yes	❏ No
Are social workers on site?	❏ Yes	❏ No
If not, do they visit regularly or are they available on call?	❏ Yes	❏ No
Are there volunteers who regularly assist in the care of residents?	❏ Yes	❏ No

How many registered nurses (RNs) are on duty during the day and at night? _____

_____

What is the ratio of RNs to residents? _____

How many certified nursing assistants (CNAs) are on duty during the day and at night? _____

What is the ratio of CNAs to residents? _____

How many other staff, such as aides, are on duty during the day and at night? _____

_____

What is the ratio of aides to residents? _____

What are qualifications for staff, including aides? _____

_____

What background checks are performed on staff? _____

_____

What are the ongoing training requirements for aides and other staff? _____

_____

Does the staff receive special abuse prevention training? ❑ Yes ❑ No

What are the procedures for notifying families of changes in a resident's
health or plan of care? _____

Who makes the decision to send a resident to a hospital for emergency care? _____

_____

Administration

Who are the owners? _____

Is it for-profit or nonprofit? _____

Is it owned by a chain of nursing homes, or is it independent? _____

_____

What is the community's philosophy? _____

_____

Is it Medicare and Medicaid certified? ❑ Yes ❑ No

Other

Is there a residents' council? ❑ Yes ❑ No

Is there a family council? ❑ Yes ❑ No

Are pets allowed? If so, are there restrictions on kind, breed, and size? _____

_____

Is smoking or vaping allowed? ❑ Yes ❑ No

How many rooms are there? Residents? Couples? _____

_____

What were the opinions of the residents and their families that you talked with? ____

_____

How does the management respond when residents become romantically or sexually
attracted to one another? _____

Nursing Home Contracts

Lawyer who reviewed contract: _____

Date resident signed contract: _____

Person who signed contract on behalf of the resident: _____
in the legal role of _____
(agent with power of attorney or guardian)

Person liable for payment of fees: _____

Term (length) of the contract: _____

Contract can be reviewed/renewed on _____

Move-in date: _____

Intent to terminate requires _____ days' notice.

Conditions for termination by resident: _____

_____

Conditions contract can be terminated by management:

- ❏ Necessary for the resident's welfare
- ❏ Skilled care is no longer required
- ❏ Health and safety of others is endangered
- ❏ Failure to pay for services
- ❏ Ceases to operate

Medicare certified ❏ Yes ❏ No

Accepts Medicaid ❏ Yes ❏ No

Levels of care licensed to provide: _____

_____

Procedure for change in level of care: _____

_____

Fee schedule for each level of care provided ❏ Yes ❏ No

Basic daily rate includes:

- ❏ Room
- ❏ Meals
- ❏ Housekeeping
- ❏ Linens
- ❏ General nursing care
- ❏ Medical records services
- ❏ Recreation
- ❏ Personal care
- ❏ Other: _____

Price list for extra services not included in the basic rate provided ❏ Yes ❏ No

Procedure for change in price lists: _____

_____

Application fee: $_____

Refundable ❑ Yes ❑ No

Conditions for refund: _____

Private room ❑ Yes ❑ No

Private bath ❑ Yes ❑ No

Maximum number to share a room: _____

Procedure for selecting or changing rooms or roommates: _____

_____

_____

Furnishings provided by management: _____

_____

_____

Furnishings provided by resident: _____

_____

_____

Responsibility for lost or damaged personal property: _____

_____

Overnight guest policy: _____

_____

_____

Guest meal policy: _____

_____

_____

Visitation policy: _____

_____

_____

Grievance procedure: _____

_____

_____

Statement of residents' rights provided ❑ Yes ❑ No

Requirement of private pay ❑ Yes ❑ No

Right to apply for Medicare and/or Medicaid ❑ Yes ❑ No

Bed hold policy consistent with Medicare/Medicaid requirements ❑ Yes ❑ No

Limits on liability for resident's injury	❑ Yes	❑ No
Arbitration required	❑ Yes	❑ No
Requirement to have an advance directive	❑ Yes	❑ No
Requirement to have a power of attorney	❑ Yes	❑ No
Requirement to have a do not resuscitate order	❑ Yes	❑ No

CHAPTER 12

ALL IN ONE: CONTINUING CARE RETIREMENT COMMUNITIES

"My parents' six years in a CCRC were the best years of their lives," a colleague told us. A CCRC—continuing care retirement community—offers residents a place to live with graduated levels of support for the rest of their lives. It's often called a continuum of care or a life plan community, meaning the CCRC provides the various levels of personal assistance and health care that residents need throughout their lifetimes.

When you are healthy, you move into an apartment, townhouse, or small house within the CCRC complex, where you live independently. If you need help with some of your personal care needs, you move to the assisted living section (see Chapter 9). If your care needs increase, you may move to the CCRC's memory care (see Chapter 10) or skilled nursing care section (see Chapter 11). Of course, you may never need to move beyond independent living. But if you do, you stay on the same campus and sometimes even the same building or floor.

A CCRC was ideal for our colleague's parents. Her mom had dementia, so she lived in the memory care unit. Her father, right down the hall in assisted living, could walk to visit his wife whenever he pleased. She thrived under the routine, eating and staying hydrated, which had been a concern. Without the stress of caring for his wife, her father became involved in the community and, as he told his daughter, never had so many friends in his life.

There are many kinds of CCRCs. The cost and financial arrangements vary a great deal. You generally pay an admission fee—often fairly hefty, anywhere from $50,000 to $1 million—plus monthly fees from $1,000 to $5,000. Some CCRCs are privately owned, while others are affiliated with a religious organization, university, or hospital. There are nonprofit and for-profit CCRCs. You will find them in rural settings, in the suburbs, and in high rises downtown. This chapter can help you decide whether a CCRC is right for you and, if so, how to pick the best one for your situation.

What You Might Find at a CCRC

CCRCs vary so much that it is difficult to generalize, although the levels of care are usually the same:

- independent living
- assisted living, with personal care for residents who need help with bathing, dressing, and taking their medications
- sometimes memory care, for those with cognitive issues
- skilled nursing care, for residents who need medical care or rehabilitation

The CCRC probably also provides health services, meals, housekeeping, transportation, and emergency help.

Because the CCRC offers care to meet the changing needs of its residents, you can expect to live in the same community for the rest of your life. And you (and your family) never have to worry about moving again.

There are some high-rise CCRCs in urban areas, but most CCRCs are just a few stories tall or sprawl across a campus-like setting. They feature independent living units in small, connected townhouses or even single-family homes. Almost all have a central building that contains the assisted living units that are studio or one-bedroom apartments and the skilled nursing care center that may have single or shared rooms arranged around a central nursing station.

The central building will also contain the dining hall, which is often quite luxurious. Because the residents eat at least one meal a day there, CCRCs generally feature a restaurant-style dining room with a warm and welcoming atmosphere. You might see tables for two, four, and more; chandeliers; waiter service; a salad bar; and three or four entrée options. Larger CCRCs often have a smaller, more informal dining spot where residents can purchase breakfast, lunch, or snacks.

The CCRC may also have a separate dining room for residents in assisted living. This arrangement allows the staff to provide them with more attention and help. Residents with dementia and memory problems may also eat their meals there or live in a memory care wing or floor. The residents receiving skilled nursing care typically eat in their rooms.

Gathering together for meals promotes socialization and friendship among the residents. It is also a means of monitoring the residents' health. If without warning a resident fails to appear for dinner, the CCRC staff generally will go to the resident's unit to see that he or she is okay.

The CCRC is almost certain to offer on-site cultural, social, and recreational activities and programs. Most CCRCs offer common rooms for socializing: a card room, computer room, and recreational facilities, such as an indoor swimming pool or a putting green. Most have exercise rooms equipped with treadmills and other machines. You might find a small branch bank, convenience store, and hair salon or barber shop. Interested in organized square or line dancing, yoga or stretching classes, and shuffleboard or bocce competitions?

You'll have a wide choice of activities. The CCRC may organize bus trips to the theater, movies, or museums and have a van that takes residents to the mall, grocery store, and bank.

Some CCRCs have a limited number of small garden plots that are assigned to individual residents. Others feature walking trails around the grounds. A small library, often stocked with books donated by residents, is common, as are creative art studios, club rooms, and even a media room that looks like a small movie theater. Some have private lounges that residents can rent for dinner parties, family holiday gatherings, or other special celebrations.

In independent living, CCRCs often offer a variety of floor plans, different numbers of bedrooms, and even different styles, such as freestanding units and apartments in a central building. CCRC units often have balconies or small private patios. Some permit pets such as small dogs. We've even heard of some CCRCs where community dogs live with a staffer but spend their days at the CCRC. Many have units that come with garages or have access to central parking, with space for residents and staff. Residents are promised a carefree and convenient new lifestyle as they live in a safe and secure home with a 24-hour emergency call system.

New residents typically move into an independent living unit, where they carry on their life as independently as before. (Our colleague's parents were lucky to find a CCRC that accepted them at higher levels of care.) Most have a car. The unit will probably have a full kitchen, a living room, and at least one bedroom, which residents furnish and decorate as they wish. Many CCRCs permit new residents to customize their home. You may be allowed to install quartz or granite countertops and wood flooring, put in new carpets, paint the walls, change up the cabinets or the hardware, and install new appliances.

The independent living units will have regular housekeeping that usually includes linen service. Typically, the residents are provided an evening meal in the CCRC dining room. And they have no maintenance worries. All of that is handled by the CCRC.

What to Consider before Moving to a CCRC

When you read the brochures and look at the pictures of the residents, you see active, happy, healthy people. Sure, they're probably stock photos, but our experience is they're fairly accurate. CCRCs strive to create vibrant communities with active, involved residents. Imagine yourself living in a small community of others who are about your age. You can interact with your neighbors by sharing the evening meal in a gracious dining room. You may gather with others for an evening glass of wine. Although your living unit will have a kitchen, you may increasingly find that you take your lunch in the dining hall. In time, you may even go there for breakfast.

You need not to be a joiner to enjoy CCRC living. You can pick whatever activities interest you or stay in your unit other than for the evening meal. But if joining a club or gathering with others to engage in a game of tennis, a hand of bridge, or a discussion of current events sounds appealing, you are a good fit for a CCRC.

CCRCs appeal to those who are realistic about aging. Yes, today you are in fine health, or mostly fine health, but if your health declines, is your present living situation appropriate for your abilities? You drive everywhere today, but what if that becomes difficult? If you live in a CCRC, you won't have to drive much. It may be a relief to know that the CCRC can arrange for your transportation, such as trips to a doctor or local concerts.

Most CCRCs will be glad to have you stay on campus in a guest suite for an overnight or weekend stay. When you are at the CCRC, envision yourself living in the independent living unit, perhaps having a more compact kitchen, eating your dinner every night in the CCRC dining room, and living in a community filled with older residents—not even middle-aged adults and definitely no children, unless they are visiting. Will you be happy with that? Is it close to shopping, entertainment, and restaurants? Is your place of worship nearby?

When you visit a CCRC, don't focus just on the independent living units, dining areas, and recreational facilities. Spend some time visiting the assisted living and skilled nursing care units. You want to make sure you'd be satisfied living in each of the levels, should you ever need them.

Ask how the CCRC involves residents in its operation. Is there a residents' council that regularly meets with the CCRC staff and management? How is that council selected? How long can they serve? What kind of issues does management bring to that council? Is there a group similar to a homeowners' association that has a say in how the community is run? Are there resident committees to plan social functions, recreation, on-site entertainment, lectures, and off-site travels? Do residents have a say about the evening meal menu?

Pros and Cons of CCRCs

There are two good reasons for moving into a CCRC: (1) You want to live in a retirement community that has amenities and facilities that make your life better. (2) You want to make a final move where you can get the personal assistance and health care that you may need someday if you decline physically or mentally. If those benefits seem compelling, and you can afford it, then a CCRC may be the choice for you.

The younger and healthier you are when you move in, the longer you will be able to enjoy the virtues of an active retirement community. Rather than mowing a lawn, you may be practicing golf on a putting green, making pottery, or organizing volunteer activities. You may have to leave your church choir, but the CCRC is likely to have a resident chorus. No more driving across town for rehearsals. If you bring your dog with you, you can walk her on the CCRC grounds rather than up and down busy streets. Your exercise facility is just across the road, filled with others like you. No more hunting for a parking place at the Big Muscle Gym that is full of spandex-wearing young folks. And now you don't have to cook dinner every night. You walk across the campus or take the elevator down to the dining room where you can either eat alone or join others.

You have always wanted to improve your French. Now you join the French club dining table that meets every Thursday. The book club meets in a cozy room in the main building. You enjoy the bridge club sessions on Friday afternoons. The monthly lecture series in the main auditorium features speakers on a variety of interesting subjects. You join the residents' council or other committees that advise the CCRC on all sorts of matters. You even organize a new committee to discuss, for example, how to better conserve energy throughout the community. Every Wednesday morning you drive the short distance to the nearby college town and take a painting course. In short, you have never been busier or happier.

No matter how appealing the active life in independent living, the motivating reason for entering a CCRC is the availability of continuing care. CCRC residents understand that the reason for that high fee is that they have chosen where to receive assisted living, memory care, or skilled nursing care should they need them.

We know of older people who have declined physically or mentally but continue to live in their home or apartment. When their children recognize that a parent can no longer live safely without assistance, they undertake the task of finding assisted living or skilled nursing home for them. Many who enter a CCRC do so to save their family from having to make those difficult decisions. You proactively pick where you may later get assisted living or skilled nursing care. Your children can focus on spending time with you rather than searching for somewhere for you to move.

For some, a CCRC may be a possibility but not just yet. There is no right age to move into a CCRC. You must be in good enough health to pass the admission test. But beyond that, it is up the individual and the CCRC to decide if the person is too old to be admitted. It is reported that the average age of admission is about 80 and the average resident age is around 85. If you are in your early 70s and uncertain about whether a CCRC is right for you, just wait a few years. Of course, you take the risk that you might not meet the admissions requirements. You may decline too much physically, have contracted a fatal disease, or be unable to pass a mental acuity test. If you think a CCRC may be right for you in the future, consider putting your name on a waiting list. Even if you are not sure you will want to move there, it can't hurt being on a waiting list. By the time your name comes up, you may be ready to move in.

CCRCs are not for everyone. Many cannot afford the high admittance fee. Others don't see the value in the monthly occupancy fee. Why pay $4,000 a month—or $48,000 a year—to live in a small apartment and be provided an evening meal? Some want to live near family, and there is no acceptable CCRC in the area. Others prefer to move to a retirement community in a pleasant climate and, should they ever need personal care, move back closer to where their children live. CCRCs are also not for people who have arranged to have a family member care for them or would prefer (and can afford) to hire in-home assistance.

You'll want to review the process for decisions concerning changes in levels of care. We've heard complaints of CCRCs unilaterally deciding to move a resident to a higher level of care, despite the resident's and family's protest and even doctor's recommendation.

If being alone is what you like, perhaps a CCRC will just seem too busy or too social to appeal to you. From what we've seen, life in a CCRC may appeal more to extroverts or at least those who like spending time with others.

What CCRCs Cost

CCRCs are financed by charging the resident an initial admission fee and a monthly occupancy fee. As mentioned, the admission fee can be hefty. How much varies greatly: from $50,000 to $700,000 and more. To some extent, you are prepaying for your residential living costs and personal and health care for the rest of your life. The original insurance model for CCRCs to be economically viable was to charge an admissions fee that was high enough to pay for the additional costs of the assisted living or skilled nursing care because the monthly fee did not increase even when the resident moved into assisted living or skilled nursing care. CCRCs reckoned that some residents would never use the assisted living or skilled nursing facilities, some would use them moderately, and a few would spend considerable time there. For many residents, the admission fee would exceed the benefits received. But for a few, the fee was far less than the benefits they received. Just as with any insurance, many pay but only a few collect more than they pay.

Many CCRCs no longer follow that traditional model. Prospective residents did not like paying an admission fee of $500,000 with the idea of moving into the CCRC's independent living unit and then ten months later dying suddenly of a heart attack. In short, they didn't want to bet on their living a long time and eventually needing assisted living or skilled nursing care. The result is that most CCRCs now offer contracts that refund part of the admission fee if the resident dies or moves out within a set number of months after moving in; six months is common. Others refund a percentage that declines by some amount each month. For example, if the refund declines 2 percent per month, and the resident dies after ten months, the CCRC will refund 80 percent of the admission fee to the estate of the deceased resident.

Even if the admission fee is partially or totally refundable, the insurance concept is still at work. To cover the costs of those residents who eventually need assisted living or skilled nursing care and to allow refunds, a possibly refundable admission fee must be set higher. Some CCRCs that provide for some refund of the admission fee also increase the monthly fees for residents living in assisted living or in skilled nursing. For many potential residents, paying more for assisted living or skilled nursing care makes more sense than paying a large admission fee. Some CCRCs offer a choice: pay a nonrefundable admission fee or elect a refundable admission fee and, should the resident eventually need assisted living or skilled nursing care, pay a higher monthly fee.

The refund may also be linked to whether the resident rented the unit or purchased it as a condominium. If the unit was rented, as is usually the case, some contracts make the refund contingent on whether the CCRC can find a new resident to move into the unit within a set number of days, such as 30. If the unit was purchased as a condominium, the resident may not get the refund until the unit is sold.

In addition to the admission fee, the resident must pay a monthly fee, perhaps from $1,000 to $5,000. The amount depends on the type of contract and how much you prepay for future services. Usually the fee pays for all utilities (except your phone), cable, house-cleaning, maintenance and repair of the unit, appliances, landscaping, snow removal, linen service, recreational facilities, organized group activities, some on-site entertainment, and the evening meal. Breakfast and lunch may be available by a daily payment. The fee may also pay for on-site shuttle service and transportation to medical appointments, houses of worship, banks, and grocery stores. Increasingly, for an extra fee CCRCs will provide some personal care for residents in the independent living units.

Whether a resident's monthly fee increases as a result of moving into assisted living or skilled nursing depends upon the admissions contract. Some CCRCs maintain a fixed monthly fee regardless of the level of care they provide to the resident. Even so, the monthly fee can be, and often is, raised annually. Be aware that you are likely to face annual monthly fee increases even if you stay in the same level of care.

Admission and occupancy fees are commonly a bit higher for couples receiving the same level of care. You should also ask about how a couple is charged if one of them needs to move into assisted living or skilled nursing care and one remains in independent living. Does the monthly fee increase? Does that affect the possibility of a refund of the admission fee?

Keep in mind that the percentage of your CCRC fees, both the admission and monthly fees, that pay for health care may be deductible on your federal income tax return. If you're 65 or older, you can deduct unreimbursed medical expenses that exceed 10 percent of your adjusted gross income (as of 2019). To claim the deduction, however, you must itemize and not claim the standard deduction. Check with your tax advisor.

Today there are three basic forms of admission contracts. Because there are so many options and variables, you may want an experienced elder law attorney to review the agreement with you before you sign.

- *Life care or extended contract.* This is the most expensive option. It promises that the monthly fee will stay the same even if the resident needs assisted living, memory care, or skilled nursing care. The admission fee will be high, but it may be partially refundable under specific conditions. The percentage of the refund is often based on how many days the resident spent in the more costly, higher levels of care.

- *Modified contract.* This option provides for an admissions fee plus a monthly fee for a set of services beyond the independent living level for no additional cost but for only a set length of time. For example, the resident may have the right to 30 days of assisted living care. After that, the resident's monthly fee increases to pay for the cost of such care. These contracts vary greatly on the number of days covered before the monthly fee is raised.

- *Fee-for-service contract.* The admission and monthly fees cover independent living but not any assisted living, memory care, or skilled nursing care. The resident is charged a daily rate for that care in addition to the monthly fee.

Admission Requirements

Before deciding on a CCRC, make sure you fit its requirements. To be financially viable, CCRCs need residents who live for some time in the independent living units and need assisted living or skilled nursing care only in later years. Some CCRCs will admit only people who can demonstrate they are in good health and can live independently; other CCRCs may not admit residents over age 85. Because the CCRC has a limited number of beds in its assisted living, memory care, and skilled nursing care units, it must take care not to have too many residents who need that level of care. The CCRC may deny admission if the applicant has a preexisting medical condition. If the resident did not disclose a preexisting condition and then needs more care as the condition worsens, the CCRC may have the right to evict the resident or charge an additional fee.

Prospective residents must also demonstrate that they will be able to pay the initial admission fee and the monthly occupancy fee for the rest of their lives. Typically, applicants must have total assets equal to twice the admission fee as well as monthly income that is one and half times the monthly fee. Residents age 65 and older must be enrolled in Medicare and may be required to have a supplemental medical insurance policy. If not, they must have enough income and assets to pay for non-Medicare-reimbursed health care. New residents also will likely be required to have advance directives for their health care and financial powers of attorney. A CCRC wants to be sure that someone has the authority to pay the monthly fees and other expenses and make necessary health care decisions should the resident become unable to do so.

How CCRCs Are Operated

CCRCs are owned and operated by either a nonprofit entity or a for-profit corporation. Many of the nonprofit CCRCs have a religious affiliation. Others are owned by fraternal organizations or other secular entities. A Roman Catholic–affiliated CCRC near Larry is located next to a monastery and offers a daily morning mass. Other CCRCs with religious affiliation may operate more like secular communities but reflect some religious values. A national group of CCRCs originally organized by the Society of Friends, the Quakers, operates CCRCs consistent with Quaker values and principles that include showing deep respect for the individual and creating a sense of community.

A nonprofit CCRC may extend a preference to co-religionists or members of the fraternal society if there is a waiting list for admission. (Many CCRCs do have a waiting list, although with the growing number of CCRCs, this is less true than in the past.) For-profit CCRCs and most nonprofits, however, simply use a waiting list of first come, first served.

Whether owned and operated as a nonprofit or a for-profit, what is most important to a prospective resident is the financial stability of the CCRC. It must be managed professionally and efficiently to fulfill all that it has promised to its residents. Even if the admission fee is refundable, the combined pool of admission fees must be enough to pay for the future care of residents. If the admission fees are set too low or must be refunded too soon, the CCRC may not be able to pay its bills.

How can you determine a CCRC's financial stability and long-term viability? Review the licensing and financial statements. Ask all CCRCs you are considering for the audited financial statements and a recent actuarial study, which will help you determine whether the community has sufficiently funded its future obligations to residents.

For nonprofit CCRCs, you'll want to look at their Form 990, which tax-exempt organizations must file with the IRS. Find an organization's Form 990 at www.Economicresearch .com, www.Guidestar.com, or www.Propublica.org. The 990 will show the organization's net assets—the difference between assets and liabilities.

Ask for occupancy rates as well as the amount of increases in the monthly fee for the last five years. Annual increases are common. If the fees have been rising steeply, you might want to look elsewhere unless the CCRC has a good explanation. Don't rely on assurances that future fees won't rise as much. Oral reassurances are not legally binding.

Another concern is the amount of debt the CCRC owes. The typical CCRC gets started by borrowing the amount needed to construct and furnish the buildings, to be paid off over 20 or 30 years. Ask the CCRC how much it originally borrowed, how much has been paid off, and whether it has borrowed or expects to borrow additional amounts to finance new construction or to rehabilitate the existing buildings.

While there are stand-alone CCRCs, most are owned by an entity that operates multiple CCRCs. If the CCRC you are interested in is owned by a larger entity, find out where the other CCRCs it operates are located. Being owned by a larger entity has advantages. It may mean that if the local CCRC has financial difficulties, the larger entity will see to it that the CCRC does not fail. The larger entity may also have more experience with how to operate a CCRC, use economies of scale to operate at less cost per resident, and be more knowledgeable about ways to enhance the residents' lives.

For tips on sizing up a CCRC's financial status, see the free guides under the "Resources" tab at www.carf.org, the website of CARF International, a CCRC accreditation organization. At www.myLifeSite.net, you can run side-by-side comparisons of financial ratios and other factors for CCRCs in 12 states, for a fee of $29 per month. The state where the CCRC is located may be able to provide you with financial information. For example, California requires each CCRC to submit an annual report of its financial condition. The reports can be seen at https://cdss.ca.gov/inforesources/Community-Care /Continuing-Care/Annual-Reports.

Choosing the Right CCRC

If you think a CCRC is the right choice, you need to decide which CCRC is best for you. You might want to start by thinking about the community involvement you now enjoy and how much you will still be involved in the coming years. But that's only part of it. Some folks move to a CCRC because they are planning for the time they are less mobile, less capable of driving, less interested in going out, and happy to spend more time at home.

You may also want to consider how you'll see your children and grandchildren. Is it close enough to drive, or are there airports with direct flights to visit them? Perhaps you'll choose a location with a better climate or nearby attractions such as amusement parks, museums, or sports teams that your family may enjoy while visiting you.

Creating a home in a CCRC does not mean less activity or seeing others less, unless that is what you prefer. One of Sally's friends who moved from Virginia into a CCRC in Massachusetts reported, "Our neighbors are super nice, and meeting people has been very relaxed and fun. I actually think we already know more people here than we did in the 11 years in our old neighborhood. With 1,300 residents, it's hard to not find the ones you want to hang out with. There's no pressure to socialize, and privacy is respected; it's just easier to get to know people. We are 40 minutes from [our son] and his family. It's really nice to be so close. Moving to be near grandkids is a very usual motivation here."

Before making your decision, you may want to spend time visiting several CCRCs. Talk to some current residents about how they like living there. Be sure to talk to some random residents, not just those referred to you by the CCRC.

If you want some extra space, look for a CCRC that features cottages surrounded by grass and walking paths. Or you may prefer a townhouse that is a short walk to the central common areas. There are in-town high-rise CCRCs for those who enjoy apartment living and want to live near the amenities of a city. Can't part with your dog? Some CCRCs permit the residents to bring their pets. If you like to garden, if only in a small flower bed, find out if the CCRC has small gardens available.

The following checklists are in Chapter 12:

- ❏ *What to Look for in a CCRC*
- ❏ *CCRC Contracts*

What to Look for in a CCRC

General community

How many independent living homes or units are there? What is the configuration?

_____

How many independent living homes or units are available at this time? _____

_____

How many units are there for those who require assisted living? _____

How many are available? _____

How many skilled nursing beds are there?_____

How many are available? _____

_____

Is there a waiting list? ❑ Yes ❑ No

If so, how long might it take to be accepted and admitted?_____

_____

How old is the CCRC? _____

What are the plans for expansion or updates? _____

_____

If major rehabilitation is planned, will that require relocation of any residents? _____

_____

What is the amount of the long-term debt? _____

What is the asset-to-debt ratio? _____

Is the admission fee kept in a reserve account? ❑ Yes ❑ No

Does the CCRC have a residents' council or association? ❑ Yes ❑ No

What would happen if the CCRC should merge with another CCRC or be bought out by a larger organization? _____

_____

Under what conditions can a resident revoke the contract? _____

_____

Grounds and location

Are the grounds well maintained and easy to navigate? ❑ Yes ❑ No

Are there places to walk? ❑ Yes ❑ No

Are there bike lanes or paths? ❑ Yes ❑ No

Is the neighborhood desirable? ❑ Yes ❑ No

Are there ample conveniences (such as stores, banks, libraries, and restaurants) in and near the community? ❑ Yes ❑ No

Are medical professionals on site, such as a physician for a day
each week? ❏ Yes ❏ No

Is a hospital nearby? ❏ Yes ❏ No

Is bus or mass transit available nearby? ❏ Yes ❏ No

Is this a smoke-free community? ❏ Yes ❏ No

Are there designated spots for smokers? ❏ Yes ❏ No

Is there adequate security? ❏ Yes ❏ No

Are parking areas and walkways well lighted? ❏ Yes ❏ No

Are security personnel on site or on call 24/7? ❏ Yes ❏ No

Staff

Does the staff seem professional and happy to help? ❏ Yes ❏ No

Does staff treat residents with dignity and respect? ❏ Yes ❏ No

Do residents seem happy and engaged? ❏ Yes ❏ No

Are residents social and interacting with one another? ❏ Yes ❏ No

What credentials do staff members hold? _____

_____

What ongoing training do staff members receive? _____

_____

What is the hiring procedure for aides, doctors, nurses, and other staff? _____

_____

Are CCRC administrators usually available throughout the day? ❏ Yes ❏ No

Independent living units

Do the housing options meet your needs? ❏ Yes ❏ No

Are there different floor plans available and options to choose from? ❏ Yes ❏ No

Are floor plans efficient and pleasing? ❏ Yes ❏ No

Are all layouts wheelchair and walker friendly? ❏ Yes ❏ No

Are residences equipped with modern conveniences such as laundry
and dishwasher, full kitchens, and individual thermostats? ❏ Yes ❏ No

Are common areas properly cooled, warmed, furnished, and clean? ❏ Yes ❏ No

Do homes or units have outdoor living spaces for residents to enjoy? ❏ Yes ❏ No

Is there ample light? ❏ Yes ❏ No

Are there fire suppression systems and emergency exits? ❏ Yes ❏ No

Are there emergency alert systems in each unit/home? ❏ Yes ❏ No

Is each residence equipped with handicap bars, nonslip floors,
and other safety features? ❏ Yes ❏ No

Do multilevel residences have elevators? ❏ Yes ❏ No

Are furnished residences available?	❏ Yes	❏ No
Can residents customize their units?	❏ Yes	❏ No
Can the interiors of rooms or homes be painted?	❏ Yes	❏ No
Are there decorating rules?	❏ Yes	❏ No
Are cable and telephone services available?	❏ Yes	❏ No

What utilities are included in monthly fees, and which are residents responsible for paying? _____

Is parking available for residents?	❏ Yes	❏ No
Is parking available for visitors?	❏ Yes	❏ No
Are parking areas well lit?	❏ Yes	❏ No
Are pets allowed?	❏ Yes	❏ No
If so, are there any limitations on type, size, and breed?	❏ Yes	❏ No

What levels of personal care are provided in the independent living units? _____

_____

Is staff available to help residents with personal care and activities of daily living?	❏ Yes	❏ No
Can residents hire outside help for personal care?	❏ Yes	❏ No
Are there good motels nearby where guests can stay?	❏ Yes	❏ No
Is there adequate storage space or extra storage lockers for infrequently used items such as luggage or holiday decorations?	❏ Yes	❏ No

Assisted living, memory care, and skilled nursing care units

What are the policies about how the decision is made to move to a higher level of care? _____

What happens if one spouse needs a higher level of care than the other spouse? _____

_____

If spouses live in different units, such as one in independent living and one in skilled nursing care, how does that affect the monthly occupancy fee? _____

_____

If spouses live in different units, does the CCRC provide transportation or assistance for one spouse to visit the other?	❏ Yes	❏ No

What levels of personal care are provided? _____

_____

Are in-room meals offered?	❏ Yes	❏ No
Does the CCRC provide special dementia care?	❏ Yes	❏ No
Is the dementia center in a separate wing or building?	❏ Yes	❏ No

What is the staffing ratio? _____

What types of rooms are offered in assisted living? Single rooms? Double rooms? Shared bathrooms? Rooms with a bathroom in the suite? _____

_____

What types of rooms are offered in skilled nursing care? Single rooms? Double rooms? Shared bathrooms? Rooms with a bathroom in the suite? _____

_____

Does the skilled nursing care center accept Medicare or Medicaid reimbursement?   ❏ Yes   ❏ No

Medical services

What health care services are available for each level of care? _____

_____

What health care services are covered by the admission and monthly fees? _____

_____

Do residents have to stay within the CCRC network for health care?	❏ Yes	❏ No
Can they see health care providers outside of the community?	❏ Yes	❏ No
Is there specialized care for those with dementia, Alzheimer's disease, and other health conditions?	❏ Yes	❏ No
Is there a pharmacy on site?	❏ Yes	❏ No
Is medication monitoring available in independent living and assisted living?	❏ Yes	❏ No
If so, is medication dispensed by a qualified staff member?	❏ Yes	❏ No
Are physical, occupational, and other therapies offered on site?	❏ Yes	❏ No

Personal services

What transportation services are offered? _____

_____

Are there on-site hair salons, cleaners, and other conveniences?	❏ Yes	❏ No
Are any types of housekeeping, laundry, or linen service offered?	❏ Yes	❏ No
Are these services included in the monthly fees or at an additional cost?	❏ Yes	❏ No
What other personal services are available? _____		

_____

Is there an indoor swimming pool?	❏ Yes	❏ No
Is there a gym?	❏ Yes	❏ No
Are there organized exercise classes?	❏ Yes	❏ No
Are there houses of worship on campus?	❏ Yes	❏ No
Is transportation to houses of worship provided?	❏ Yes	❏ No

Social activities

What kinds of social events are planned? _____

Is there a monthly schedule of activities?   ❑ Yes   ❑ No

Who organizes social and recreational activities? _____

_____

What is attendance like at social events? _____

_____

What events or activities are included in the monthly fee? _____

What events or activities cost extra? _____

Are off-site day trips planned?   ❑ Yes   ❑ No

If so, to where and how often?   _____

_____

Is there ample notice for upcoming events?   ❑ Yes   ❑ No

Can all residents participate?   ❑ Yes   ❑ No

Are these events and activities capped at a certain number
of residents?   ❑ Yes   ❑ No

How do residents sign up? _____

Is there a common social area that is open at all times for residents?   ❑ Yes   ❑ No

If so, are games, cards, TVs, movies, and other supplies available?   ❑ Yes   ❑ No

What classes are offered on site?_____

Is there a forum in which residents can suggest activities and events?   ❑ Yes   ❑ No

Is there a planning committee that residents can join?   ❑ Yes   ❑ No

Meals and meal programs

What meal programs are offered? _____

_____

Are special diets catered to?   ❑ Yes   ❑ No

Can residents make special requests?   ❑ Yes   ❑ No

How many entrée choices are offered daily? _____

What is the meal schedule, and can mealtimes be flexible? _____

_____

Are snacks included in any of the meal plans?   ❑ Yes   ❑ No

Can guests dine with residents?   ❑ Yes   ❑ No

If so, is there a fee?   ❑ Yes   ❑ No

Do menus offer a variety of meals?   ❑ Yes   ❑ No

Admissions and contracts

What information must be provided by a potential resident in the application process?

_____

What is involved in the assessment process? How are potential residents assessed?

_____

What are the contract options? _____

_____

Are residences owned or rented? _____

What is the admission fee? _____

Is it refundable? ❑ Yes ❑ No

What are the limits or conditions for a refund? _____

How much is the monthly fee? _____

How much has the monthly fee been raised in the past five years? _____

What is the CCRC's estimate of whether and how much the monthly fee may be raised in the next three years? _____

What is the payment schedule? _____

What services are included in the monthly fee? _____

_____

What is the breakdown of any additional services for which there is a fee? _____

_____

Does the CCRC accept Medicare reimbursement? ❑ Yes ❑ No

Does the CCRC accept Medicaid reimbursement? ❑ Yes ❑ No

If a resident has long-term care insurance, does it cover any
of the care provided by the CCRC? ❑ Yes ❑ No

What happens when one member of a couple needs the next level of care? _____

_____

What happens if a resident decides to move? What is the refund policy? _____

_____

What happens when a resident dies? What is the refund policy? _____

_____

What happens in the case of death of a spouse or marriage of a single resident? _____

_____

Who makes the decision to move a resident into the next level of care—the resident, the resident's family, or the CCRC? _____

_____

What medical care, if any, is paid for by the entrance and monthly fees? _____

_____

What happens when a resident requires assisted living or nursing care, but no rooms are available within the community? _____

_____

Is the CCRC accredited by the Continuing Care Accreditation Commission?	❑ Yes	❑ No
Is the skilled nursing center certified by Medicare?	❑ Yes	❑ No
Is the skilled nursing center certified by Medicaid?	❑ Yes	❑ No
Is there an ombudsman or an organization of residents who can help raise issues with the staff and management?	❑ Yes	❑ No

CCRC Contracts

Lawyer who reviewed the contract: _____

Date resident signed the contract: _____

Person who signed contract on behalf of the resident:_____

in the legal role of _____ (agent with power of attorney, guardian)

Type of contract:

    ❏ Life care

    ❏ Modified

    ❏ Fee-for-service

    ❏ Other: _____

Admission fee: _____

Monthly fee: _____

Services included in monthly fee:

    For independent living unit: _____

    For assisted living unit: _____

    For memory care unit: _____

    For skilled care unit: _____

Refund policy: _____

Meal plan

    ❏ Seven-day evening meal

    ❏ Fewer than seven-day evening meal plan. If so, how many evenings? _____

    ❏ Breakfast

    ❏ Lunch

    ❏ Snacks for purchase

Physical examination required before acceptance   ❏ Yes   ❏ No

Immunizations required: _____

Tuberculosis test required   ❏ Yes   ❏ No

Advance directive required   ❏ Yes   ❏ No

Power of attorney for finances required   ❏ Yes   ❏ No

Move-in date: _____

Assigned unit: _____

Furnishings provided by the CCRC:

    ❏ Stove

    ❏ Refrigerator

    ❏ Dishwasher

    ❏ Microwave

❑   Washer/dryer

❑   Other: _____

Permitted modifications by resident: _____

_____

Renter's or homeowners' insurance required	❑ Yes	❑ No
Medicare certified	❑ Yes	❑ No
Medicaid certified	❑ Yes	❑ No

Procedure for change in level of care: _____

Procedure to appeal a proposed change in level of care: _____

Procedure for change in level of care when spouses need different levels of care:

_____

Assisted living unit shared	❑ Yes	❑ No
Assisted living units for couples	❑ Yes	❑ No

Maximum number to share a room in assisted living: _____

Maximum number to share a room in skilled nursing care: _____

Procedure for selecting or changing rooms or roommates: _____

Responsibility for lost or damaged personal property: _____

Overnight guest policy: _____

Visitation policy in assisted living: _____

Visitation policy in skilled nursing care: _____

Grievance procedure: _____

Residents' council	❑ Yes	❑ No
Statement of residents' rights provided	❑ Yes	❑ No
Privacy right to personal unit	❑ Yes	❑ No
Requirement to apply for Medicare	❑ Yes	❑ No
Requirement to have advance directive	❑ Yes	❑ No
Requirement to have power of attorney	❑ Yes	❑ No
Limits on liability for resident's injury	❑ Yes	❑ No
Mandatory arbitration provision	❑ Yes	❑ No

CHAPTER 13
PAYING FOR CARE

Paying for care, whether at home, in assisted living, in memory care, or in a nursing home, is expensive—very expensive. The median annual cost for a home health aide is $52,620, according to Genworth's 2019 survey of long-term care costs. Assisted living costs $48,612 a year. A private room in a nursing home topped $102,204 a year and, for a semiprivate room, $90,156. For a married couple, the cost of paying for care for one spouse in a facility can mean the at-home spouse has much less money to live on. To calculate costs in your area, see Genworth's cost calculator at www.genworth.com/cost-of-care.

For most of us, these costs would soon exhaust our savings. This chapter covers three ways to possibly mitigate those costs: long-term care insurance, Medicare, and Medicaid. As always, it's best to contact a financial expert for personal guidance.

Long-Term Care Insurance

To help protect your home against fires or floods, you buy homeowners' insurance. Similarly, you can buy long-term care insurance to help protect your family from going broke paying for long-term care. The exact definition of "long-term care" is determined by the insurance policy. Policies will generally pay some benefits if the individual qualifies and lives in a nursing home, in assisted living or memory care, or at home. You generally have to meet at least one of the following three conditions:

1. You cannot perform two (sometimes three) "activities of daily living."
2. You need supervision because of a cognitive impairment, such as dementia.
3. You need long-term care because of a medical necessity, such as congestive heart failure.

The activities of daily living that you need help with will be spelled out in the policy. Usually they are defined something like this:

- dressing: the ability to get dressed without help from another person
- eating: the ability to feed oneself
- bathing: the ability to use a bathtub or shower to keep clean

- toileting: the ability to use the toilet, including getting on and off, and performing associated personal hygiene

- continence: the ability to maintain control of bowel and bladder function, and perform associated personal hygiene

- mobility: the ability to move around where the individual lives on foot, with a walker, or in a wheelchair

- transferring: the ability to get in and out of a bed, chair, or wheelchair without help from someone else

Like other insurance, you, the insured, purchase a policy from an insurance company—the insurer. You pay premiums to the insurer, which in turn agrees to pay you a daily benefit amount for each day it pays for your long-term care, up to a dollar limit, for a set number of days. Simple, right? Unfortunately, no. You have to crunch the numbers to decide whether it's right for you.

One reason people buy long-term care insurance is to avoid the possibility of spending a lifetime of savings on care. Long-term care insurance, they believe, is a good investment. Those without much savings and with limited incomes, however, can't afford the premiums. Some in this category will have their long-term care costs covered by Medicaid (see the discussion on Medicaid on page 235). Others who have substantial assets and can afford the premiums may decide it's more advantageous to pay directly for the cost of care rather than paying years—perhaps decades—of monthly premiums. And, in the end, many may pay premiums for years and die without ever collecting any benefits because they never need long-term care.

Types of Long-Term Care Policies

If you decide to consider long-term care insurance, your first step is to research the type of policy you want. Three types of policies are currently available: traditional, short-term, and hybrid.

Traditional stand-alone policies reimburse the insured for long-term care expenses up to a fixed benefit amount and duration (more on that on the next page). A traditional policy, for example, might reimburse an individual $200 per day for up to three years.

Short-term policies offer benefits for up to one year at lower premiums. This type of scaled-back policy might pay enough benefits to cover a short stay in a facility or a few hours of home care a day. For example, a policy might pay a daily benefit of $200 per day for 180 days. Experience with short-term policies is limited, so be sure to check with a trusted financial advisor to decide whether such a policy is right for you.

Hybrid policies link long-term care benefits with an annuity or life insurance. The idea is that the insured will collect long-term care benefits, or heirs will collect a death benefit, or possibly both. These policies come in many forms. Many are basically life insurance policies that pay a death benefit, but if the insured needs long-term care, the policy will pay out a daily benefit amount like a long-term care policy.

Suppose that the insured owns a hybrid policy that will pay $200,000 upon death or in long-term care benefits. At age 87, the insured moves into a nursing home. The policy pays

$200 a day in long-term care benefits. The insured lives in the nursing home for 200 days and collects $40,000 in benefits. She then dies. The policy will pay the named beneficiaries $160,000: the $200,000 death benefit less the $40,000 already paid out for long-term care.

The premiums on a hybrid policy are typically higher than either a traditional long-term care policy or a pure life insurance policy. But at least the insured is guaranteed to collect benefits as long as premiums are paid. With some hybrid policies, you can pay a large, one-time lump-sum premium payment and get a guaranteed return.

Long-term care insurance policies can be complex; be sure you fully understand what you are buying.

Applying for Long-Term Care Insurance

For traditional and short-term policies, most companies require that you answer a set of written questions about your health plus pass a physical exam. People who buy traditional long-term care insurance are generally in their fifties or sixties, although some companies sell policies to people up to age 80. The older you are when you take out the policy, the higher the annual premium. If you have a preexisting medical condition, the company may not sell you a policy or if it does, it may charge a higher premium and delay benefits for care related to that condition until a specified period, such as six months, has passed. Common reasons to deny coverage are if you currently use long-term care services; need help with activities of daily living; have Alzheimer's disease or other dementia, multiple sclerosis, Parkinson's, or metastatic cancer; or had a stroke within the past year or two. For hybrid products, you may need to provide only basic medical information and not undergo a medical exam.

Traditional Policy Options

If you decide on a traditional long-term care policy and are accepted by the insurance company, you have several options to consider.

- *Daily benefit.* First, you must decide on the dollar amount of the daily benefit. You will have several choices. The policy will pay the lesser of your daily cost of care or the daily benefit limit. Say your policy pays $225 a day, but the daily cost of your nursing home is $275 a day. The policy will pay $225 a day, and you must pay out of pocket $50 a day or $18,250 a year. That's a lot, but it's still far less than the $100,375 ($275 × 365 days) you'd pay without the insurance. If you want to reduce the amount you pay each day, you can choose a higher daily benefit. But the higher the daily benefit, the higher the policy premiums. Note that the policy pays the daily benefit up to the cost of the care. So, if you are living in a facility at a cost of $130 a day and the policy says it will cover up to $225 a day, the policy will pay only $130 a day.

- *Years of coverage.* Second, you must decide how many years of coverage you want. The more years you choose, the higher the premiums. Policies will pay the daily benefits for a limited time, such as for three, four, or five years. (In the past, insurance companies sold policies that would pay the daily benefit without any time limit—called benefits for life policies—but these policies are rare today.)

- *Inflation clause*. Third, look for an inflation clause. Most policies include a provision that the daily benefit limit rises with time, such as 5 percent a year. The idea is that because long-term care costs steadily increase, so should the daily benefit limit. A policy with a $200 limit in the first year and a 5 percent inflation rate would pay $210 a day in the second year. Every year, the daily limit would increase by 5 percent. The higher the inflation rate increase, the higher the premiums.

- *Joint coverage*. Finally, if you are married, ask about a joint policy that covers both of you, which may be called a shared care or shared benefit rider. Such coverage is typically less expensive than two individual policies. Just be sure that you understand the benefits available to each spouse. You probably want a policy that will pay adequate benefits for both spouses—not one that limits the benefits in a way that most of the benefits could be used up by the first spouse to need care.

Qualifying for the Daily Benefit

Policies pay the daily benefit only if the insured meets the specified physical and mental requirements set out in the policy. These are often called medical or functional thresholds, or benefit triggers. As mentioned earlier, the policy will pay benefits if the insured cannot perform a specified number of activities of daily living, perhaps because of a physical condition or dementia, as defined in the policy. Alternatively, the insured may qualify for benefits because of a mental condition, the most common being dementia, that is so severe that the insured cannot take care of him- or herself. The policy will likely refer to this as the insured having a "cognitive impairment" that requires supervision and personal care. Or the insured must be physically in need of care, such as having had a serious illness or injury, or having a chronic health condition, such as being partially paralyzed by a stroke. The policy will likely refer to this as the insured having a "medical necessity" for long-term care.

Where Care Is Provided

Most policies currently sold cover care provided in assisted living or memory care, in a nursing facility, or at home so long as care is provided by professionals. Some older policies limit where you must live to receive coverage. Some policies will allow you to pay family members for at-home care if they meet certain qualifications. (See the discussion of family caregiving agreements in Chapter 5.) The policy may pay a different daily benefit amount based on where you receive care, such as less for care provided in the home. Ideally, the policy will pay the same daily benefit amount no matter where it is provided. Read the policy carefully. If the policy pays only if you are in a state-licensed nursing home and your nursing home is not licensed by the state, no benefits will be paid.

Deductibles

Like many insurance policies, long-term care policies often won't pay benefits until the insured has paid a certain amount out of pocket. The deductible for long-term care is called the "elimination" period. When you purchase a policy, you choose how long the elimination period will last. The longer the elimination period, the lower your premium. Many insureds select an elimination period of 90 or 180 days. If, for example, you own a policy with a 90-day elimination period and enter a nursing home on June 1, the policy will begin to pay benefits on August 30 after you have paid out of pocket for the first 90 days of your care.

A Lifetime Commitment

Before you buy any long-term care insurance policy, keep in mind that it is a lifetime commitment. If you buy a policy at age 65, you can expect to pay premiums for many years. A 65-year-old man has about a 40 percent chance of living to age 85 and a 20 percent chance of living to age 90. If you are a woman who is age 65, you have over a 50 percent chance of living to age 85 and a 30 percent chance of living to age 90. Our point is that this adds up to a lot of years of paying premiums.

If you stop paying the premiums before you need the benefits, the policy lapses and will pay no benefits—ever. Letting the policy lapse means you are losing the investment just when you are older and more likely to need the benefits.

If you do qualify for benefits, most policies suspend the payment of premiums while the policy is paying benefits.

If you are considering buying a long-term care policy, you should do some simple math. For example, a policy that pays $225 a day for up to four years will pay a maximum of $328,500 over four years—a lot of money. And, as we said, the average cost of a nursing home is $100,375 a year.

But you may never qualify for benefits. And the odds are that you won't need four years of long-term care benefits. The average length of stay for those currently in nursing homes is 2.44 years, according to the National Nursing Home Survey.

The question to ask is whether the risk of possibly paying $328,500 for long-term care is worth the cost of the insurance. Keep in mind that you may be paying premiums for many years or even decades before you qualify for benefits. And you may never qualify.

The cost of the annual premium is based in part on the age of the policy buyer. The younger you are when you purchase the policy, the lower your premiums will be for the rest of your life. Every year you wait, the premiums will be a bit higher. The good news is that once you purchase a policy, the annual premium stays the same—except when it doesn't.

Unfortunately, if the insurance company finds that it set the premium levels too low, meaning that the company is paying out more benefits than it anticipated, it may be allowed to raise premiums. Most policies offer a level premium that won't increase as a result of individual circumstances, but companies may increase premiums for entire classes, say for all policyholders over age 75. Prior to the last five or ten years, insurance companies badly underestimated how high the premiums should be. As a result, the companies have been losing money on older policies. At least one company had to declare bankruptcy because it lost so much money. In response, insurance companies have asked the state insurance regulatory agency to approve significant increases in the premiums for existing polices. Companies have raised premiums for the policies that they are selling now. Whether those premiums will also need to be significantly raised is uncertain.

Where to Purchase a Policy

There are several places to buy long-term care insurance.

- You can buy through an insurance agent who is trained in long-term care insurance. Be sure that the agent is licensed to sell insurance in your state. Your state's department of insurance can tell you if the agent is properly licensed.

- Your employer may offer group long-term care insurance or individual policies at a discounted group rate. If you sign on for the group policy and later retire, you may be able to convert the policy to an individual policy without having to answer questions about your health or pass a physical examination.

- Some professional and service organizations offer group-rate policies. Just be sure you know what happens to your insurance coverage if you should leave the organization or if the organization stops offering the group policy.

- Some states operate "partnership" programs with long-term care insurance companies to encourage people to plan for long-term care. To find out whether your state has a long-term care partnership program, check with your state's insurance department. The insurers agree to offer policies that meet certain quality standards, such as providing cost-of-living adjustments for benefits to protect against inflation. In return for buying a partnership policy, you can keep assets you would normally need to spend down to qualify for Medicaid, up to the value of the insurance benefits you received and still qualify for Medicaid. (See a discussion of Medicaid on the next page.)

Read the Fine Print

Be aware that insurance companies strictly enforce policy requirements. Policyholders have been denied benefits because they did not meet the specific requirements of the policy. A few have sued to get benefits. They usually lose. For example, insureds have lost and not received benefits when the court found that their medical condition was not severe enough to meet the "medical necessity" requirement of the policy.

Medicare

Medicare may pay for some of the cost of nursing home care or care in a rehabilitation facility for a limited time—not for the long term—and only for skilled nursing care, not custodial care.

If you are enrolled in Medicare Part A, you qualify for Medicare payment of care in a skilled nursing or a rehabilitation facility for up to 100 days, if you meet all three of these conditions:

1. You have moved to the facility from a hospital after three consecutive days of inpatient care as a formally admitted patient (not under observation status).
2. Your care in the facility is medically necessary as determined by a doctor.

3. Your stay in the facility began within 30 days after the date of your discharge from a hospital.

If you meet these requirements, Medicare will pay for the entire cost of the first 20 days. It will continue to pay for days 21 through 100, but you must pay a daily copay that in 2020 was $176. Medicare does not pay for any additional days of care. Because it covers only nursing and not custodial care, moving into a nursing home solely for care for dementia may not qualify.

As mentioned in Chapter 5, Medicare may also cover some home health care services, again with limits. For more on Medicare home health care benefits see www.medicare.gov /coverage/home-health-services or AARP's *Medicare for Dummies* by Patricia Barry.

Medicaid

Unlike Medicare, Medicaid pays for both health care and custodial care of individuals who qualify for the program. A limited amount of Medicaid funding is available in many states to pay for long-term care provided at home or in an assisted living facility. Most Medicaid dollars, however, are spent on nursing home care. Medicaid pays some $60 billion a year for nursing home care for older Americans. In fact, it covers six out of ten nursing home residents—more than 800,000 people nationwide.

Eligibility requirements for Medicaid are complex. While Medicare is a federal program, Medicaid is run by the states but partly financed by the federal government. Each state operates its Medicaid program a little differently, and regulations can change every year, but a few rules apply in all states.

To be eligible for Medicaid, the individual must be a U.S. citizen, a lawful permanent resident, or in another covered group. An individual usually is eligible for Medicaid in the state where he or she lives, which includes the state where the nursing home is located.

Medicaid is a need-based program. It pays for the cost of care only for those who cannot afford it. To be eligible for Medicaid to pay for nursing home care, an individual must meet two requirements: an income test and an asset (net worth) test.

The income and asset requirements vary by state. In some states, if you receive Supplemental Security Income (SSI), you are eligible for Medicaid payment of your nursing home care. SSI is a monthly payment from the federal government to people with limited incomes who are blind, disabled, or age 65 or older. In 2020 the maximum monthly SSI payment was $783. (Amounts listed here are based on 2020; rates are adjusted every year for inflation.)

Most nursing home residents who are eligible for Medicaid don't receive SSI. They are eligible under different requirements, called the "medically needy" standard. To be medically needy, the individual must first meet an asset test, which in many states means not having more than $2,000 in savings. A few assets, like the home, its furnishing, and a burial plot, are not included in the limit. Many individuals meet the asset test by paying for their nursing home care until they have spent their savings down to the amount required by the state in which they live.

Individuals who meet the asset test must use their income, such as a pension or Social Security benefits, to help pay for the cost of their care to the extent that they are able. This is called spending down their income. For example, say Anne has no savings and her only income is her monthly Social Security benefit of $1,500. She moves into a nursing home that costs $250 a day or $7,500 a month. Even if Anne turns over her entire Social Security benefit of $1,500, she is $6,000 short. Therefore, she is eligible for Medicaid. She gets to keep a personal needs allowance of at least $30 (more in most states) a month. The result is that Anne pays $1,470 and Medicaid pays the rest, $6,030, of her $7,500 nursing home bill.

Many states do not use the medically needy standard. Instead, they use what is called the "categorically needy" standard that has an income cap. In these states, individuals who meet the state asset test must also meet an income cap test, which means that their income is not more than 300 percent of the maximum SSI benefit paid to an individual, or $2,349 (in 2020).

Different eligibility rules may apply if you need Medicaid assistance to pay for some of your care outside of a nursing home—for example, at home or in assisted living—which falls under what is known as the home- and community-based services waiver program. To qualify, you must need nursing home–level care and be otherwise financially eligible. Medicaid will not pay for the expenses of board and room but may cover some of the costs of your care, depending on the regulations of the state where you are receiving care. The waiver programs are federally approved and state-specific, and they have limited enrollments, so you can be financially and functionally eligible and still not be able to enroll. Many have waiting lists.

Married Couples

The Medicaid eligibility rules for married couples are complicated, and they depend on whether both spouses apply for Medicaid. In the typical situation where one spouse needs nursing home Medicaid benefits and one spouse will be staying at home and does not need benefits, the couple must meet an asset test and income test. Fortunately, the eligibility rules do offer some relief for the spouse who is not applying for Medicaid—called the community spouse. Here are the basics:

- *Income.* Only the income of the spouse going into the nursing home is counted to determine eligibility. The community spouse staying at home can keep all of his or her income.

- *Assets.* For assets, the rule is just the opposite. It doesn't matter who owns what; all the assets are counted. The community spouse, however, can keep the house. It is not counted as an asset so long as it is worth less than $585,000 or $878,000, depending on the state. Plus, the home furnishings and one car may not be not counted. The community spouse can keep assets (no matter who owns them) up to a limit that varies from state to state. This is called the "community spouse resource allowance." In all states, the community spouse can keep at least

$25,728. Most states allow the community spouse to keep one-half of the couple's assets up to the maximum amount of $128,640 (in 2020). Here's how that works in most states. If the couple has $20,000 in assets (not counting the home), the community spouse can keep the entire $20,000. If the couple has $40,000, the community spouse keeps the minimum of $25,728. If the couple has $100,000, the community spouse keeps one-half, or $50,000. If the couple has $300,000, the community spouse keeps the maximum allowed, or $128,640.

Be warned that this is only a quick overview of the rules. For more information and guidance, contact an elder law attorney with expertise in your state's Medicaid program.

The following checklist is in Chapter 13:

❑ *What to Look for in Long-Term Care Insurance*

What to Look for in Long-Term Care Insurance

Insurance agent/agency/company

Does the agent and agency have a good reputation?	❏ Yes ❏ No
Is the agent licensed in your state?	❏ Yes ❏ No
Have complaints been lodged against them?	❏ Yes ❏ No
Is the insurance company financially secure?	❏ Yes ❏ No

Policy options and costs

Is the policy traditional, short term, or a hybrid? _____

_____

If a hybrid policy, what are the provisions for unused benefits to pass to a named beneficiary? _____

_____

How does the cost of a traditional policy compared to a hybrid policy? _____

_____

What is the maximum payout of the hybrid policy? _____

What is the premium?_____

What does the agreement say about premium increases? _____

_____

What is the history of premium increases over the past ten years? _____

_____

What is the likelihood of a premium increase in the future? _____

_____

What are the daily benefit options? _____

_____

What are the differences in premium costs for each daily benefit option? _____

_____

What are the duration options?_____

_____

What are the differences in premium costs for each duration option?_____

_____

What are the inflation options? _____

_____

What are the differences in premium costs for each inflation option?_____

_____

What are the elimination period options before benefits begin? _____

_____

Is the elimination period based on consecutive days, or can these days be accumulated over time? _____

_____

What are the differences in premium costs for each elimination
period option?_____

_____

Where can care be provided? Are there any restrictions? _____

_____

What are the benefit changes, if any, depending on where care
is provided? _____

_____

What care services can be covered? Excluded?_____

_____

Can a family member be compensated for providing care?	❏ Yes	❏ No
Can unused benefits be carried over?	❏ Yes	❏ No

Spousal coverage

Is a "shared care" rider available for couples wanting coverage?	❏ Yes	❏ No
Is a spousal discount available for couples wanting coverage?	❏ Yes	❏ No

What are the benefit options?_____

_____

What are the benefit protections for the second spouse needing benefits? _____

_____

Coverage eligibility

What are the medical requirements or restrictions to be able to purchase
a policy?_____

_____

Is a medical examination or evaluation required?   ❏ Yes   ❏ No

Benefit eligibility

What are the benefit triggers, or medical or functional thresholds, to be eligible to
receive benefits?_____

_____

What criteria are used to determine benefit eligibility?_____

_____

What is the necessary level of cognitive impairment to receive benefits? _____

_____

How are activities of daily living defined?_____

_____

How many deficits in activities of daily living are required to receive
benefits? _____

_____

Who evaluates eligibility for benefits?_____

_____

Who develops a care plan for benefit eligibility?_____

_____

Under what circumstances can a claim be denied? _____

_____

What is the recourse for appealing denied claims? _____

_____

CHAPTER 14
TWICE AS NICE: SECOND HOME

Want to stay where you've been living for decades but also need a change of pace, scenery, or weather? If there are good reasons to stay where you are and good reasons to live somewhere else, and you have the means, consider taking advantage of the best of both by splitting your time between the two locations. That second home could be a condo in a warmer climate or a summer cabin in the cooler mountains. It could be a little place where you can get some quiet time over long weekends or a family compound where generations share extended vacations.

In this chapter we explore the ins and outs of the two main ways to acquire a second home: through a purchase or a timeshare. Both have advantages and disadvantages that we walk you through.

When considering a second location, keep in mind the financial issues, which we go over in detail—including finding ways to pay for the extra expenses of owning two properties. Renting out your home (or homes) while you're away is a growing trend. Airbnb, VRBO, and other online rental services are thriving. We help you consider whether that's a route you want to take.

And we explore the legal issues. Legally, you can have only one primary home, called a domicile, even though you live in more than one place. You can change your domicile as circumstances change, but you need to do so intentionally. We'll help you figure out which home is the better choice.

Finally, we delve into timeshares, including the pros and cons, how to find one, and how to sell one.

Purchasing Your Second Home

Buying a second home is similar to buying your main home. You need to find the place that fits your tastes and needs, although your needs for a second home can vary drastically from those for your main home. Instead of the distance to work and the quality of the schools, for instance, you may be more interested in the time to drive there, the quality of the skiing, or the number of close-by golf courses. Maybe you'll use your second home as a getaway for one or two seasons, a source of short-term rental income when it's not occupied by family, or a fix-it-upper to be flipped for profit. Sally's second home in rural West Virginia, about an hour's drive from her main home, was her weekend haven where she puttered with DIY projects, worked on a garden, and just relaxed on the front porch.

Whatever your plan for your second home, you need to keep in mind the IRS's plan for it. You can deduct interest on up to $1 million of qualified mortgage debt on both your primary and secondary homes—but that depends on when the loans were taken out. You also can deduct the real estate taxes you pay on both properties up to a total of $10,000. To claim the deduction, you must itemize your deductions rather than take the standard deduction. (See Chapter 4 for more information about tax deductions and be sure to consult with a tax adviser.)

Sally knows from experience that having two residences has practical complications. To a degree, it means having two of everything: two sets of pots and pans, two vacuum cleaners, two hammers, and two sets of toiletries. Typically, whatever you need seems to always end up in the other place, so you buy a duplicate. A second home, however, can become the repository for other-season clothes, extra beds, and furniture you aren't using in your primary home.

Technology has made it easier to manage your homes from afar. With Internet-connected thermostats, you can turn on the air conditioner on your way to the beach house so it's cool when you arrive. Today's home security systems can be easily installed with wireless components so you can use your phone to monitor who is at your front door. Some smart locks allow you to remotely unlock the door to give access to a service provider, neighbor, or invited guest. To ward off burglars, Sally used simple plug-in timers on the front porch light and upstairs lamps to turn on and off at various times when she wasn't at home. Her sister installed a standby generator at her second home in ski country. It would automatically kick in if there was a power outage to prevent frozen pipes while she was away.

Another factor to consider in having a second home is medical coverage. You'll need to make sure that your health insurance plan will cover you in both locations. If you have coverage through a health maintenance organization (HMO) or Medicare Advantage plan, find out if in-network doctors are in both locales. With today's electronic medical records, it's a lot easier to transfer medical files among health care providers, but you'll probably want to have a primary care doctor in both locations. Check out the availability of medical specialists for any chronic condition you have and get referrals to doctors in your second location before you need them. Refilling prescriptions is easy with electronic records, especially at national chains. Sally's mail-order drug service has an option to list alternate mailing addresses for different times of the year.

While it may not be a primary factor in determining where you want your second home, you may want to take a look at the cost of medical care. The difference in cost for routine care and elective procedures can be huge. According to www.fairhealthconsumer.org, a nonprofit that tracks health care costs, a dental crown in a Midtown Manhattan zip code would cost $2,200, while one hundred miles north in Red Hook, New York, that same crown would be $1,350. Assuming medical insurance, an in-network colonoscopy in Midtown Manhattan would run $5,111 and $2,710 in Red Hook. Not all differences are as dramatic when compared to Manhattan, but some are. An in-network mammogram in Sarasota, Florida, runs $1,397; in Minneapolis, Minnesota, it's $584.

Renting out Your Second Home

Renting out your second home when you are not using it can help it pay for itself. If you rent it for less than 14 days, you don't have to report the rental revenue as income. If you rent it out for 14 or more days, you do need to report the income, but you can deduct rental expenses such as housecleaning services or advertising costs. You will need to document your rental income, rental expenses, the days you personally used the home, the days it was vacant, and the days it was rented.

On the other hand, if your second home is used as rental property, it's not a "second home." Under IRS rules, if you don't use the home for enough days, it is considered rental property and not a second home. To deduct mortgage interest, according to IRS publication 936, you must use it as your second home more than 14 days or more than 10 percent of the number of days during the year that the home is rented at a fair rental, whichever is longer.

No matter how many days you rent it, you should get the advice of a tax professional about the income tax consequences of owning and renting it out.

If you rent your second home, also factor in extra possible costs such as damage to your property through accidents, misuse, or abuse. Your best protection is to buy adequate insurance. Your homeowners' policy may need to be converted to a landlord's policy. Those premiums can be roughly double those on a normal home insurance policy. Again, consult with a professional.

Short-Term Rentals

Another way to profit from your second or even primary residence is to post it as a short-term rental on Airbnb, VRBO, or another online locator. The short-term rental business is booming. Airbnb boasts listings of three million accommodations in 65,000 cities worldwide. VRBO claims two million rentals at vacation spots in 190 countries.

The first consideration before posting is whether you can legally use your property as a short-term rental. You must comply with zoning regulations, which are becoming tighter in many jurisdictions. Some localities prohibit having paying guests in private homes. Some laws require you to be on the premises during the rental period if it is less than 30 days. Others require you, like a hotel, to pay sales or occupancy taxes, get a permit, or have a business license.

If you want to rent out an apartment or condominium, check to see if you are permitted to sublet the premises. Landlords and condominium associations often have rules to prevent owners from renting out their units. Renting out your apartment without your landlord's approval can get you evicted.

Relations with the neighbors are also a major consideration. A few noisy or inconsiderate guests can quickly turn your neighbors against your new enterprise. You'll need to take care that guests comply with parking restrictions and understand the rules about common recreational facilities.

Posting your home as a short-term rental can be a big commitment. You should make sure you have smoke and carbon monoxide detectors, fire extinguishers, and first aid supplies readily available along with emergency contact information for local hospitals or police. You should post house rules for parties, noise, quiet hours, pets, check-in and check-out hours, and maximum occupancy. Consider how you are going to separate your private space and personal valuables from guests. Will you need additional security measures as guests come and go through your front door?

You also need to check with your homeowners' or umbrella insurance policies to make sure you have adequate coverage against potential liability to your paying guests. Airbnb and VRBO provide up to $1 million for property damage done by guests booked through their systems, but cash, artwork, jewelry, and pets are excluded.

Airbnb handles the online credit card payments, charging you a fee of 3 percent for each reservation and charging your guests 6 to 12 percent. It will provide an account of your earnings each year via 1099 and 1042 IRS forms. VRBO also handles the online payments to you but doesn't charge guests a booking fee. VRBO hosts pay an annual subscription fee, instead of Airbnb's pay-as-you-go system.

Selling Your Second Home

The IRS distinguishes primary residences from second homes in significant ways. If you bought your second home to use for a few years and then decide to sell it, the IRS wants to know how much time you spent there. If you lived in it for more than 14 days a year, it's a residence and not an investment property. That means when it comes time to sell, you won't be able to take a tax deduction for a capital loss, but you will have to pay tax on capital gains. Sally's excitement over a good price for the sale of her second home in West Virginia was dampened when she realized she had to pay capital gains taxes, since she'd lived there more than 14 days a year.

As discussed in Chapter 4, when you sell your primary residence, you can take advantage of the capital gains exclusion when you sell it for a profit—up to $500,000 when you file a joint return or $250,000 when you file as an individual. For purposes of federal and state taxes, you can have only one primary residence. When you sell your second home, you get no exclusion. Be sure to maintain complete documentation on which home is your domicile.

What's Your Domicile?

Once you've picked your home away from home—be it a cabin in the wood, city highrise, or beachfront condo—you need to determine how long you'll stay in each location. Are you splitting your time 40–60? 50–50? We ask because there are complicating legal and tax consequences for living in two homes. Yes, when it comes to death and taxes, your domicile is important.

Death and Domicile

It's a basic legal concept that you can have more than one residence but only one legal domicile. Questions about where you are domiciled can arise after your death because the state where you were domiciled is where your will is probated. If it is not clear where to probate a will, the court has to try to figure that out after that person is dead. They start from the premise that you don't change your domicile unless you intend to do so. Deciphering intent after you have died and can't tell the court what you had in mind—when you probably never thought about it in the first place—gets tricky.

Some of the subjective factors that indicate you intend to make one place your permanent home are where you spent most (more than 50 percent) of your time, where you voted, what driver's license you had, where you registered your car, where you banked, the address on your federal tax return, where your dog was licensed, where you paid personal property taxes, how involved or connected with the new community you were, and where you had your church and gym memberships.

Taxes and Domicile

The state where you have your legal residence—that is, your domicile—is going to expect you to pay state income taxes. Even if you are not domiciled in the state, you may have to pay taxes on the income you made in that state. And you may have to pay taxes in more than one state. When Sally was on a national advisory group based in California, the organization withheld California income taxes. To get a refund, she had to file state tax forms and prove that she didn't live there and did no work there. In many cases, states provide credit for taxes paid in another state, but details vary case by case.

One reason Florida is so popular for snowbirds is that it has no state income tax. You can become an official Florida resident by filing a declaration of domicile with the clerk of court with proof of your intent to make Florida your predominant and principal home. You'll need to document that you have a job (with a paystub or W-2), have a Florida driver's license or Florida tags for your car, or are registered to vote. California, on the other hand, taxes the income of nonresidents who stay for more than six months, earn any income, or make mortgage payments. The District of Columbia has for years tried to tax the income of nonresidents who work in the District and live in Virginia or Maryland, but Congress doesn't allow it to tax nonresidents. Check with a CPA or lawyer in both states about state taxes you might have to pay if you are living in more than one state.

If one residence is in a high-tax state and the other is in a low-tax state, the high-tax state may demand that you document exactly how many days you were in each state. Some taxpayers rely on handwritten diaries, folders of receipts, and toll booth records to show where they were on every day. Now there are apps that automatically track your cellular network, Wi-Fi, and GPS. Check out https://Monaeo.com and www.TaxDay.com to track how many days you spend in each state.

One other consideration when choosing your domicile is the $250,000 capital gains exemption on the sale of your primary residence. The exemption is available only if the property has been your primary residence for two out of five years prior to the sale, which you'll need to be able to document. When you are considering which house to be your domicile, you should keep that exemption in mind.

Thirteen states impose state estate taxes. If you were domiciled in one of those states, your survivors may have an estate tax bill to pay that they wouldn't have to pay if you were domiciled in a non-taxing state. State estate tax laws frequently change, so check with a tax professional for current laws, exemptions, and rates.

Make Your Intent Clear

If it isn't clear which state is your domicile, pick one and take consistent steps to show your intent. You can have more than one mailing address, but you should use the address of your domicile, which is your permanent legal residence, on these major documents:

- federal tax return
- passport
- Social Security
- bank and brokerage accounts
- will
- advance directives
- powers of attorney

You can always change your mind about your domicile, but if you do, you need to change all your documentation. If you live in one place for five months, in your second home for five months, and travel for the other two, proving your domicile can be complicated unless you have taken consistent, positive steps to stick with one state as your domicile.

Acquiring a Timeshare

Based on their marketing materials, timeshares seem to be a great opportunity that shouldn't be passed by. Who wouldn't want to stay in a beautiful resort for a week or two at what seems to be a bargain price? The industry boasts of incredible vacation experiences for the whole family, often in spaces more luxurious than hotels. What's not to like? Well, some love their timeshares, but many others don't and wish they'd never bought one.

Sally has a friend in Florida who says he uses his timeshare to great advantage, staying in choice accommodations all over the country. Although the timeshare works for him, you should be aware that owning a timeshare can be complicated. You must be certain you know how the plan you are considering works, where it has units, and all the costs involved.

We have other friends who complain bitterly about owning a timeshare. If you get into a plan that doesn't fit, the financial obligations can be a nightmare, they say, and it can be devilishly hard to get out of a timeshare contract. Many complain that even if they want to sell and can find a buyer, the money they get back is far less than any money they put into the deal. We address that issue and discuss exit options, along with the shady routes you want to avoid.

How Timeshares Work

Let's parse the terms used so you can fully understand how different timeshares work.

There is the *unit timeshare*, where you purchase a specific unit at a specific resort. You own the unit. You and the other unit owners together own the resort property. You share in the use and the cost of maintaining the common grounds. This is a real estate transaction for real property just like purchasing any other real estate. You'll get a deed to a *timeshare estate*, which you can rent, sell, exchange, or pass on to your family. You'll pay a purchase price plus an annual maintenance fee. You will be a member of a homeowners' association that elects officers, manages expenses for the upkeep of the property, and probably hires a management company.

The other main type of timeshare usage is an *interval plan*, sometimes called a *vacation club*. Under this arrangement, you purchase the right to use space in the resort for some set time determined by your *right-to-use contract*. This contract treats the timeshare as personal property, not real property. The contract can be a *fixed time* option, where you have the use of a fixed unit for a specific week each year for the rest of your life. Or it could be a *floating time* option, where you have the right to use any available unit in the resort on a first-come, first-served basis to get your pick of dates. You might also have biennial ownership, accessing the property every other year, as an "odd" or "even" year user.

A variation of the interval plan is the *points-based* system. You buy "points" that give you the right to use any available unit within the resort's affiliated properties for a period of time that is referred to as an *interval*. The number of points needed to use a unit depends on how long you stay, when you stay, and where the resort is located. Some resorts have unit intervals available around the world that you can choose from.

Most resorts use an exchange company that tracks the pool of available properties and interval points. You deposit your interval points into the exchange company's inventory of available weeks. You then go through the exchange company to find the interval you want to use at the place where you want to stay. Some exchange companies let you save up unused points from prior years, and others force you to use the points within the year. Companies may also let you pay for extra points to make up any difference in point value. The exchange company charges you a processing fee each time you select an interval from its inventory.

Sally's friend Robert has had a unit timeshare for more than 30 years. He learned about timeshares through a friend, who was promised a $100 gift certificate for recruiting a prospect to visit her timeshare resort on Longboat Key, Florida, not far from Robert's home. After checking out the resort, Robert persuaded his reluctant wife that by having a set week at the timeshare, they'd be forced to take at least a one-week vacation every year. They bought a studio unit for the first week in June for $2,800 with a $400 annual maintenance fee. For that then-princely sum—remember, this was in the 1990s—they also got two beach towels plus a $5,000 bond set to mature in ten years.

The very first year, they couldn't get away the week they were committed to using the timeshare. They realized that they were just two days past the rescission date to get out of their contract. A panicky call to the resort resulted in a deal to use their unit another week. So off they went on their first vacation at the timeshare, working the whole time and even driving to their nearby respective offices midweek. They decided that this was not going to work, and they were never going back. To this day, they haven't gone back to their unit on Longboat Key.

Sounds like a disaster, but it didn't turn out badly. To recover on their investment, they placed their unit into an exchange, trading their Longboat Key unit the first week in June for other units available in the exchange for that week. Over the years, they have traveled to New Orleans, Louisiana; Vail, Colorado; Lake Tahoe, California; and Nantucket Island, Massachusetts, among other vacation spots. In 33 years, they used their timeshare week 30 times—paying the annual $400 maintenance fee and forfeiting three of their vacation weeks. About six years ago, they transferred into another exchange program that switched from a set week to points that they could use for any available unit in the exchange at any available time.

Today, whenever they travel for conferences or pleasure, they reserve a timeshare in the exchange and use their points. In 2018 they spent a total of six weeks in different timeshares across the country. Robert calculates that for 2018 alone, at $239 in exchange fees times six weeks (a total of $1,434 in exchange fees) plus his annual Longboat Key maintenance fee of $480 (that fee increased several years ago), he spent a total of $1,914 on 42 nights of lodging. That works out to a cost of $45 a night. With comparable hotels costing over $200 a night, he considers his timeshare to be extremely cost effective.

What to Consider before Buying a Timeshare

These are the key points to consider before buying a timeshare:

- Take your time to comparison shop among different resorts and the various exchanges. There are many options and details to consider.
- A better deal may come if you wait—or if you patiently negotiate.
- How useful will your timeshare be, not just this year and next year but a decade from now?
- Be strategic about the resort's location. Is it too far away or, as in Robert's first experience, too close to be a real vacation getaway? Do you love the weather? Are there activities you'll want to do every year?
- If you buy a unit timeshare, be careful about the week you pick. Make sure it will remain workable for you and your family for many years. Will that week be attractive for other users if you want to rent it out or when you want to sell it?
- You might get a better deal by buying directly from an owner who wants to exit. Be sure that you know all the details and are getting what you want, not just a bargain that you may later regret.

Timeshare Marketing

If you are not already a timeshare owner, you may have been urged to become one. Marketing of resort properties is ubiquitous and intense. Sally got a call out of the blue from a major company with a great incentive—roundtrip airfare for two to Hawaii and three nights' accommodations at the resort. All she had to do was bring her spouse and commit to a tour of the property. She and Art went. Once on site, the sales reps worked hard to convince them that this was the deal of a lifetime. When they protested that Hawaii was too far and expensive to repeat on an annual basis, they were encouraged to consider their other resorts stateside. They successfully resisted the sales pitch and had a lovely Hawaiian vacation.

In another encounter with a different company, Sally stayed a couple of nights in a rental unit she found online, unaware that it was a timeshare operation. Once the company had her name and number, its representatives were relentless. She got more than a dozen calls over the following months—despite repeatedly saying she wasn't interested. The concept doesn't fit her lifestyle or budget. Larry has no interest in owning a timeshare. When a timeshare salesperson calls, he just says, "Not interested," and hangs up. Then he blocks the number on his cell phone.

There are other ways to explore timeshares than trying to resist a high-pressured sales pitch during a free vacation or meal. Skip the presentation by the skillful salesperson by renting a unit directly from an owner at a resort you're considering. Try it out to see how you like it and enjoy your vacation without the pressure to buy or the complications of conducting a business deal in the middle of a holiday. If you like it, buy it directly from an owner who wants out. Check on eBay, Craigslist, or timeshare listing sites, where you might find intervals offered for as little as $1 or at other steep discounts.

Costs of Owning a Timeshare

If you think a timeshare would suit your lifestyle, you'll want to crunch the numbers to see if a timeshare is worth the investment.

Factor in all the costs, which may include these:

- The entry fee, payable in one lump sum or financed, averaging around $20,000 in 2018.
- Annual maintenance fees, averaging $970 a year in 2018. Because fees are bound to increase every year, you need to know if there is a cap on how quickly or how much they can rise. Note that you'll need to pay the annual fee even if you don't use your unit or interval. Ask how the money is spent. Request a copy of the maintenance budget and review expenses. How much goes into repairs and routine maintenance?
- Financing costs, if you finance the entry fee. Because of the steep loss of value in a timeshare, most major banks are reluctant to finance a timeshare, at least at the same rate as a regular home mortgage. The resort will likely offer you financing, but consider the interest rate. It will probably be pretty steep.
- Closing costs.

- Broker commissions.

- Property taxes. They may be a separate cost on unit-type plans where you have a timeshare deed.

- Special assessments for major repairs or renovations. For properties you're considering, find out what's scheduled to be replaced or renovated. Look to see if the property is showing signs of wear and ask how much a renovation might cost.

- Travel to and from your resort. That was the key deal breaker for Sally's Hawaiian offer. She'd be paying thousands for her and Art for airfare from the East Coast, plus far more if she wanted to bring along kids and grandkids.

Once you've totaled the costs, compare them against what you would pay for a similar vacation, for that length of time, at a similar hotel. Think about how much you spent on your last vacation and if the timeshare arrangement would supplement or replace it. Here's an example:

Let's say the entry fee is $23,000, which is financed over ten years at 4.5 percent interest. With monthly payments of $238 and an annual fee of $970, the annual cost is $3,826. For a one-week stay, it works out to about $550 per night. Over the ten years, the total investment will be $40,244, or $575 per night for 70 days in the timeshare. Not exactly a bargain.

You can negotiate the price for a better deal. Patience can bring significant reductions in the initial offering. In one of Sally's timeshare conversations, the more reluctance she showed, the lower the price. During the negotiations, the rep kept redoing the calculations and adding incentives until the final deal was thousands of dollars less than the starting price. She still declined.

If the budget works out for you, and you are considering buying, experts recommend looking at several possible timeshares. The timeshare industry is very competitive. A better deal might be just down the beach.

Investigating the Resort

Before signing up for one plan, investigate. Search for online reviews and read them carefully. Check out the developer and management company with the state attorney general and local consumer protection agency for any complaints. If you are looking at a timeshare in Florida, be sure to check with the Florida Attorney General's office, which receives complaints about timeshare sellers and resellers. You might want to talk to a local real estate agency about the reputation of the resort.

Talk to current owners, too, about their experience. Break loose from the sales rep to talk with a resident in the elevator or by the pool. Don't be shy about asking the sales rep for a private moment with a current owner so that you can get a candid response.

Reviewing the Agreement

No matter what the sales rep says, you *don't* have to sign the sales agreement right away, and you *can* walk out of the room with a copy. Read it carefully, in private, away from the sales office. As with any contract, consider having an attorney review it. You must make sure that everything the sales rep promised is written into the contract.

A key provision to look for is your ability to get out of the contract. Your right of rescission—commonly called a cooling-off period—is governed by state law, if it is not specified in the contract. How long you have to change your mind varies from state to state, but it is short, such as 3 to 15 days. When the days start counting and whether the count includes business days or weekends also varies. Your right might even expire before you get back home from your vacation. The website www.NOLO.com has a chart that sets out all the states' rescission laws for timeshare contracts. If you decide you have buyer's remorse and want out of the contract—and you're within the time frame—send a letter to the resort by certified mail with a return receipt, so you can prove you cancelled within the deadline.

Selling Your Timeshare

Let's say you no longer want to use your timeshare. Maybe the kids, who loved a week at the resort's beach, have grown up and scattered; your week doesn't work into your current schedule; you're frustrated with trying to schedule an exchange when and where you want to go; or you inherited your parents' timeshare that was great for them but doesn't interest you.

Welcome to the wild world of reselling. Getting rid of a timeshare is fraught with difficulties. Be resigned to the fact that you'll get less money back than you paid. A timeshare is not an appreciating investment; don't even expect to recoup your purchase price.

Sell Back to the Resort

The first step in trying to sell a timeshare is to check with your resort to find out if it will take back your timeshare. Because of the profit motive in selling brand-new units to new owners, the resort is often not interested in purchasing your unit. Still, if it's paid off (no mortgage) and you're in good standing with the company (no delinquent fees) you may be able to negotiate a deal.

You should find out if the resort will let you return your timeshare by using a "deed back." This is sort of like a quit claim deed, in which you relinquish any interest you have in the property. With a deed back, you give up any equity in intervals or points you have built up, but you also get rid of your maintenance fees or any special assessments. If the resort will take a deed back, you'll get no money or perhaps a small fraction of your investment and you'll have to pay transfer or closing fees. But at least it plugs the drain on your budget.

The resort has no obligation to accept your offer. The decision to take back your unit will probably be up to the homeowners' association or board of directors. You may have more success convincing them to take it back if you have a "good" reason, such as the death of a spouse, serious illness, or sudden change in financial circumstances. You may have to be persistent in convincing them that it is in their best interest to work with you and take back your ownership. Once they have your interval back, they can resell it. This works only if there is high demand at the property. Another option to explore with your resort: Will it rent out your unit and apply the rent to your management fee? Or can you rent it on your own? If it is in an exchange, however, you can't rent it.

The major resorts recognize that there can be reasons to terminate a timeshare and may work with you. Marriott Vacation Club, for example, has "exit specialists." Wyndham has an "Ovations" program. Diamond Resorts has "Transitions" to work with members who want to get out of their programs.

Sell on Your Own or through Resellers

If your resort won't buy it, a second option is to try selling on your own. You might run a classified ad in the major newspapers where most of the owners in your resort live. Try eBay or Craigslist. There are also free online timeshare listings. On www.RedWeek.com you can pay $59.99 a year to list your timeshare for sale or rent.

Be sure you have all the information and documents you'll need to sell your timeshare:

- name, address, and phone number of the resort
- deed
- your membership contract
- your financing agreement, if you have an outstanding loan on the timeshare
- maintenance fee schedule and the date of your last payment
- real estate tax amount and due date, if the tax is not included in maintenance fees

One of the biggest risks in advertising that you want to sell is the barrage of scamming resellers who promise to take it off your hands—of course for an up-front fee. The fee may be called any number of things—advertising fee, listing fee, appraisal, marketing analysis. Whatever it's called, don't go with any company that asks for an upfront fee. Be forewarned that there are lots of reselling scams. Don't believe the so-called guarantees of quick sales or refunds! The Internet is full of claims by resellers that the market is "hot" right now for your unit, that they have a ready buyer, or that they've sold dozens of units just like yours in the last month. For a small up-front fee to place an ad, you'll soon be rid of your timeshare. Douse those claims with a bucket of saltwater!

Florida had so many complaints about resellers' deceptive activities that in 2011 it passed laws designed to rein in the scams. The Florida Timeshare Resale Accountability Act includes the following provisions, which also offer a cautionary tale for sellers and buyers alike:

- A timeshare resale advertiser may not misrepresent a preexisting interest in the owner's timeshare.
- It may not mislead a customer as to the success rate of the advertiser's sales.
- It must honor a cancellation request made within seven days following a signed agreement.
- It must provide a full refund to a timeshare owner within 20 days of a valid cancellation request.
- It must not collect any payment or engage in any resale advertising activities until the timeshare owner delivers a signed written agreement for the services.

- It must provide a full disclosure statement printed in bold type, with no smaller than a 12-point font, that's printed immediately above the signature line for the timeshare owner.
- A timeshare advertising agreement must be in writing.
- There is up to a $15,000 penalty per violation.

How do you know the realistic asking price? Try to find out what other weeks like yours are selling for. There are several ways to do this:

- Ask your resort about recent sale prices.
- Look at current and completed eBay auctions.
- Check real estate records in the county where the resort is located.

It is important to look at actual resale prices—"comps" in real estate lingo—not ads, which can list prices you'd like to get but may not. Make sure your comps are similar to your timeshare: age of unit, season of the year, location, number of bedrooms, and resort amenities. Keep in mind that buyers are looking for the best deal, so price your time-share accordingly. You may want to get an independent appraisal. But be sure the appraisal comes from a licensed agency independent from the resale service.

Before listing your timeshare with any reseller, check for complaints lodged with the agency with the state attorney general or consumer protection agency. Search the agency's name online for consumer comments. Verify with the state Real Estate Commission that the agency is licensed to sell real estate in the state where your property is located. The American Resort Development Association website lists licensed brokers who adhere to a code of ethics.

If you do go with a reseller, find out the resell details—and get them in writing:

- How is your unit going to be promoted?
- How frequently you will get progress reports?
- How long is the listing agreement in effect?
- Can you sell or rent the unit on your own?
- How much will you pay in commissions, and are there any other costs?
- How can you get out of the listing agreement, and is there a cooling-off period?

If You Can't Sell

What if you can't find a buyer? Can you just abandon your timeshare and stop paying the annual maintenance fee? Not really, without serious damage to your credit score. The management company will either turn your debt over to a collection company or sue you for a civil judgment for the unpaid amount. With a civil judgment, the company can garnish your wages or seize your bank account. If you have a mortgage on the property, foreclosure is likely. That will take the property off your hands, but you can still be held liable for any deficiency if the foreclosure sale doesn't bring enough to cover all you owe.

Another weak option is to donate the timeshare to a charity. You might offer your week to a local charity to auction as a fundraiser. Or offer to donate the timeshare to a charity and ask the charity to take over the payments—although few charities will want to take over the financial obligation that you are trying to get rid of. If you are considering donating, keep in mind IRS rules. If you just donate your week to be auctioned off, you can't take any deduction at all because you have only made a partial transfer of the use of the property, and there's no deduction for a partial transfer. IRS publication 526 even uses that example for what's not deductible: a charitable auction of the use of a property for a week. If you donate the timeshare to a charity, you can deduct the fair market value of your gift. If your timeshare has no value, you have nothing to deduct.

The following checklists are in Chapter 14:

❑ *Proof of Domicile*
❑ *Timeshare Checklist*
❑ *What to Look for in a Timeshare*

Proof of Domicile

Residence #1:   Residence #2:

Address: _____   Address: _____
             _____   _____

Date acquired: _____   Date acquired: _____

Purchase price: _____   Purchase price: _____

Dates occupied: _____   Dates occupied: _____
                _____   _____
                _____   _____

Dates vacant: _____   Dates vacant: _____
                _____   _____
                _____   _____

Indicate which address(s) you use for each item. If you have inconsistencies, take steps to document which residence you intend to be your domicile.

	Residence # 1	Residence # 2
Driver's license	❑	❑
Car(s) titled or licensed	❑	❑
Voter registration	❑	❑
Passport address	❑	❑
IRS filing address	❑	❑
Personal property taxes	❑	❑
Social Security address	❑	❑
Health insurance policies address	❑	❑
Medical insurance coverage area	❑	❑
Address on bank and brokerage accounts	❑	❑
Address on credit cards	❑	❑
Address on insurance policies	❑	❑
Residency stated on last will and testament	❑	❑
Residency stated on durable power of attorney	❑	❑
Residency stated on health care power of attorney	❑	❑
Residency stated on trust documents	❑	❑
Location of house of worship	❑	❑
Membership in civic/service organizations	❑	❑

Timeshare Checklist

Name of development company or resort: _____

Website: _____

Contact information: _____

Sales agent: _____

Management company: _____

Unit owners' council ❑ Yes ❑ No

Affiliated exchange company: _____

Total number of available ownership units: _____

Timeshare costs:

Entry fee: _____

Financing terms: _____

Sign-up incentives/rewards: _____

Closing costs: _____

Broker commission: _____

Real estate taxes: _____

Maintenance fee: _____

Special assessment: _____

Right of rescission/cancellation: # days: _____

Total start-up cost: $_____

Total cost over ten years: _____

Average cost per week: _____

Timeshare option:

- ❑ Deeded unit
- ❑ Right-to-use contract
- ❑ Fixed week
- ❑ Floating week
- ❑ Week by advance reservation
- ❑ Biennial use
- ❑ Points based
- ❑ Other: _____

Building type:

- ❑ High-rise
- ❑ Garden
- ❑ Villa
- ❑ Mixed

Specific unit:
- ❑ Bedroom(s)
- ❑ Bath(s)
- ❑ Kitchen
- ❑ Living area
- ❑ Balcony
- ❑ Patio
- ❑ Elevator
- ❑ Other amenities: _____

Resort amenities:
- ❑ Pool
- ❑ Beach
- ❑ Golf
- ❑ Tennis
- ❑ Skiing
- ❑ Water sports
- ❑ Watercraft
- ❑ Spa
- ❑ Exercise equipment
- ❑ Restaurant
- ❑ Bar
- ❑ Entertainment
- ❑ Children's activities
- ❑ Other: _____

What to Look for in a Timeshare

What is the demographic profile of the resort—young families, retirees, singles, etc.?

_____

How long have timeshare holders been vacationing at the resort? _____

What are the annual maintenance fees? _____

What has been the increase in the maintenance fees from year to year? _____

Is the resort all-inclusive? _____

Are other mandatory fees charged (cleaning, utilities, occupancy taxes, energy surcharges)? If so, how much are these charges? _____

What is scheduled for major repairs and renovations, and what are projected assessments? _____

Are any activities or amenities available free or at a reduced rate, such as golf, skiing, water sports, children's programs, spa visits, and entertainment passes? Are they transferrable? _____

Is a specific exchange company affiliated with this resort? _____

Is there a mix of timeshare programs (points-based, fixed-week) within the resort?

_____

What is the variety in unit amenities, such as the type of building, view, size, number of rooms, or quality of unit? How many of each type of unit does the timeshare program own? _____

Does the resort rent units on behalf of owners? At what charge? _____

Is it easy to trade this resort for another location? _____

How do the annual fees compare with fees charged by other resorts in the area? ____

_____

What are the plans to improve the overall appearance of the property? _____

_____

Is adequate insurance in place for recovery from major weather events? _____

How long does it take to travel there? _____

What is the cost to travel there? _____

Will the property be adversely affected by climate change? _____

Resident I spoke with: _____

Feedback: _____

_____

_____

Resident I spoke with: _____

Feedback: _____

_____

_____

Resident I spoke with: _____

Feedback: _____

_____

_____

Resident I spoke with: _____

Feedback: _____

_____

_____

CHAPTER 15
LIVING ABROAD

More and more Americans are opting to pull up stakes and live in another country. According to the U.S. State Department, an estimated nine million Americans live abroad, with Mexico and Canada being the most popular destinations. Many are retirees, with over half a million people who live outside the United States receiving monthly Social Security Administration benefits.

Living in a different county can be a fresh start, full of adventure and travel, and often at a lower cost of living. Whether you are planning on living there a short time, several months a year, or permanently, this chapter is for you.

Embracing a new culture, and perhaps learning a new language, is a big move. It takes a lot of time, energy, and effort to do all the research and planning involved in making the decision and, eventually, the move. It also takes a serious dose of self-reflection to decide whether this is right for you. You need to carefully weigh the pros and cons and make some wise decisions about where you'll go and what you'll do once you get there. This chapter helps you sort through some of the things you need to consider and, if you do decide to make the move, how to prepare to leave.

Pick and Choose

Perhaps the most fun and easiest thing to do is to explore all the possible locations in other countries that seem to offer what you are looking for. A quick search online for best places to live or best places to retire abroad turns up dozens of sites willing to help you choose where you might enjoy living. *International Living*'s 2019 Annual Global Retirement Index put Panama and Costa Rica in the top spots. Panama has a tropical climate and offers retirees significant discounts on everything from health care and energy bills to entertainment and plane fares. Costa Rica also boasts a tropical climate along with a low cost of living, top-notch and affordable medical care, bargain real estate, and natural beauty. *Live and Invest Overseas* picked Algarve, Portugal, as the best place to retire in 2019 for its natural beauty, weather, welcoming vibe, world-class health care, and affordable housing. For more ideas, check out the AARP website at www.aarp.org/retirement/planning-for-retirement/info-2017/top-ten-countries-to-retire-se.html.

While websites give glowing descriptions for almost every hamlet on earth, take some of the promotional hype with a grain of salt—or sand. Find out as much as you can about the new destination. Dig deep. You *must* spend time in a location before you even think about moving there. Go at least once, if not more often. And stay for a while. It's a good idea to rent for a season or two so you can get a better sense of what it's like to live there and what it costs day-to-day. Try it out during the worst weather season!

If you're considering a tropical climate where air conditioning is essential, you'll find out how much electricity costs and whether there are frequent power outages. If you're planning on having a car to travel around the country or continent, you'll discover whether you can deal with the traffic, street signs in another language, and the cost and availability of gasoline. Track down people who live or have lived there to get candid impressions of what it's really like after a year or two. Check out websites, such as https://international living.com and www.expatinfodesk.com, that offer information and insight from people living overseas.

Factors to Consider

Only you can determine the most important factors to consider in a move abroad and choosing your overseas destination. But here are some things you might want to look at. We've listed them alphabetically; you'll need to figure out how much weight to give each one. See the Choosing My Destination checklist to help with your decision-making process. Be sure to talk it through with your partner or anyone who'll be making the move with you.

- *Accessibility to family and friends.* How close do you want to be to loved ones back home? How frequently do you plan on returning to the States or having people visit? Where is the closest international airport? Are there nonstop or direct flights? What's the cost?

- *Activities.* Are activities you enjoy available? If you like good restaurants or cultural attractions, will there be enough of these to keep you busy six months or a year after the newness has worn off?

- *Affordability.* How does the cost of living stack up with your income and budget? Are expenses—housing, utilities, food, and transportation—comparable to what you now pay, or will they take a bigger or smaller bite out of your budget? What is the exchange rate for U.S. dollars? What about taxes—sales tax, property tax, income tax? Take into account the cost of moving as well as visiting family and friends or having them visit you.

- *Climate.* Are you looking for four seasons or year-round warm weather? Have you spent time there during the worst weather season, so you'll know what to expect? How long is the rainy season? How hot or cold does it get and for how many months? How variable is the weather from season to season? What is the risk for natural disasters such as typhoons, tsunamis, earthquakes, or volcanic eruptions?

- *Cultural differences.* Do you like the music, the holidays, the traditions, the lifestyle, the pace? Do you look forward to making new friends among people who may be very different from you? Do you want a vibrant expat community to help with the transition? Are the natives welcoming to foreigners? Can you live without familiar stores, items, and brands? What are you willing to change, and what can't you live without?

- *Health care.* Will you have access to adequate and affordable health care? Are specialists available for any chronic health condition you have? Is emergency care accessible? Will your health care insurance pay for your care? Are you eligible for the country's national health care insurance?

- *Housing.* Are homes or apartments for rent or sale at a reasonable price? Can you, as a foreigner, legally own property? If you buy a property and later change your mind, will you be able to sell it quickly? For more on this, see the housing section on page 265.

- *Language.* Can you get by just speaking English? Or will you need to learn a new language, and if so, are you ready and able to do so? Some languages are much more difficult to learn, and some people are more proficient at learning a new language than others. Will you feel comfortable in a country or neighborhood where you do not speak the language?

- *Safety.* How safe is the country and the specific area you're thinking about? What is the political situation? The crime rate? You can check the U.S. State Department website for up-to-date travel advisories. If a tense situation arose, would you be able to get away safely? Will your home be secure from trespassers or property damage while you are away?

- *Taxes.* You may also have to pay taxes in your new country. In Spain, for example, you need to file a Spanish income tax return if you reside in Spain for more than six months of the tax year and if your income is above $24,000, or if you receive rental income of more than about $1,100 or have capital gains or savings income of more than $1,700. The income tax applies even if your income comes largely from U.S. accounts. You may get credit on your U.S. tax return for the taxes you pay in the other country, but it is complicated. Some countries have reciprocal tax treaties with the United States. Find them at www.treasury.gov/resource-center/tax-policy /treaties/Pages/treaties.aspx. Sally's high school classmate who has lived in France for many years tells her that figuring out the taxes she must pay in the United States and in France is a nightmare.

- *Transportation.* Is there reliable public transportation? How are the roads? The traffic? If you are considering driving in your new location, what are the licensing requirements? What are the requirements for vehicle registration? Are you fit enough to ease into a lifestyle that may include more walking or biking to get around?

- *Visa, residency, and work requirements.* Immigration and residency laws differ greatly from country to country. Do you need a visa to enter and reside in the country you're considering? If you are planning on working, how do you get a work permit? See the next section for more on this.

Here we walk you through a few of these factors.

Health Care

Depending on the country you are going to, health care may be excellent and affordable, or it may be extremely limited. Expect that the health care system will be different than in the United States—for better or worse. Medications may have different names, wait times to schedule appointments may be shorter or longer than at home, and language barriers may make communicating with medical providers difficult.

On the other hand, the cost of care may be less expensive, even if you have to pay out of pocket. As a tourist in Finland, Sally dislocated a finger when she slipped while boarding a train in Helsinki. By the time the train arrived in Kuusamo, she knew she needed to see a doctor before setting out on a week-long backpacking trip. She was seen immediately at the small hospital by a doctor who had interned in the United States, spoke excellent English, and fixed her finger. There was much discussion in the billing office when it came time to check out. Because she wasn't a citizen of a European Union country and didn't have a European health insurance card, the billing office wasn't sure how much to charge her. They seemed almost apologetic that she would have to pay about €100 (just under $100 at the time) for the entire visit—X-ray, emergency room fee, doctor fee, splint, and medications. She could not have gotten better care and would have paid much more at home in Virginia.

Check any health insurance policy you have to determine coverage for emergency, hospital, and general health care while you are abroad. If you receive Medicare, be aware: Medicare covers *no* medical costs outside the United States. Medicare supplement (Medigap) policies may cover 80 percent of medically necessary emergency care that you need within the first 60 days of your travel, with an annual $250 deductible, with a lifetime cap of $50,000. Those Medigap policies won't give you protection after the first 60 days or for general health care.

If you move permanently outside the States and have a Medicare Advantage Plan or Part D drug coverage, you will need to cancel those plans and stop paying the premiums. Both require you to live inside the service area of the plan. If you think you may come back to the States frequently for visits or move back at some point in the future, you may want to keep your Medicare Part B (physician) coverage and pay the monthly premiums ($144.60 per month in 2020). This ensures that you have medical coverage during your visits back home and avoids potential gaps in coverage or the costly late enrollment penalties when you return. If and when you come back, you'll be able to re-enroll in a Medicare Advantage plan or Part D during your Special Enrollment Period: a short window of the month before and two months after your return. If you know you are permanently moving, it's not worth paying the Part B premium because it won't cover any of your costs outside the States.

You may want to investigate travel health insurance that would cover you during an extended stay out of the United States. Travel health insurance is typically just for unexpected medical costs for emergency care due to injury, illness, or death. Food poisoning or a broken bone from a fall or automobile accident would be covered; routine medical care won't be. Emergency transportation to get to care or to get home may be included. When considering medical evacuation coverage, be sure you understand the coverage scope. Some policies will pay for transport only to the closest hospital, not to your choice of hospitals in the United States. The premiums will be based on the length of time you want coverage, your age, and the limits on medical and evacuation coverage. Emergency health insurance also may come as part of a travel vacation package plan that has other benefits such as trip cancellation, trip delay, or lost baggage coverage, but that won't help for a lengthy stay.

Some major health insurance companies also offer international or expatriate health insurance. These policies are like major medical policies that cover preventive and routine care, hospitalization, dental, and prescription drugs, in addition to emergency care. Preexisting conditions may not be covered; check with the various companies for exclusions. As when purchasing any type of insurance, compare terms and prices among all available plans to get the coverage you need and can afford.

Depending on where you relocate, if you become a legal resident, you may be able to join the national health care insurance system or purchase private health care insurance. Before you leave, find out the options and requirements at that country's embassy in the United States.

Preventive Care

Before you leave the United States, get any recommended immunizations that are required in your new location. You can check on any health issues you need to be aware of by going to the Centers for Disease Control Travelers' Health Center at www.nc.cdc.gov /travel/destinations/list. Make copies of any prescriptions for your medications. Carry a list of all medications you take and transport your prescription medications in the original containers. Bring along your immunization record and health history. If you use a mail-order service, find out if your meds can be mailed to your new address. Stock up on vitamins, over-the-counter medications, and medical supplies you rely on in case they are not readily available when you arrive.

Also bring prescriptions for your eyeglasses or contacts. You may want to take multiple pairs with you or leave an extra pair with a friend who could mail it to you in an emergency. Bring extra hearing aid batteries, too.

Housing

One other matter to check on with the embassy is any restrictions on owning property. For example, non-citizens can't own land in Thailand. Foreigners in Mexico cannot own property within 62 miles of any border or 31 miles of the coastline. In those areas where foreigners cannot contract to buy real estate, you must have a bank act on your behalf and set up a real estate trust, called a *fideicomiso*, that holds the title for you. Setting up that transaction can cost a couple thousand dollars, in addition to annual management fees. Some report that the process can take months to finalize. Costa Rica also has restrictions on ownership near its coastline.

The International Living website has country-specific information on owning real estate at www.internationalliving.com/global-property-ownership. It may not be up to date for all countries, so verify the specifics with the embassy or local professionals. Always get advice and have an independent, licensed, in-country real estate attorney review all real estate transactions. You don't want to buy a property and then find out it's not yours.

Financing the transaction can also be difficult. U.S. banks may be unwilling to give you a mortgage for property in another country. Going through a foreign bank may not be easy either: The legal requirements may be very different, large down payments may be the norm, and extra sales taxes may be imposed on foreigners. Property insurance can be hard to come by in some countries.

Visa, Residency, and Work Requirements

Although some countries encourage U.S. citizens to settle there, it's still important to check with the country's embassy for any requirements for residency permits, work permits, or retirement visas. Be prepared to provide all the required documentation—and it may be lots—and know where and when to apply. It might be at that country's embassy in the United States before you leave or with the local immigration office after you arrive. You can find information on how to contact a foreign embassy at www.usembassy.gov.

Each country has its own immigration laws and requirements depending on why you want to come to the country—whether to live, work, study, or retire—as well as what country you are leaving from and how long you plan to stay. Spain, for example, has two different types of visas. There's a long-stay visa (*visado nacional*) that allows you to live, work, study, or retire. You need to stay for at least six months to maintain your visa and renew it annually. The other visa, the *visado residencia*, does not permit you to work, but you don't have to renew it very year.

Some countries may require a health examination or criminal background check. Most will require proof of income and will not allow you to work if you are planning on retiring there. You may need a written statement from a financial institution showing that you have a regular source of income. Countries typically require a minimum of $2,000 per person per month, although the amount could be higher or lower, depending on the country. Panama, for example, requires retirees to have a monthly income of $1,000 to receive its *pensionado* (retired) visa. England requires people over age 60 who want to live there to have £25,000 annually to obtain an Independent Means Visa. For the Spanish *visado residencia*, you need proof of about $2,500 in monthly pension or investment income.

Other countries have different requirements. If you plan to stay more than 90 days in Germany, you must obtain a residence permit before you leave the United States. Germany requires a bank statement covering the last three months plus proof of medical insurance and a copy of the rental agreement where you will be living to obtain a temporary residence permit. This permit must be renewed annually. Later during your stay, you can apply for a settlement permit, *Niederlassungserlaubnis*, which requires you to demonstrate basic knowledge of the German language, political system, and society, plus other requirements.

Finances

With today's ease of online banking, managing your finances while living abroad is fairly simple, but you need to plan in advance. If you haven't already, you'll want to set up direct deposits of your income and arrange for automatic payment of your regular bills. As long as you have Internet access, you can check bank balances from just about anywhere in the world, although you'll want to avoid using public Wi-Fi, which may not be secure. ATMs provide ready access to the local currency.

If you're keeping your U.S. bank accounts, check your bank's foreign ATM and transaction fees. These fees can typically run around $2.50 per ATM withdrawal or 3 percent per foreign transaction, plus any fees the foreign bank charges. While this may not seem too bad, over time these charges can pile up, taking a chunk out of your funds each year. Also check your credit cards. Some will charge a foreign transaction fee; some won't. If your card doesn't charge international transaction fees, financial experts generally recommend that you pay in the local currency to avoid conversion fees. But check with your credit card companies before you go.

One way to avoid multiple transaction fees is to set up a bank account in your new location. That way you can transfer funds from your U.S. bank account for day-to-day expenses. But beware of how much you transfer at any one time. If on any day in the year you have more than $10,000 on deposit in a foreign bank account, you will need to file the annual Report of Foreign Bank and Financial Accounts, called the FBAR, with the U.S. Treasury. The penalty for not doing so is steep. You also should be aware of the Foreign Account Tax Compliance Act, which requires foreign financial institutions to report to the U.S. Treasury on the foreign assets held by U.S. account holders. To thwart the financing of terrorist activities, the USA Patriot Act restricts some financial transactions between U.S. and foreign banks. If you no longer have a stateside address, you may run into bureaucratic difficulties with the foreign bank.

Don't forget the IRS. U.S. citizens with income generated in the United States need to file federal income tax returns, and possibly pay taxes, no matter where they live in the world.

Plan for how you are going to prepare your taxes and how you will receive various tax reporting documents such as W-2s or 1099s that need to be attached to your returns. Be sure to get expert tax advice from a tax advisor who specializes in international taxation issues.

You may be able to receive your Social Security retirement, disability, or survivor's benefits when you live abroad, although there are some restrictions depending on the country. Use the tool at www.ssa.gov/international/payments_outsideUS.html to find out if your benefit payments will continue indefinitely, if they'll stop after six consecutive calendar months, or if certain country-specific restrictions apply.

Social Security considers being "outside the United States" to be away from the United States or its territories for 30 days in a row. You can use direct deposit to a bank in any country that has an international direct deposit agreement with the United States. Survivors or dependents getting benefits on someone else's account have special rules for payments outside the United States.

While you are living outside the United States, Social Security will periodically send you a questionnaire to determine if you still are eligible for benefits. If you don't return it, your payments will stop.

Read the Social Security publication *Your Payments While Outside the United States* (Publication 05-10137) for all the details about moving abroad or go to your local Social Security office before you depart.

Legal Affairs

Seek legal advice before settling abroad to make sure you have the right legal documents. You may find that the documents you created here, such as wills, trusts, and powers of attorney, are not enforceable in other countries. Some countries have signed the Hague Convention on the International Protection of Adults that addresses how powers of attorney are recognized and enforced in another country, but not all countries have signed it—including the United States.

If you are permanently changing your residence, the probate laws of the new country will determine how your property is distributed at your death, so you may need to draft a new will according to its laws. If you own property in two countries at the time you die, the legal issues get complicated. In addition to needing a will, lawyer, and executor in the United States, your estate may need a lawyer there as well to handle the distribution of your foreign assets. The U.S. embassy or consulate can provide you with a list of local English-speaking lawyers willing to assist U.S. citizens. You may also want to contact a member of STEP, the Society of Trust and Estate Practitioners, www.step.org/step-directory. It is important to understand any contracts you are asked to sign—particularly in local real estate matters. Be especially thorough in reviewing documents not in English.

Before You Leave

Before you get set to leave, you have a long list of details to take care of. The decisions you make may depend on how long you intend to stay abroad. Whether your plan is to stay for a year, permanently, or only for as long as it works out, you'll need to think about what happens to your home and stuff, what important documents to take with you, and how you will stay in touch.

Home

If you are currently renting, check to see when the lease term is up, how far in advance you need to give notice that you are vacating, and whether you'll pay an early termination penalty. If you own your current residence, will you rent or sell it? Property management companies can help you find and screen tenants, collect rents, and do repairs or maintenance. They typically charge 7 to 10 percent of the monthly rent.

The sale of your home involves getting the house ready to sell, determining the sale price, working with a real estate agent or selling it yourself, negotiating the sale terms, and all the other legal details that accompany any real estate transaction. There is an important tax twist to keep in mind if you are selling your home and not buying another one in the States. (Review the legal issues of primary residence and domicile in Chapter 14.) If you sell your home for more than you originally paid for it (plus the amount of any major improvements), you may have to pay capital gains tax. If you have owned your home and used it as your main residence for two of the five years prior to the sale date, you can exclude $250,000 of any capital gains, or $500,000 if you file a joint return with your spouse. If you decide first to rent your home while you are living abroad and then later decide to sell it, don't get tripped up by the two out of five years' requirement that you used the home as your principal residence. For more information on the tax consequences, refer to IRS publication 523, *Selling Your Home*.

Possessions

What to do with a lifetime of possessions, from furniture to pots and pans, out-of-season clothing to sports equipment? Some options: have a humongous yard sale or whole house auction, store your possessions in a rental storage unit or a friend's garage, or ship items to your new location. Shipping is the most expensive option, so you'll want to carefully plan what you absolutely need in your new place. If you need sage advice on downsizing and moving, check out AARP's *Downsizing the Family Home* by Marni Jameson.

Vehicles

What do you want to do about your car? You can lend or give it to someone else, sell it, store it, or ship it. The answer may depend on how long you plan to be gone. Check with your state's department of motor vehicles about what you need to do if you are going to store your car for a long time. Do you need to renew registration or undergo safety inspections before you leave? Is the place you are storing your car secure? Will someone periodically start it to keep the battery charged and drive it to avoid flat spots on your tires? For long-term protection, keep your car under cover in a garage or enclosed storage unit and check with your insurance company about lowering the premium.

If you decide to take your car with you, the logistics depend on where you're going. Of course, if you're moving to Canada or Mexico, the logistics aren't as complicated as shipping it overseas. In Canada, you just register the car. In Mexico, it gets a bit more complicated.

Under Mexican law, any vehicle in the country for more than 180 days must be imported, licensed, and insured in Mexico. You will need to hire a customs broker, who will handle the transportation of your car across the border. You'll also pay an import duty tax based on your car's value. Your car needs to be completely empty and then cleared through U.S. Customs, which can take up to a week to make sure it is not stolen and is properly exported. You'll need your U.S. title, registration, and driver's license. Take photographs to show the condition of the car and remove your U.S. plates. Then wait for the broker to tell you where to pick up your car across the border. Once you have imported your car, you need to fax or e-mail copies of the *Hojas de Pedimiento de Importacion*, called the "green sheets," to the insurance broker to activate your Mexican insurance. Next you need to register the car in the area where you live. To legally drive your vehicle without plates from the border to where you'll register it, you should go to the *Transito* to obtain a temporary

30-day permit. To finish the registration process and obtain permanent plates, you will need to have a *comprabante* (a bill from your Mexican residence to prove your legal address), copies of your driver's license, your immigration documents (tourist card, temporary or permanent resident card), the importation papers (green sheets), and the *factura* (invoice) the importer gave you when you picked up your car.

The process for shipping your car overseas depends on the size of your car, where you ship from and to, and how soon you want it. Work with a shipping agent to explore the options and get several quotes for each option. You'll need to decide how you are going to get the car to the ship and from the ship after it arrives, whether you want it to be packed in its own crate, to roll-on and roll-off (RoRo) a vessel equipped to transport wheeled vehicles, or to be in a shared container to wait for a ship with a load to your destination port. You can get door-to-door service at a steep price. How much you'll pay in import duties and what you need to do to register the car once it is shipped depends on where you are headed. The shipping company will have that information.

Driver's Permit

If you plan to drive in your new location and already have a valid state driver's license, you should apply for an international drivers' permit (IDP). The only two sources of IDPs in the United States are the American Automobile Association (AAA) (www.aaa.com/vacation /idpf.html) and the American Automobile Touring Alliance (AATA) (http://aataidp.com). Both accept online and walk-in applications. The State Department says never purchase a permit from any other place because it would be illegal to carry or use and won't be recognized. Your IDP will be valid for up to a year or until your stateside license expires. You may want to renew your state license before applying for your IDP so it has a fresh expiration date. You'll need to provide original passport photos, a copy of your valid driver's license, and a fee (about $15). Always carry your U.S. driver's license along with your IDP, as both are necessary.

Once you are in your new country, you will need to find out what you must do to get a local driving permit. The American embassy should be able to tell you the requirements.

Stay Connected

E-mail, texts, Skype, social media, WhatsApp, and many other apps make it easy to stay in touch with friends and family back home. Be sure to find out if your texts will go through and if your e-mail service is going to work where you relocate. There are web-based accounts and addresses that you can access wherever there's Internet service. Depending on where you are going, you may want to purchase a SIM card in your new location so your phone will work in that country's network. When Sally traveled to South Korea, she found many booths just outside international arrivals where she could rent SIM cards that worked for a week, month, or year.

And don't forget your regular mail. You can file a change of address with the U.S. Post Office. Once you are settled, you can selectively notify those businesses or people you want to hear from of your new mailing address. You can try using the Direct Marketing Association's "do not mail" service at www.dmachoice.thedma.org/ to cut down on junk mail, but it can take a very long time to get off some lists! Cancel or forward your magazine subscriptions.

The following checklists are in Chapter 15:

❑ *Choosing My Destination*
❑ *Residency Requirements*
❑ *Pre-departure Preparation*
❑ *Documentation Checklist*

Choosing My Destination

This checklist is designed to help you clarify your priorities for where you want to live out-side of the United States. You may like a variety of the options, but to give you the clearest picture of your priorities, be realistic about your desires and your resources. Your spouse or others who would move with you should separately fill out this worksheet. Then compare and negotiate any differences.

	Most prefer	Neutral	Least prefer
Relationships			
Near people I know	❑	❑	❑
Where I can make new friends	❑	❑	❑
With those who speak English	❑	❑	❑
With those who speak a language other than English	❑	❑	❑
Other: _____			
Location			
Close to current location	❑	❑	❑
Accessible to current location	❑	❑	❑
Where I can get to other countries	❑	❑	❑
Four seasons of weather	❑	❑	❑
Warm weather	❑	❑	❑
Cold weather	❑	❑	❑
Urban	❑	❑	❑
Rural	❑	❑	❑
Mountains	❑	❑	❑
Ocean	❑	❑	❑
River, lake, or pond	❑	❑	❑
Africa	❑	❑	❑
Asia	❑	❑	❑
Australia/New Zealand	❑	❑	❑
Canada	❑	❑	❑
Central America	❑	❑	❑
Europe	❑	❑	❑
Mexico	❑	❑	❑
Middle East	❑	❑	❑
South America	❑	❑	❑
United Kingdom	❑	❑	❑
Other: _____			

	Most prefer	Neutral	Least prefer
Community and culture			
Walk or easily get to shops and services	❏	❏	❏
Slower pace of life	❏	❏	❏
Active lifestyle	❏	❏	❏
Secure community	❏	❏	❏
Food I like	❏	❏	❏
New cuisine	❏	❏	❏
Outdoor activities	❏	❏	❏
Cultural activities	❏	❏	❏

Other activities I enjoy: _____

	Most prefer	Neutral	Least prefer
Resources			
Cost of living is lower than now	❏	❏	❏
Cost of living is higher than now	❏	❏	❏
Cost of living is same as now	❏	❏	❏
Access to hospital	❏	❏	❏
Access to affordable health care	❏	❏	❏
Access to public transportation	❏	❏	❏
Access to international airport	❏	❏	❏
Access to Internet	❏	❏	❏
Stable utilities	❏	❏	❏

Other: _____

Residency Requirements

Embassy: _____

Contact person: _____

Address: _____

_____

_____

Telephone: _____ E-mail: _____

Website: _____

Residency permit

Resident permit required   ❑ Yes   ❑ No

Requirements: _____

_____

_____

Location to apply: _____

Deadline to apply: _____

Apply before departure   ❑ Yes   ❑ No

Retirement visa

Retirement visa required   ❑ Yes   ❑ No

Requirements: _____

_____

_____

Location to apply: _____

Deadline to apply: _____

Apply before departure   ❑ Yes   ❑ No

Required immunizations: _____

Health examination required   ❑ Yes   ❑ No

Criminal background check required   ❑ Yes   ❑ No

Proof of income required   ❑ Yes   ❑ No

Income documentation required   ❑ Yes   ❑ No

Property ownership restrictions   ❑ Yes   ❑ No

Acceptance of same-sex partnerships   ❑ Yes   ❑ No

Pre-departure Preparation

Rental property

Lease term: _____

Notice to vacate required	❑ Yes	❑ No
Early termination penalty	❑ Yes	❑ No
Security deposit returned	❑ Yes	❑ No

Homeownership

Engage real estate agent	❑ Yes	❑ No
Sale by owner	❑ Yes	❑ No
Hire lawyer	❑ Yes	❑ No
Consult tax professional	❑ Yes	❑ No

Personal possessions

Make a list of all your possessions and what you are going to do with them, putting them into the categories below:

Yard sale: _____

Discard: _____

Give to family/friends: _____

Donate to charity: _____

Store with family/friends: _____

Self-storage unit: _____

Warehouse storage: _____

Ship to new location: _____

Insurance for items in storage: _____

Vehicle #1: _____

Sell	❑ Yes	❑ No
Loan to family/friends	❑ Yes	❑ No
Store	❑ Yes	❑ No
Ship to destination	❑ Yes	❑ No
Registration/inspection	❑ Yes	❑ No
Insurance	❑ Yes	❑ No

Vehicle #2: _____

Sell	❑ Yes	❑ No
Loan to family/friends	❑ Yes	❑ No
Store	❑ Yes	❑ No
Ship to destination	❑ Yes	❑ No
Registration/inspection	❑ Yes	❑ No
Insurance	❑ Yes	❑ No

Health

Prescriptions for medications	❑ Yes	❑ No
Prescriptions for glasses/contacts	❑ Yes	❑ No
Personal medication record	❑ Yes	❑ No
Health history	❑ Yes	❑ No
Immunization record	❑ Yes	❑ No
U.S. health insurance	❑ Yes	❑ No
International health insurance	❑ Yes	❑ No

Financial

Social Security	❑ Yes	❑ No
Direct deposit of income	❑ Yes	❑ No
Auto-payment of bills	❑ Yes	❑ No
U.S. bank account	❑ Yes	❑ No
Foreign bank account	❑ Yes	❑ No
U.S. income taxes	❑ Yes	❑ No

Passport

Expiration date: _____

Extra copies	❑ Yes	❑ No

Location of extra copies: _____

Documentation Checklist

You'll want to take copies of important papers, scan them, and store them in the cloud and on your smartphone. You may want to leave copies with someone you trust and can get in touch with in case of an emergency.

- ❏ Vehicle insurance
- ❏ Homeowners' insurance
- ❏ Personal property insurance
- ❏ Important contacts
- ❏ U.S. driver's license
- ❏ International driver's license
- ❏ Vehicle title and registration
- ❏ Credit cards (front and back)
- ❏ Bank account information
- ❏ Investment advisor information
- ❏ Investment accounts/mutual fund information
- ❏ Digital assets/PINs/passwords
- ❏ Travel rewards accounts
- ❏ Camera serial numbers
- ❏ Electronics serial numbers
- ❏ Funeral/burial plan

If I should die while outside of the United States, I wish my body to be

Buried at _____

Cremated and ashes buried at _____

Cremated and ashes scattered at _____

SELECT RESOURCES

2018 Home and Community Preferences Survey: A National Survey of Adults Age 18-Plus, www.aarp.org/content/dam/aarp/research/surveys_statistics/liv-com/2018 /home-community-preferences-survey.doi.10.26419-2Fres.00231.001.pdf

AARP Home Fit Guide (www.aarp.org/homefit)

AARP Livability Index (www.aarp.org/livabilityindex)

AARP Livable Communities website (www.aarp.org/livability)

Disrupting the Status Quo of Senior Living: A Mindshift, by Jill Vitale-Aussem (Health Professions Press/AARP)

Get the Most Out of Retirement: Checklist for Happiness, Health, Purpose, and Financial Security, by Sally Balch Hurme (American Bar Association/AARP)

Housing America's Older Adults 2018, by the Joint Center for Housing Studies of Harvard University

Medicare for Dummies, by Patricia Barry (Wiley/AARP)

Navigating Your Later Years for Dummies, by Carol Levine (Wiley/AARP)

Residence Options for Older and Disabled Clients, by Lawrence A. Frolik (American Bar Association)

ABOUT THE AUTHORS

Sally Balch Hurme has led the national conversation on many issues critical to older people and their families, from planning for retirement and care to making decisions for others. During her almost 25 years with AARP, she advocated on a wide range of issues, including consumer fraud, elder abuse, surrogate decision making, advance care planning, and financial security. Because of her wealth of knowledge on elder law issues, Hurme is quoted frequently in national media, is in demand nationally and internationally as a speaker, and is a Great Courses lecturer on *Getting Your Legal House in Order.*

Hurme is the author of the award-winning ABA/AARP *Checklist* book series, including *Checklist for My Family: A Guide to My History, Financial Plans, and Final Wishes*; *Get the Most Out of Retirement: Checklist for Happiness, Health, Purpose, and Financial Security*; *Checklist for Family Caregivers: A Guide to Making It Manageable*; and *Checklist for Family Survivors: A Guide to Practical and Legal Matters When Someone You Love Dies.*

Hurme was an adjunct professor at American University's Washington College of Law and at George Washington University Law School. She is a member of the National Academy of Elder Law Attorneys, the American Bar Association, and the Virginia and District of Columbia bars. Hurme has served multiple terms on the boards of the National Guardianship Association and the Center for Guardianship Certification, and she participated in the drafting of uniform guardianship laws and the International Convention on the Protection of Incapacitated Adults. She was honored by the National College of Probate Judges with the William Treat Award for excellence in probate law.

Hurme received her B.A. in political science from Newcomb College of Tulane University and her J.D. cum laude from the Washington College of Law, American University. She lives in Bridgewater, Virginia, with her husband, Art, and near her daughter, son-in-law, and two grandchildren. When not watching the grandkids' sporting events, she can be found in her vegetable and flower gardens or kayaking on the beautiful Shenandoah River.

Lawrence A. Frolik is Professor of Law Emeritus at the University of Pittsburgh School of Law. For more than 40 years, he has taught and written extensively about later-life legal issues. A passionate advocate for older Americans, he believes that as we age, knowledge and planning are the keys to making life fulfilling and rewarding.

A nationally recognized author and speaker, Frolik has given hundreds of talks to lawyers and the public on issues of aging and disability. He is the author of 15 books, including *Residence Options for Older and Disabled Clients* and *Elder Law and Later-Life Legal Planning*.

Frolik served on the Executive Council of Pennsylvania AARP and on the Board of Directors of the Kendal Corporation, which oversees a number of continuing care retirement communities. He was chair of the Pennsylvania Bar Association Elder Law Section, a congressional delegate to the White House Conference on Aging, an advisor to the Pennsylvania legislature on issues of guardianship and powers of attorney, and a member of the Executive Committee of the Council of Advanced Practitioners of the National Academy of Elder Law Attorneys.

Frolik received his B.A. with honors from the University of Nebraska and his J.D. cum laude from Harvard Law School. He lives with his wife, Ellen Doyle, in Pittsburgh, Pennsylvania. They love to hike and travel—particularly if there are wild animals to be seen. When forced to be indoors, they enjoy art museums and classical music concerts.